UNIVERSITY OF KNOWLEDGE

GLENN FRANK, B.A., M.A., Litt.D., L.H.D., LL.D., *Editor-in-Chief*

PRINTED AND BOUND IN THE UNITED STATES
OF AMERICA BY THE CUNEO PRESS, INC.

Every Branch of Knowledge
Man Possesses
May Be Applied To Some Good
Purpose

Black Star photo By Fritz Henle

"LIBERTY ENLIGHTENING THE WORLD"

THE UNIVERSITY OF KNOWLEDGE
WONDER BOOKS
GLENN FRANK, EDITOR-IN-CHIEF

JOURNEYS IN NORTH AND SOUTH AMERICA

Written and compiled by
NUMEROUS WORLD TRAVELERS
under the direction
of
MASON WARNER
World Traveler—Foreign Newspaper Correspondent
Member
Adventurers' Club of Chicago

•

UNIVERSITY OF KNOWLEDGE, INCORPORATED
CHICAGO - 1940

GLENN FRANK
Editor-in-Chief

INTRODUCTION

This is the first of three volumes of highly concentrated travelogues which are included in this series alike for those readers who can and for those readers who cannot travel extensively.

For those readers who can now or may be able later to travel extensively these volumes constitute an indispensable key to their explorative wanderings.

Since, through pictures and text, the world is so completely swept by these three volumes, the treatment of any one city, country, or region is necessarily confined to matters of major interest. This fact is a merit, for the prospective traveler can here pick his way through to the places of real significance to him, with his sense of selection unconfused by a mass of details that might otherwise blur his judgment respecting the places that might matter most to him. Once he has decided where he wants to go and what he wants to see, he can then supplement his reading with whole volumes devoted to the particular places he intends to visit.

These three volumes are, in effect, a kind of airplane flight over the world with gifted authors, who have themselves trotted the globe, showing the reader far more than he could possibly see from an actual airplane flight. A million details are passed by, but a sentence here and a paragraph there illuminate, as by a flash of lightning, a land, its people, their traditions, their social habits, their institutions, their problems, and the varied factors that give distinctiveness to this or that city, country, or region. And it is all done with an amazing economy of words and with a minimum demand upon the reader's time.

May I say again that these volumes do not attempt to deal with any single country exhaustively. Readers may readily find whole volumes or series of volumes devoted to each of the many countries here dealt with. The attempt is to put together a broad outline of the whole round world which beckons to the traveler and to help him decide where he may, with greatest interest or profit, spend his free time in travel.

But too many of us are so tied to our jobs or so limited in our resources that extensive travel is out of the question. These three volumes of concentrated travelogues are designed for these of us as well. It is possible, by reading such books as these, to be an armchair traveler, to realize much of the joy, the widening of interest, the enrichment of knowledge, and the insight into the point of view of other men and other peoples which travel gives, without leaving job or home.

Mark Twain, half in jest and half in earnest, once told how he became an arm chair mountain climber. This gifted man of letters believed in economy of physical effort. It would be ungracious to say he was lazy in the light of his massive literary output. But it would be just to say that he agreed with the man who said he never believed in standing when he could sit down or in sitting down when he could lie down. Twain was in the hotel at Chamonix. A party of fellow guests set out one morning to climb to the most challenging peak visible from the hotel. Twain declined to join them. Instead, as they climbed the mountain, he seated himself in a comfortable chair in the yard of the hotel and, through a telescope, watched his fellow guests in their arduous climb. He said that without moving from his chair he got all the thrill and exhilaration they experienced in their climbing. As he watched them struggle upward, he said, he felt his muscles go tense. When he saw them slip near a menacing crevasse in the ice, he held his breath in fear. When they reached their goal, his spirit pulsed with a sense of achievement as he applauded vigorously.

There was, I am sure, a twinkle in his eye as Mark Twain told this, but there is an element of veracity in his story. The editor and publisher of this series would be the last to say that the reading of these three volumes of tabloid travelogues is the equivalent of travel in the many countries with which they deal. But it is accurate to say that, for those who cannot afford to travel or for any one of many reasons cannot travel, the reading of these three volumes and still other special volumes the reading of these may suggest is the next best thing to extensive traveling.

And, it should be said in passing, that all the other volumes in this series prepare the actual or armchair traveler to get the utmost possible benefit from these three volumes of travel. For, after all, what we get out of traveling in other lands or of reading of other lands depends upon how much knowledge of varied lands and peoples and problems we bring to our travel or to our reading.

GLENN FRANK,
Editor-in-chief.

ACKNOWLEDGMENT

For several months we have been very busy collecting pictures from every part of the world and have received the kindest consideration and co-operation from many individuals and groups.

We desire to express our gratitude to the following organizations:

Methodist Book Concern, Chicago
Australian National Travel Association, Los Angeles Calif.
The Alaska Railroad
Illinois Central System
Canadian National Railways
National Railways of Mexico
Northern Pacific Railway
Canadian Travel Bureau, Ottawa
Union Pacific Railroad
Chicago & Northwestern Railway Co.
The Art Institute of Chicago

Without the invaluable help, too, of Chambers of Commerce throughout the North and South American continents and their neighboring islands, this volume would lack many of its best illustrations.

J. Bradford Pengelly
Picture Editor

TABLE OF CONTENTS

Drawing by Raeburn Rohrbach

THE WHITE AREAS REPRESENT COUNTRIES DESCRIBED IN THIS VOLUME

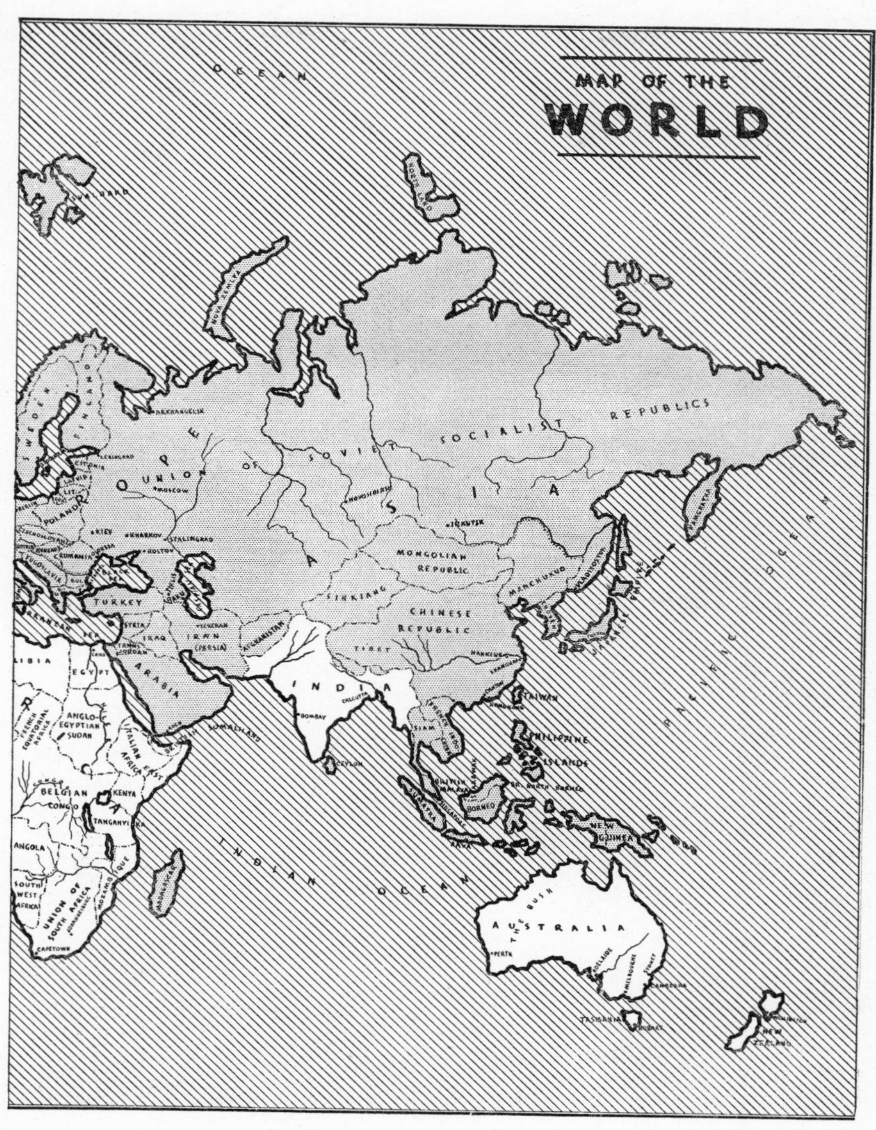

THE SHADED LAND AREAS ARE DESCRIBED IN COMPANION VOLUMES

Black Star photo By Gerstenberg

GREENLANDERS REJOICING IN THE RETURN OF THE SUN AFTER THE LONG ARCTIC NIGHT

"GREENLAND'S ICY MOUNTAINS"

GREENLAND, the second largest island in the world, lies north and east of the North American Continent in the North Atlantic Ocean. More than seven-eighths of Greenland's 830,000 square miles are covered with snow and ice.

The coast of Greenland is picturesque with majestic fiords, some of the walls of which tower hundreds of feet in height. Because of the continuous outward movement of the vast glacier which covers a large part of the island, huge masses of ice break off in the fiords and become icebergs. Only after the *Titanic* was sunk by one of these dreaded wanderers was a sea patrol stationed in the northern reaches of the ocean to chart the bergs and warn the shipping world of their approach.

Black Star photo By Gerstenberg

THREE TYPICAL NORTHLAND WINTER HOMES
Left to right: Earth hut, skin tent, and cloth tent.

Of the sixteen thousand people inhabiting this country, about three hundred are Danes. The rest are pure-blooded Eskimos on the east coast and in the Etah tribes, but mixed with Danish blood elsewhere. Their time is occupied with fishing and seal hunting. Hundreds of years of hunting have decimated the wild game. A few herds of reindeer still roam the country, while in the few mountainous districts occasional hares, ermine, polar bears, musk ox, and lemmings run wild.

THE STRANGE LEMMING

The lemming incidentally is a most peculiar animal. Stemming from the rat family, it has the size and outward characteristics of a mouse. A huge army of these furry rodents, comprising millions, may suddenly gather out of nowhere and start a relentless journey to nowhere. Nothing can stop them in their blind march to limbo. Crops and all forms of vegetation are damaged. But on go the lemmings, and, when they finally reach the edge of a sheer fiord wall of ice, even that does not deter them. Over the top creep countless millions of them, to drown in the icy seas below.

EARLY HISTORY

Eric the Red, that intrepid Norse explorer, discovered the island in about the year 982. Sporadic attempts at settlement were made, but, because of the severity of the climate and the uncertainty of livelihood, little was accomplished. During the fourteenth and fifteenth centuries, when Norway was undergoing a siege of the dreaded Black Death, Greenland was forgotten, and in time all of its settlers died. From the sixteenth to the nineteenth century various European explorers charted the coasts of Greenland in their search for the Northwest Passage to India. Up to 1933 the Norwegians were still claiming part of the east coast as belonging to them, but in that year the World Court declared all of Greenland to be Danish territory.

A HALF-DEAD WORLD

With the advance of science, together with the improvement of arctic travel and exploration, Greenland may yet become a valuable piece of property; but at present it is a forbidding country of ice chasms and desolation, barely supporting the few who are able to live in its rigid isolation.

Courtesy Alaska Steamship Company

Courtesy Canadian National Railways

HISTORIC ST. LOUIS GATE, CITY OF QUEBEC

CANADA

Courtesy Canadian Travel Bureau, Ottawa

HIGHWAY MARKER AT TOP OF GREAT DIVIDE, YOHO NATIONAL PARK, B. C.

THE DOMINION OF CANADA is the largest unit in that group of nations known as the British Commonwealth of Nations. It occupies the northern half of the continent of North America and comprises about 3,500,000 square miles. Young, energetic, and separated from old-world influences, the people of Canada have the material for making their country the greatest and most influential of all the British nations.

RESOURCES

When the facts of Canada's resources are examined carefully, it is not difficult to foresee its vast possibilities. One-fourth of the entire country is available for agricultural development. These areas when fully developed will help to make the British commonwealth agriculturally self-sufficient. From the Canadian Yukon and from British Columbia, more than $22,275,000 worth of gold was mined during the year 1900 alone. But since 1900 Northern Ontario has become the second largest gold-producing

A SALMON CATCH FROM A NEW BRUNSWICK RIVER

Courtesy Canadian Travel Bureau, Ottawa

area of the world, exceeded only by the Union of South Africa. In 1935 Northern Ontario produced more than $60,000,000 of gold. Silver, copper, lead, and zinc are being mined in prodigious quantities. The province of Ontario produces about ninety per cent of the world's supply of nickel. There is enough coal stored below the earth of Nova Scotia, Alberta, and British Columbia to furnish the needs of the British Empire for years to come.

Vast timberlands contain enough timber to supply all of the lumber demands of the country and provide for a big export surplus. Fur-bearing animals abound in these forests. The fur-farming industry started on Prince Edward Island, has spread over the country and has produced rich results. The waters that surround Canada, particularly around British Columbia, where the yearly salmon catch is tremendous, and along the Atlantic coast, where cod, halibut, and lobsters are caught, have made Canada one of the largest fishery countries in the world. Manufacturing plants are on the upgrade; and trade and commerce are increasing to a point where, instead of standing in sixth place in aggregate volume of trade, it appears possible for Canada to rise to her rightful place in the sun among the leading nations.

"BLOWS HOT AND COLD"

Extending from Boothia Island in the north, far above the Arctic Circle, to the city of Windsor in the south, which is across the river from Detroit, Michigan, the Canadian mainland is in a position to experience diversities of climate. Naturally, its more northern stretches suffer from severe winters. But, on the whole, with the exception of the extreme arctic north, Canada's climate is comparable to that of the United States. The year is ushered in with a short, mild spring, which is followed by another short period of summer when the temperature sometimes goes as high as 90 degrees. The autumn is a delightful period of what we know as "Indian Summer;" but winter is quite severe and long, and is subject to heavy snowfalls. The cold in the western provinces is of the dry kind, that crackles, and is exhilarating. Winter

Courtesy Canadian Travel Bureau, Ottawa

ALONG SKI TRAILS, MOUNT ROYAL, MONTREAL

hunting in Canada is a sport that not only appeals to the sporting blood in a man but invigorates him with that sense of physical well-being that can be obtained only from winter exposure.

THE INDIANS

The Indians were the first people to live in Canada. Scattered widely from coast to coast were tribes of Chippewa, Blackfeet, Ottawa, Cree, Iroquois, Huron, and other Indians. In the beginning they were hostile to the advent of the whites and fought them bitterly. Then, as the French began to penetrate deeper into the interior, they bought over the friendship of the Indians, mainly with "firewater." This practice of achieving the aid of the Indians was bitterly condemned by Laval-Montmorency, a puritanical, zealous prelate, who had been sent over by Cardinal Richelieu to convert the savages. He threatened to excommunicate those who gave brandy to the Indians; but the practice continued. From time to time, both the British and the French used Indian warriors to fight their battles. When the English won out, a number of treaties were made with the Indian tribes, reservations were allocated for their homes, and money was set aside for their use. Nowadays, the Canadian Indians are in somewhat the same position as are their American brothers. They act as guides in the mountains and forests, tend their farms in some communities, and make baskets and Indian mementoes on their reservations. In the far west they are employed in the salmon fisheries, the saw-mills, and the fur-seal industry. Many are still hunters and trappers, retaining the habits and customs of their ancestors.

EXPLORATION

It was the hardy Norsemen who were the first white men to discover Canada. In about 1000 A.D. a band of them under the leadership of the redoubtable Leif Ericsson sailed from Greenland and landed somewhere on the shores of what is now Nova Scotia. They did not remain long enough to form a settlement, but continued down the coast to what is now New England which they called Vinland. Not until 1497 did another white man set foot on Canada; then John Cabot embarked from Bristol, England, and arrived in Canada in that year. It was because of the glowing reports he brought back that English fishermen dared the perilous voyage across the Atlantic, to fish for cod and halibut in Canada's fish-filled waters. But these fishermen were not interested in exploration and made no attempt to investigate the mainland that bulked in the distance far from their fishing grounds.

The first real explorer of Canada was a Frenchman, Jacques Cartier, with a commission from Francis I to discover a new northwest passage to the East. He set sail from St. Malo, France, and arrived in the New World in 1534. Eventually, after a number of voyages, he sailed up the St. Lawrence River as far as Montreal, where he was prevented from continuing by the Lachine Rapids. It was Cartier who first called the country Canada, evidently using the Indian word, *kannatha*, which means a village, as the reason for his choice.

Until 1603 Canada remained merely a new, wild country, full of valuable fur-bearing animals and fierce Indians, and surrounded by waters abounding with fish. But in 1606 another great French explorer, Samuel de Champlain, sailed up the St. Lawrence River and founded the first French colony in North America, Port Royal, now called Annapolis, Nova Scotia. But he was not interested in colonizing. He, too, as was the case with all of the early explorers, was seeking only to establish a new northwest passage to India. Incidentally, it was for this reason that the natives of North America were originally called Indians by the Europeans. The first explorers, believing that they had landed on the far eastern shores of India, called the copper-colored natives Indians.

BRITISH VS. FRENCH

French companies were soon chartered to exploit the commercial possibilities of Canada. In 1613 British soldiers from Virginia raided Port Royal and annihilated it. In 1629 Champlain surrendered Quebec to a British fleet. But France regained her holdings in the treaty of St. Germain-en-Laye. It was then that Cardinal Richelieu, of France, began to colonize Canada of his own accord, and missionaries were sent by the Church to convert the Indians. Exploration continued, by both the Church and the State, which competed with each other and sometimes engaged in bitter struggles regarding the policies of governing New France, as they termed the country. After La Salle had made his trip up the St. Lawrence river, across the Great Lakes, and down the Mississippi, the French evolved the daring plan of conquering the interior of North America, so that in a process of attacking from the rear they could eventually push the British colonies out of Virginia on the east coast. Meanwhile, the British had made a number of attacks on Quebec, without being able to take it. But in the end, after France had experienced disastrous losses in its European war with England, it ceded the regions of Hudson's Bay, Nova Scotia, and Newfoundland to the British, after Nova Scotia had been captured by the British.

THE BATTLE OF QUEBEC

The French then continued their explorations of the lower Mississippi, still hoping to form a net around the eastern British colonies in America; La Vérendrye, a French-Canadian, pressed westward as far as the Rocky Mountains, which barred his way to the Pacific Coast. Finally, in 1759, in what was the decisive battle between the two nations, the British general, Wolfe, defeated the French under the generalship of the Marquis of Montcalm on the Plains of Abraham, above the city of Quebec. Both generals died in the battle, and with Montcalm died the influence of the French in Canada. In 1763, in Paris, Great Britain was given a free hand in Canada, and France relinquished all rights in the new territory.

THE CANADIAN CONFEDERATION

Originally there were five separate and distinct British colonies in North America. Nova Scotia, New Brunswick, upper Canada (Ontario), and lower Canada (Quebec) agreed, by the British North America Act of 1867, to unite into a single federation, called the Dominion of Canada. Manitoba and British Columbia in 1870 and Prince Edward Island in 1871 joined the federation. In 1905 Saskatchewan and Alberta, comprising the land that separated Manitoba and British Columbia, formed two provinces and completed the roster of nine provinces which, with the Yukon and the Northwest Territories, now make up the Dominion of Canada.

Courtesy Canadian Travel Bureau, Ottawa

LOBSTER POTS ON NORTH BAY, NOVA SCOTIA

NOVA SCOTIA

Nova Scotia, the first of the provinces to be colonized and the first to be seen by the Atlantic traveler on his way to Canada, is one of what the natives call "the maritime provinces." Almost surrounded by sea, it is no wonder that its inhabitants were, and still are, sea-faring people. In olden days when square-rigged sailing ships went scudding around the seven seas of the world, Nova Scotian vessels and sailors were well represented. Practically the entire coast is studded with fishing villages, of which Lunenberg is perhaps the most representative and picturesque. In the "Ovens," near Lunenberg, the ocean pounds so mightily that, during a heavy sea, its effect is as though the low rumble of heavy guns were sounding. The Lunenberg fishing fleet is the largest of its kind in North America and uses the famed Grand Banks as the center of its operations.

"THIS IS THE FOREST PRIMEVAL"

Nova Scotia, translated, means New Scotland; and it was so called by Sir William Alexander, a Scottish courtier of King James I, who granted the country to his court favorite. At present there are about half a million people in the province, mostly of Scotch stock. In Nova Scotia, especially in the Cape Breton Island section, Gaelic is occasionally spoken. There are also a scattering of French Acadians, the residue of those unfortunate Frenchmen of the Grand Pré region, the Evangeline country, as it is termed, and of which Longfellow wrote so feelingly. It was from this paradise that its inhabitants were exiled to Louisiana. The site of the original Acadian village in Grand Pré is designated with signs in French and English, as is the well from which Evangeline drew her water, and the original site of the Acadian Church, over which a Memorial Chapel has been built. A statue of Evangeline graces the front lawn of the chapel. Pubnicos, on the southern coast of Nova Scotia, and the countryside about Cheticamp, Cape Breton, still retain many of the old customs and relics of the Acadians. Some of the villages in this region are so quaintly old-world that, were you to be led into them blindfolded, and the blinder removed, you would easily imagine yourself to be in a seventeenth-century French village.

PICTURESQUE PICTOU

Pictou, on the north coast, is another city with an interesting historical background. Between the years 1765 and 1773, a number of British colonizations were attempted here. But it took a New England group, the Philadelphia Company, to accomplish the founding of a successful colony. Benjamin Franklin was financially interested in this venture. One of his printing presses is still on display in the Chateau de Ramazay in Montreal. The *Royal William,* an early steamship, crossed the Atlantic from Pictou to Gravesend, England, in 1833. The waters of Pictou furnish the night clubs of the world with millions of lobsters. It is a common sight to see dozens of old men seated in front of their houses, whittling out the wooden plugs that are inserted into the joints of the lobsters' claws to prevent them from biting each other and those who handle them.

HALIFAX

The capital city of Nova Scotia is named after the Earl of Halifax, who presided over the Board of Trades and Plantations. Because it possesses one of the finest natural harbors in the world, it attracts a great deal of Canada's shipping. In the winter, when the St. Lawrence River is icebound and closed to shipping, it becomes Canada's chief port. The Canadian Pacific and Canadian National railways have their eastern terminals here. Originally it was intended to be a naval base for British ships. The Citadel, an imposing fortress, still squats on the hill, around which the city is built. From it a marvelous view of the harbor can be obtained. As is the case with the British fortifications in Gibraltar, modern long-range guns ominously await the approach of a marauding enemy warship or airplane.

THE HALIFAX DISASTER

During the World War a frightful catastrophe occurred at the Halifax wharves. A boat loaded with high explosives, bound for France, was accidentally rammed by another boat in the harbor. Eighteen hundred people were killed, twenty thousand more were injured, dozens of boats moored in the harbor sank to the bottom of the ocean and almost a third of the city of Halifax was razed to the ground.

The Province House in Halifax is one of the finest examples extant of Georgian architecture. Old St. Paul's Church has been a landmark since 1750, when it was erected as a gift from George II, then ruler of Great Britain. The oldest newspaper in Canada, the *Halifax Gazette*, begun in 1752, is still being published as the *Nova Scotia Royal Gazette*.

CAPE BRETON ISLAND

Nova Scotia furnishes Canada with a considerable amount of its coal. Cape Breton Island is the center of the coal fields. Here is located one of the largest under-water coal mines in the world and, naturally enough, wherever coal deposits are plentiful, Canada's largest steel and iron works are located. Hunting and fishing facilities are available all over Nova Scotia, particularly in Cape Breton, where The Three Sydneys and Bras d'Or Lakes furnish the onlooker with scenic views incomparable for sheer loveliness. A trip down the La Have River is likewise so rich in scenic beauty that, in spots, it is almost breath-taking.

Courtesy New Brunswick Bureau of Information

PULPWOOD COMING DOWN THE MIRAMICHI RIVER NEAR NEWCASTLE, NEW BRUNSWICK

BAY OF FUNDY

Nova Scotia is attached to Canada proper by an isthmus which connects it with the Province of New Brunswick. Its coast line is dotted with fishing villages and seaports. The interior is forested with immense trees and broken up occasionally by stretches of well-cultivated farms nestling in fertile valleys. The province is interlaced with rivers and lakes and has an extensive coast line that is washed by the waters of the Gulf of St. Lawrence and the Strait of Northumberland on the north, and the Bay of Fundy on the southeast. Curiously shaped, intricate caves and hollows have been carved out of the rocks on the Bay of Fundy coast by the action of waves and tides. The tide in some sections has a rise of over fifty feet!

For natural beauty in scenic sites, the Baie de Chaleur is considered of primary importance. Bathurst with its surf bathing;

Caraquet, Shippegan, and Tracadie with their fishing, salt-water bathing, and duck hunting; Jacquet River, Chatham, Newcastle, Charlo, and Dalhousie all afford the tourist and vacation seeker ample pleasures.

NEW BRUNSWICK

At the head of the St. Johns River, where it empties into the Bay of Fundy, is St. Johns. Established by the French in the sixteenth century as a fishing village, it is still the center of the Newfoundland fisheries. To the canneries here the fishermen bring in their catches of halibut and cod, for eventual distribution to the world. Having been destroyed by fire a number of times and rebuilt, the newer town does not have the quaint appearance of most old Canadian cities. Instead, there are modern buildings, examples of which are an Athenaeum, Catholic and Anglican cathedrals, and several modern educational institutions. Its charm, however, is heightened by the hills on which the city is built, together with the backdrop of hills surrounding it and rising in some spots to heights of 600 feet.

MONCTON

The city of Moncton is the second largest city in New Brunswick and, like St. Johns, is a focal shipping center of the province. About twenty miles from the city are the famous Rocks of Hopewell Cape and The Bore. The latter is an odd rock formation, caused by the erosive effect of the high Bay of Fundy tides, which rush into the narrow Petitcodiac River and course madly through the rocks, shaping them into seemingly hand-carved formations. The entrance to The Bore, for instance, is an almost perfectly shaped minaret. Another natural wonder near Moncton is the "Magnetic Hill," which because of its unique position in a number of other hills causes one riding up the hill to imagine that he is going up backward. A large part of the population speaks French, having been descended from the early Acadians who found a place of refuge there when they were exiled from their homeland.

FREDERICTON

Fredericton, the capital of New Brunswick, is the center of the province's timber activities. Overlooking the city on its necklace of hills are the University of New Brunswick's buildings. In the city proper are quiet, elm-shaded streets, quaint churches, and a modern cathedral. At one time the city of St. Johns was the capital of the province, but in 1786 the governmental activities were shifted to Fredericton, evidently because it was not as vulnerable to attack as St. Johns, which had been a war football between the French and the English a number of times.

PRINCE EDWARD ISLAND

Since 1887 Prince Edward Island has been noted for its breeding of black foxes, farms for which abound over the island. The entire northern stretch of the island is a beach of about ninety miles in length. The water deepens only gradually, so that bathing can be enjoyed along the full length of the strand. The sea winds are deflected by a buffer of high sand dunes. Invigorated by the tangy sea air, hungered by a dip into salt water, tired by a tramp over the sun-drenched dunes, a tourist would find a dinner of Prince Edward Island lobsters or milk-fed chickens a gourmet's delight.

Courtesy Canadian National Railways

PERCE VILLAGE AND ROCK, GASPÉ PENINSULA, QUEBEC

Black Star photo

CHATEAU FRONTENAC, QUEBEC

QUEBEC

The Province of Quebec, adjoining New Brunswick, is a paradox. Along its southeastern border and the St. Lawrence River where the cities of Montreal and Quebec are located, it is the most populated and most historical portion of Canada. But stretching northward from this section is a region of wild, unexplored territory that has seldom been visited by a white man. Its virgin fastnesses, hitherto unexploited, offer opportunities and inspirations that urge Canada on to heroic achievement in future developments. Even now most of the world's supply of asbestos comes from Quebec. Hydro-electric power more than compensates for its lack of coal deposits. The St. Lawrence River, which cuts off its southeastern corner, is one of the greatest commercial waterways in the world. When the great plans for a direct route from the Atlantic Ocean are realized, the St. Lawrence River will be one of the most important links in one continuous waterway, joining Europe and the cities of Quebec and Montreal, with Detroit, Chicago, St. Louis, Memphis, New Orleans, and South America.

YESTERDAY AND TODAY

On the site of the present city of Quebec there once stood the Indian village of Stadacona. Four hundred years ago Jacques Cartier saw it nestling on the shore from his boat in the river. Were he to stand today in the same boat and look at the modern Quebec, no doubt he would cross himself piously and believe that he was witnessing a mirage or that he was imagining something that did not really exist. For the Quebec of today is a thriving metropolis, having a population of more than 130,000, living in modern homes and apartments, and working in sky-reaching, cloud-scraping buildings. Yet, in spite of its apparent modernity, Quebec has been unable to throw off its old-worldliness. Here the old and the new rub elbows and jostle together in friendly proximity. Just as the Province of Quebec is a paradox, so is its city namesake a paradox. The old city wall, which defended it from hostile tribes of Indians and whites, still remains as a reminder of stern pioneering days. The calèche, which rattled over Quebec's cobblestones in its early days, is still used as a means of conveyance. All over the old city are seen similar relics of ancient days still in use: ancient customs, ancient houses, ancient streets.

Quebec is located on the steep north side of the St. Lawrence River, on a plateau overlooking the river's confluence with the St. Charles River. "Lower Town" is on the slope, while "Upper Town" is on the plateau, crowned by a citadel, fortified walls, and ramparts, standing in almost perfect preservation. The lower part contains the old Quebec; the upper part, the newer Quebec, with wide streets and modern buildings.

Because it is situated at the conjunction of two rivers, Quebec has an extensive waterfront, deep enough to accommodate the largest ocean liners. Like most large cities it is well represented commercially. When the Ocean-to-Great Lakes waterway is completed it will be in a position to become one of the greatest ports in the world. The Quebec Bridge spanning the St. Lawrence River is an architectural wonder of the world. Ten years in the making, its main span is 1,800 feet long, while its entire length is 3,240 feet. Hotel Frontenac, built in the style of a French château, is one of the city's beauty spots. The Dufferin Terrace, a spacious promenade about 1,400 feet long, attracts many sight-seers. St. Louis Gate is reminiscent of old France, as are dozens of other historical landmarks scattered about the city, particularly in Lower Town.

"PARLEZ-VOUS ENGLISH?"

The speech of Quebec is bilingual. Conductors on the street cars call out the names of the streets in both French and English. Street signs similarly are double-tongued. When Quebecians listen to their radios, they hear the announcer give his talk in both languages. In some parts of Lower Town the inhabitants speak only French and, unless a visitor can handle the language, he does not make himself understood.

THE SHRINE OF ST. ANNE DE BEAUPRÉ

About six miles from Quebec, the waters of Montmorency Falls noisily splash and supply much of the water power for the great city. Farther on, about twenty-one miles up the river from

CHURCH OF ST. ANNE DE BEAUPRÉ, NEAR QUEBEC CITY

Black Star photo

Quebec, is located the Shrine of St. Anne de Beaupré. Every year thousands of devout Catholics make their way to this hallowed chapel, to worship at a shrine that was originally built by Breton sailors, who erected it out of thankfulness for their safe arrival in the new world, after a severe storm had threatened their lives. The chapel has been twice destroyed by fire, but each time it has been rebuilt and it still contains, in addition to church relics and gifts from the French nobility, thousands of testimonies from those who claimed to have been cured of serious ailments by the intercession of St. Anne.

MONTREAL—OLD AND NEW

Like Quebec, its sister city, Montreal is a mixture of quaint medievalisms on the one hand and modernity on the other. Only a short walk from the Château de Ramezay, the fur-trade headquarters in 1705, where Benedict Arnold lived before his unsuccessful attempt to take Quebec, stand high, storied buildings housing banks, financial organizations, and insurance companies. Seventeen miles of waterfront affords Montreal ample facilities for its shipping interests, which are the largest in Canada. Its commercial life is as varied as that of any large city. Rising from the banks of the river, it is built on a long slope which culminates in Mount Royal, on which there is a beautiful park. On the slope is the Oratory of St. Joseph, and nearby the Montreal Wax Museum, a counterpart of Madame Tussaud's in London. At the peak of Mount Royal is a cross, 132 feet high, which can be seen for miles around when it is illuminated at night.

The Montreal Botanical Garden, covering 800 acres of land, is the largest in the world. Scientifically designed and operated, it should, indeed, not be missed. McGill University and Montreal University, together with a number of other educational institutions, are housed in magnificent buildings.

OTTAWA

The Province of Ontario is notable because it contains Niagara, the city, with Canada's half of the magnificent Niagara Falls, and the city of Ottawa, the capital of the Dominion of Canada. Ottawa's chief pride is its system of parks and boulevards. Thirty-five miles of tree-shaded boulevards connect the 1500 acres of Ottawa's

Courtesy Canadian Travel Bureau, Ottawa

THE CITY OF OTTAWA FROM THE AIR

twenty-seven parks, the most beautiful of which is Rockcliffe. Rideau Driveway, paralleling the Rideau Canal, is another excellent boulevard. The Parliament buildings, housing the governmental activities of the entire Dominion, rear majestically over the Ottawa River, for which the city is named. Behind them, in similar majesty, are the Laurentian Mountains, imposing in their solidity. Bronze statues have been erected in the spacious lawns that front the edifices. Pinnacling the buildings is the Peace Tower containing the Memorial Chamber, the Altar of Sacrifice, and a fifty-three-bell carillon, a splendid tribute to the 60,000 Canadians who lost their lives in the World War.

The Victoria Memorial Museum offers ample reward for a visit by the tourist; as do Rideau Hall, where the Governor General resides, the Royal Mint, the National Gallery, the Governmental Experimental Farm and Château Laurier, another modern hostelry patterned after the French châteaux. The French-Canadian city of Hull, just across the river from Ottawa, is connected with the capital by three bridges, outlets to the famous Laurentian Mountain district. Here, following the usual Canadian scheme of natural beauties, the countryside is beautiful with splendid frothy, roaring waterfalls, and churning rivers filled with fish.

NIAGARA FALLS

Of Niagara Falls, one of the world's most magnificent wonders, so much has been said that treatment here would be needless repetition. Queen Victoria Park is a beautiful repository of flowers, and the Queen Victoria Park Drive, connecting Queenston with Fort Erie, is a seventeen-mile stretch of natural beauty. A view of the scene from Table Rock gives one a panoramic grasp of the rearing, splashing grandeur of Niagara Falls.

TORONTO—THE MEETING PLACE

As the capital of Ontario and the second largest city in the Dominion of Canada, Toronto bulks large in importance. In the

Courtesy Canadian Government Motion Picture Bureau

DOMINION HOUSES OF PARLIAMENT, OTTAWA, ONTARIO

Courtesy Canadian Travel Bureau, Ottawa

PRINCE OF WALES ARCH IN TORONTO, ONTARIO

forty-acre Queen's Park, stand the provincial legislative buildings surrounded by wide lawns. Primarily a city of homes, Toronto has its share of tall, business buildings, and includes the tallest and largest hotel in the entire British Empire. Exhibition Park, covering 350 acres of ground, is the scene of the Canadian National Exposition. Two weeks out of every year, Canadians gather here to exhibit examples of their labor, and two million visitors witness the display. The Royal Ontario Museum contains one of the world's finest collections of Chinese ceramics. Certainly the city is living up to the Indian meaning of its name, "a meeting place."

FIVE LITTLE NATURAL WONDERS

It would be negligent, indeed, for the sight-seer to travel about Ontario without visiting a series of natural wonders which have drawn the attention of the world to Canada for the past three years. About 219 miles north of Toronto, on the banks of the Nipissing Lake, a preferred vacation spot of northern Ontario, is the little town of Callander, where the Dionne Quintuplets were born and now live in a completely equipped hospital. Every year thousands of curious travelers make their way to Callander to see the five tots gambol about inside their enclosure. Callander vies with even the Canadian National exhibition in attracting visitors to Canada.

ALBERTA

The most westerly prairie province is Alberta. In its eastern and northern portions the prairies are still evident, but the land

PARLIAMENT BUILDING FROM HIGH LEVEL BRIDGE, EDMONTON, ALBERTA

becomes more rolling and in the southwestern part of Alberta includes the foothills and first mountain ranges of the great Rocky Mountain chain. Wheat and mixed farm produce are grown in the arable sections. The city of Edmonton is Alberta's capital and was originally another outpost of the Hudson's Bay Company's fur interests. On the spot where the Edmonton House, the company's trading post, was built in 1795, now stands the new Parliament building on a bluff beetling over the Saskatchewan River. All expeditions into the Mackenzie territory are outfitted here, and fur trappers use the city as a center for their selling.

CALGARY ROUNDUP

Calgary is the largest city in Alberta. Begun in 1875 as a Mounted Police fort, it is now the largest city of western Canada. The surrounding ranches bring their cattle to Calgary to be shipped to the outside world. Around the city is a chain of hills through which rush the swift mountain streams. And faintly in the distance can be seen the first lofty peaks of the Rocky Mountains, snow-capped and hazy, coning up to the heavens.

BANFF THE BEAUTIFUL

The largest national park system in the world is situated in the southwestern part of Alberta. Banff, "the queen of the Rockies," is one of the most picturesque spots that bountiful nature has bequeathed to a beauty-loving mankind. Switzerland and its Alps offer nothing more beautiful. Lake Louise, a gem, nestling at the bottom of a frame of surrounding mountain peaks, is the sight that hundreds of thousands travel thousands of miles to see. Here are available all of the attractions of modern resorts: hunting, fishing, hiking, ice skating, skiing, and swimming in an outdoor sulphur pool. Jasper Park, Waterton Lakes, and Elk Island are additional vacation spots beautified by cliffs, chasms, mountain peaks, streams, and woods. Particularly wonder-stirring is "The Valley of a Thousand Falls." Grand Fork River, cascading through valleys and canyons lined with giant cedars, comes to Mount Robson. There it makes a sudden drop of 200 feet, falling from ledge to ledge, frothing, tumbling, churning itself into a lacy curtain of white loveliness. Here Mother Nature arrays herself

National Parks of Canada photo

BEAUTIFUL LAKE LOUISE SHOWING REFLECTIONS OF THE FAMOUS VICTORIA GLACIER

in one of her most charming mantles. Maligne Lake, in Jasper Park, has sometimes been called "the most beautiful lake in the world." Surrounded by mountain giants silvered over with eternal snows, the calm waters mirror their towering neighbors placidly and benignly.

BRITISH COLUMBIA

With British Columbia, we come to the last and Pacific Coast province of the Dominion of Canada. Mountainous, full of madly rushing rivers, and heavily forested, comparatively little of the land is available for agricultural purposes. Mining is its most important industry. Fishing comes next. The rivers gleam with salmon; and in their spawning season, when they race against the stream from the ocean, leaping over rocks, flashing through the fast currents, even fighting their way up rapids and low waterfalls, it is exciting to watch the fishermen spearing them out of the rivers.

VANCOUVER

In 1887, the sight of Vancouver, now an important city in the province, was devoid of population. Now, with the advent of the railroad and with the completion of the Panama Canal, Vancouver has achieved the rank of third largest city in Canada, with a population of almost 250,000. Into its harbor sail boats from all parts of the world. Its salmon-canners furnish most of the Western Hemisphere with their product. Historically the city has little to offer. Young and vigorous, it is a new city, rapidly on its way toward commercial supremacy in Canada. Stanley Park has a notable zoo and botanical gardens. The newcomer is struck by the strange presence of quite a number of Japanese and Chinese. Practically all the domestic help is oriental. In fact, so many little yellow men have infiltrated into the section that regulations have been made to restrict their entrance into the province. Another strange impression is made by the carved totem poles, many of which can be seen in the province, especially at Kitwanga and Alert Bay, where the Indians still live.

The Yukon Territory was the most advertised part of Canada during the gold rush, in 1896. At that time, Yukon was on the lips of practically every able-bodied man on the continent; and thousands of them took the hazardous trip through the wilds of Canada, lured by the one word—gold! Dawson City became a boom town of saloons, gambling halls, and civic disorder. In time, however, the gold petered out, and with it went the prospectors. Now it is the capital city of the Yukon Territory; and, with the advent of modern hydraulic methods of placer mining, the mining of gold has once more become its chief industry. Little agriculture is possible in the Yukon. Ice-locked most of the year, with short, hot summers, the Yukon is mainly a mining, fishing, and hunting country. Mount Logan is the highest mountain peak in Canada, capping the immense plateau on which the Yukon is situated. Only once has it ever been scaled, and that, in 1925, by a party with A. H. McCarthy and H. F. Lambert as leaders.

NEWFOUNDLAND

Newfoundland was the first toe hold that Great Britain obtained in America. Ever since the waning years of the fifteenth century, when it was discovered by the British, Newfoundland has been British territory, even in spite of French domination for three centuries. It, like the maritime provinces, is a region of delight for vacationists, resplendent with nature's beauties and rich in her resources. Jutting out into the Atlantic Ocean, it was chosen as the termination of the first Atlantic cable in the Western Hemisphere, thus uniting the old world with the new. Here, too, because of its extremity, Marconi received the first trans-Atlantic wireless message, when he snared the letter "s" in Morse code, which had been sent from Cornwall, England. And again, because of its extreme eastern position in the Atlantic, Alcock and Brown hopped off from St. Johns, Newfoundland, in the first trans-Atlantic flight, to be followed later by the late Amelia Earhart when she took off from Harbor Grace, on May 20, 1932. Although it is British territory it was self-governing until recently when, owing to financial trouble, it was placed under a Royal Commission appointed by the British Parliament.

Courtesy The Victoria and Island Publicity Service

PEN SKETCH OF OLD FORT VICTORIA IN 1843
This site is now the center of the city of Victoria, Capital of British Columbia.

Courtesy The Alaska Railroad. Photo by Rolphe Dauphin.

SITKA, ALASKA, SITE OF AN OLD RUSSIAN FORT

"SEE AMERICA FIRST"

SINCE THE FIRST PILGRIMS LANDED on Plymouth Rock, there has been a moving spirit in America. There is an urge to know what is going on in the world; and this curious and inquisitive spirit has led the American to the discovery and appreciation of so many wonders within his own country, that not only has he with an honest conviction adopted for himself the slogan, "See America First," but he has convinced many world travelers to visit the unique wonders offered here. Highways, railways, and airways shorten the distance across our vast continent and promptly carry the traveler to an unlimited variety of interests and scenery, whether in Alaska, in the far northwest of the continent or in the states, stretching from the Great Lakes to the Gulf of Mexico, from the Atlantic to the Pacific.

"AMERICA THE BEAUTIFUL"

In bare, rugged grandeur the Rocky Mountains unfold their dioramic spectacles. Snow in July, great river gorges with almost perpendicular walls, petrified forests, an inland salt-water sea, rock formations in weird architectural patterns, shimmering falls and graceful geysers, the breathtaking awesomeness of the Grand Canyon—all of these wonders, and many more, feed the soul of him who for the first time beholds these stupendous works of nature. Permeating the west is the magic of the rock colorings, changing from moment to moment as the sun moves through the heavens and shifts the shadows cast by each pinnacle—yellows, oranges, reds of every hue, rich purples, and blues, from the palest grayish tints to the deepest midnight shades. In the southwest lie vast desert areas, barren of vegetation except for hardy cactus and sagebrush. Uncle Sam, concerned with the richer gifts of nature, has set aside extensive areas and maintains them as national parks. Roadways leading to these preserves have been constructed; and camping and hotel facilities have been adequately provided for those who come to see and enjoy the beauties so well protected.

Not so spectacular as the great Rocky Mountain region, but fed by its melting snows and by streams from the Appalachian ranges, the mighty Mississippi River, the Father of Waters, flows peacefully for more than two thousand miles through the very center of the United States. It waters the plains and prairies which fill the granaries of the nation. At times in seeming anger it spreads its waters in ruthless destruction.

The five Great Lakes for size rank high on the list of the world's largest inland seas. Their waters supply unlimited opportunity for industrial enterprises and for a wide variety of pleasures. On their shores from Duluth to Buffalo are places of unique interest, such as the "Soo" locks, the Straits and Island of Mackinac, Chicago, Detroit, and Cleveland; and at Niagara, the gigantic Falls plunging their powerful waters over a precipice four thousand feet wide and 167 feet high. Below Lake Ontario, in the St. Lawrence River nestle the Thousand Islands, with their picturesque scenery challenging the imagination.

"America, the Beautiful," indeed! And to travelers from the four corners of the earth she opens wide her myriad doors and welcomes them to enjoy her infinite marvels and beauties.

Courtesy Northern Pacific Railway

AN ALASKA CEMETERY
Totem poles tell the family legends, and often modern granite markers are placed alongside.

THE SPELL OF THE YUKON

OUT FROM the farthest northwest corner of the North American mainland Alaska throws its vast peninsular bulk of nearly 600,000 square miles into the seas, dividing the Pacific and Arctic Oceans, and leaving only the Bering Strait to join them. From its southern coast it throws to the southwest the volcanic chain of the Aleutian Islands; and to the southeast along the Canadian coastline, a narrow strip six hundred miles long.

Alaska, pictured by such authors as Jack London, Rex Beach, and Robert Service, is a country perpetually freezing in sub-zero weather, whose turbulent rivers churn with streams of gold nuggets, and where bearded men race dog sleds over snow-slogged mountains, fighting cold, hunger, and Indians.

THE REAL ALASKA

But Alaska is more than that. With the exception of certain sections of the deep interior, inside the coastal range of mountains, where —80° winters grip the country, Alaska enjoys what is considered a moderate climate. Although the summers are cooler than in neighboring countries, the winters in the coastal regions rarely present zero weather. This phenomenon is due to the north Pacific-Japan current, which is warm most of the year, and washing the Alaskan coasts brings warmth to the center of the Bering Sea. From there northward, Alaska is locked in Arctic ice, barren, foreboding, and swept continuously by cold, wintry windstorms.

A BARGAIN

It was the dreary picture of Alaska painted by writers that caused the world to wonder why the United States purchased the territory from Russia in 1867. Other nations apparently had no interest in that desolate wasteland, which even the sturdy Muscovites had found impossible to conquer. Bought at a cost of $7,200,000. Alaska has since produced more than $320,000,000 worth of gold, more than $127,000,000 worth of copper, and millions of dollars' worth of silver, quicksilver, salmon, furs, timber, oil, and coal; altogether producing a total of more than $1,700,000,000. Countless millions still remain to be wrenched out of the earth.

Before 1841 Alaska was a wild country occupied by only Eskimos and Indians. In that year, however, Chirikov, a Russian explorer of the Siberian tundras, accompanied by Vitus Bering, a Danish explorer in the employ of Russia, visited a number of islands in the Aleutian chain and eventually located on the Alaskan mainland. The Russians continued to explore and develop the Alaskan coast until 1867, when the United States purchased the territory, mainly because of its possible development as a fishing ground.

GOLD!

For a number of years after Alaska was purchased by the United States very little was done to warrant its acquisition. Salmon, halibut, and cod were fished out of its waters and some fur trapping was done, mainly of seals, in which the coastal islands abound. But in 1896 Alaska really began to grow into what it now is. For in that year, in the Klondike region of Canada, gold was discovered and the fact announced to a gold-

Courtesy The Alaska Railroad. Photo by Rolphe Dauphin.

"SOURDOUGH" PANNING GOLD FROM AN ALASKA STREAM

hungry world. In 1897, a month after news of the discovery of gold in the Klondike had seeped into the United States, thousands of prospectors were on their way to Alaska. Into Skagway they streamed, crossing the dreaded Chilkoot Pass in the dead of winter and mushing into the upper Yukon region. There they boarded boats and descended the Yukon to Dawson City, where the gold strike had been made. Some crossed Canada by means of the Ashcroft and Edmonton trails. Others, unwilling to dare the dangers of Chilkoot, went on to Fort Hamilton, where they booked passage on a Yukon River steamer for a 1600-mile trip through the interior to Dawson City.

With this sudden influx of people, commodity prices soared to almost fantastic figures. Many made more money importing eggs and flour than did those who went digging for gold. Others were less fortunate; one speculator chartered a steamer and filled it with eggs, only to find, on delivery, that his precious cargo had spoiled in transit.

From Dawson City, where most of the land was already staked out, and where eventually the mother lode petered out, the center of the gold fields changed to Nome in Alaska. Once more thousands jammed the boats and trails, gambling halls flourished, and vigilante committees took care of the law and disorder. Wild were the tales that came out of Alaska about the rich strikes made by prospectors, which often were gambled and drunk away overnight. Tex Rickard and Wilson Mizner were two Alaskan pioneers who made fortunes in the gold rush and who returned to the United States with tall tales of their adventures.

However, as is the case with practically all boom towns, the hundreds of mushroom cities that sprang up overnight faded away just as rapidly. The feverish excitement of the gold rush passed, and Alaska and its people settled down to a period of urban development and civic enterprise that have made Alaska a favorite of many world tourists.

A MODERN COUNTRY

Travel to and in Alaska has been considerably changed since the "sourdoughs" of the gold rush mushed perilously into Dawson City. A number of steamship companies now operate modern liners, carrying passengers and freight from Seattle and Vancouver to Anchorage and other Alaskan ports. Canadian railways carry overland passengers on regular schedules. Every year more and more amateur hunters and fishers avail themselves of the tourist travel accommodations and vacation in the Alaskan wilds, hunting big game and fighting huge game fish.

HUNTING WITH GUN AND CAMERA

Jaded with the hunting of small fry rabbits, the big game hunter can go into the Kenai Peninsular field and hunt mountain sheep and bears, giant grizzly bears, both black and brown. Moreover, Kenai is loaded with moose. The Anchorage district, Matanuska, Chickaloon, Healy, Fairbanks, and Broad Pass-Cantwell are additional hunters' paradises. In the last named, where caribou mass in their annual fall migration, thousands of cows and bulls mill around aimlessly, and occasionally, if the chief bull of the herd is aged and decrepit, fierce clashes occur between the younger bulls and their leader.

Courtesy The Alaska Railroad. Photo by Rolphe Dauphin.

FLOWER GARDEN IN SKAGWAY AT FOOT OF SNOW-CAPPED MOUNTAINS

Hunters using a camera for a gun find in Alaska an endless series of exquisite photographic materials. A number of national parks have been set aside by the government for scenic perpetuation. Mt. McKinley National Park, the second largest national park in the United States, surrounds the snow-capped majesty of Mt. McKinley, the highest mountain on the North American continent, towering to a height of 20,300 feet. Immense herds of caribou graze placidly on the low, rolling hills of the eastern section of the park. The western section is mountainous and glaciered.

More than 125 varieties of flowers grow in the confines of the park. Bird life is abundant; and grizzly bears, wolves, coyotes, moose, caribou, sheep, and fox abound, feeding at roadside watering places, seemingly unaware of the hundreds of tourists who watch and photograph them at close range.

Sitka National Monument, located in the southeastern part of Alaska, is not only scenically beautifully but contains buildings and sites of historical importance. A bloody massacre of the Russian colony by the Tlingit Indians occurred at Sitka in 1802, and graves of Russian sailors who fell in the war of 1804 are still kept green. Sixteen totem poles, relics of the aboriginal Indians, rear their grotesque, colored carvings to tree-top heights. A restoration of the old Russian blockhouse used in the Battle of Alaska is another historic building to be viewed.

VALLEY OF A THOUSAND SMOKES

In Katmai National Monument Alaska possesses a national park that covers more than a million acres. Mount Katmai, an active volcano, erupted more than three cubic miles of volcanic material in 1912. In the northwestern section of the Katmai Monument is The Valley of a Thousand Smokes, so named because in a nine-mile expanse of mountain-surrounded valley millions of miniature volcanoes, called fumaroles, emit little jets of steam continuously, caused by the volcanic action seething in the bowels of the earth beneath the valley. Katmai National Monument as yet is not quite accessible to the casual tourist; but in a few years, when the harbor of Amalik Bay is developed so that boats can enter, and when a thirty-mile automobile road is completed, it will become a favorite objective for hardy globetrotters.

Courtesy Alaska Steamship Company

JUNEAU, NESTLED AGAINST THE IMPOSING BACKGROUND OF MT. JUNEAU

Paul's Photos, Chicago

AN OUTPOST OF CIVILIZATION, THE TOWN OF CARCROSS IS LOCATED ON THE WHITE PASS AND YUKON ROUTE

THE CAPITAL CITY

Juneau, the capital city of Alaska, has an average of one sub-zero day in the year. In July, its warmest month, the temperature seldom goes higher than 57 degrees Fahrenheit. January, its coldest month, averages about 27.5 degrees. Its population of about six thousand people has access to practically all the modern conveniences of most large communities, including a baseball diamond. In a new million-dollar building are housed all of the departments of both the federal and territorial governments. The Alaska Juneau gold mine, the largest in the world, employing nine hundred men and producing twelve thousand tons of ore daily, is the pride of industrial Juneau.

THE NORTHERN METROPOLIS

The city of Nome was one of the first mushroom towns of the gold-rush days, when its inhabitants lived in tents. Although its population has decreased, because modern hydraulic mining has replaced placer mining and thus uses fewer men, it is still

Courtesy The Alaska Railroad. Photo by Rolphe Dauphin.

UNITED STATES GOVERNMENT EXPERIMENTAL STATION AT THE MATANUSKA COLONIZATION PROJECT

a thriving metropolis. It is the center of the reindeer industry. Here, too, all of the conveniences of a modern city are available, including graded schools for native Indian children. In spite of Nome's thriving modernity, its environs are still pioneer territory, and the frontier spirit persists.

HISTORICAL SHRINE

The view that greets the onlooker from the city of Sitka is one that will long remain in memory. Across the sea appear outlines of the various islands that surround it, and Mount Edgecumbe, an extinct volcano with a perfect cone atop, rears its height in solemn splendor. Behind the city, in an awe-inspiring circle, the Three Sisters, Verstovia, Cross Mountain, and the Pyramid Range fling their majestic bulk into the sky.

It was at Sitka, in 1799, that the Russians established one of their first posts, in which the inhabitants were later massacred by marauding Indians. In the halcyon days of Russian rule, when San Francisco was still a solitary mission, Sitka was furnishing bells, ships, and flour to the entire western coast of the American continent. The St. Michael's Cathedral, another relic of the Russian occupation, is still one of the city's sight-seeing stops. It was in Sitka, in 1867, that the transfer of Alaska from Russia to the United States took place.

Other large cities of Alaska include Cordova, the "Copper City"; Fairbanks, "Golden Heart"; Ketchikan, the "First City"; Petersburg, the "Industrial Center"; Skagway, the "City of Romance"; Seward, the "Central Port"; Valdez, the "Key City"; Wrangell, the "Totem City"; and Anchorage.

MATANUSKA—ALASKA OF THE FUTURE

Most of the coastal activity is centered about Anchorage. Situated in the center of the southern coast, the heart of scenic Alaska, it is the starting point of the Grand Circle Tourist Route of the Golden North. Anchorage has recently taken on added importance. With the newly instituted government colonization project in Matanuska Valley, there has been built a fine road connecting Anchorage with the project.

Here two hundred families, selected by the state relief agencies of Michigan, Minnesota, and Wisconsin, have been brought from the states to fulfill a far-reaching program of rehabilitation. All of the materials necessary for the cultivation of a modern farm have been provided by the government, with the purpose that the project will not only be self-sustaining but will in the long run prove a boon to Alaska. The Matanuska Valley Project is a symbol of the indomitable will of the American people in Alaska, fighting against the odds of perverse elements, pioneering, struggling, but inevitably triumphant.

Left: Famous Inside Passage from Seattle to Skagway, longest sheltered ocean course in the world.

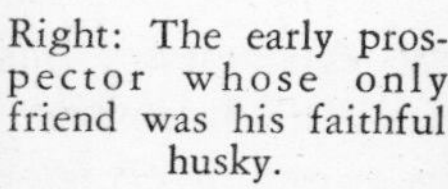

Right: The early prospector whose only friend was his faithful husky.

(Pictures Courtesy Alaska Steamship Company)

Courtesy Maine Development Commission. Photo by Robert F. Maxcy.

"THE BREAKING WAVES DASHED HIGH"
Striking view of the surf at Ogunquit, Maine.

NEW ENGLAND: EARLY AMERICAN

Forming the very northeastern tip of the United States is historic New England, a focal center of America's culture. Sea-born Massachusetts, home of clipper ships, little Rhode Island, hilly Vermont and New Hampshire, pine-clad Maine, and storied Connecticut early sowed the seeds from which sprang a great American heritage. One of our chief national traditions is the charm of New England. Its standards have become an ideal; its history, the history of a nation. Its scenery represents the rugged heart and pioneer spirit of the people. Its architectual purity and simplicity in colonial style have spread to every part of the country. Its leaders have become the nation's leaders; and this section has long been the educational center of the United States.

Every school child is familiar with the story of the landing of the Pilgrims on Plymouth Rock and the signing of the Mayflower Compact. Every American has heard tales of the first tragic winters, of friendly and hostile Indians, and of the first, fierce struggle with the mother country for what the colonists felt to be fair treatment, and of the final war for independence.

Today these six little states, proud of their history and background, venerate the deeds and perpetuate their settings. In few parts of the world can the sight-seer visit so many historic spots within so small an area.

One of the country's foremost summer and winter playgrounds, New England is as famous for her lighter moods as for her more serious aspects. Hundreds of miles of seacoast serve as a rugged front yard for the inland splendor of mountains, valleys, and lakes. Tiny villages scattered over the region have provided recreation and hospitality for the nation. Their clean white houses and steepled churches attract and satisfy the interests of an ever increasing number of visitors.

MAINE: ACADIA

Traditional paradise of sportsman and camper, Maine is the proud possessor of the only national park in the eastern part of the United States—Acadia. This, too, is the only national park in the country to include both seacoast and mountains. Extending farther north than any other state in the Union, Maine nevertheless has hardy crops. Her mineral products are varied. Mount Katahdin, Cadillac Mountain and Camden Mountains are famous summer retreats. The capital city, Augusta, is built on both sides of the Kennebec river. The State Library, located in the State House, has a valuable collection, including notable treatises by American statesmen and a rare group of Civil War battle flags.

Portland, port of entry on Casco Bay, has extensive industries, which have helped to make it the largest city in the state. With an excellent harbor, Portland is famous for her steamship-line connections.

Lewiston, situated on the Androscoggin River, just north of Portland, has a number of industries, water power for which is supplied by a fifty-foot drop of the river. This city is well over two hundred years old and has a number of interesting old landmarks in and about it.

Paul's Photos, Chicago

FERTILE VERMONT FIELDS IN WINOOSKI VALLEY, CHITTENDEN COUNTY

VERMONT: GREEN MOUNTAIN STATE

Aptly described as a "continuous natural park," the verdant charm of Vermont's famous Green Mountains surprises and delights the stranger. Over three hundred lakes and tarns dot the state-long mountain area. Thirty state parks offer the camper temporary rest and compensate for the fact that there is no seacoast for this one inland state of New England. Vermont is a friendly state. Whether the visitor chooses to make his summer home at a rustic, ivy-covered farmhouse, surrounded by a white picket fence, or at a luxurious city hotel, he is hospitably and charmingly welcomed. Satisfying to all pancake-loving Americans is Vermont's delicious maple syrup. Leading the nine maple-producing states, Vermont furnishes almost half of the country's supply.

From Ethan Allen to Calvin Coolidge, Vermont has produced personalities of notable reputation. Hardly a town in this historic little state lacks eminence. At Burlington, situated on beautiful Lake Champlain, is Ethan Allen's grave. Here also is the University of Vermont, founded in 1791 and carrying on its scholastic ideals since 1800. Great lumbering industries have been largely responsible for the city's development.

A number of important public buildings impress the sightseer and student at Montpelier, the capital of Vermont. Among these are the state capitol, the county courthouse, the public library, and the Wood Art Gallery.

At Middlebury, famous cultural center, is located the Middlebury College for Women. Rutland's natural beauty makes it a very popular resort. Marble has been quarried here for more than a hundred years. At Norwich is the oldest military school in America, excepting West Point.

NEW HAMPSHIRE: WHITE MOUNTAIN STATE

New Hampshire cities and towns as old as the colonies epitomize New England's atmosphere. There are numerous lakes, of which Winnepesaukee is the largest. The brief seacoast affords an outlet for ocean transport and offers a variety of beaches—colorful, quiet, exclusive, and popular. Called the "Granite State" for her large stone quarries, New Hampshire also holds industrial importance in the manufacture of paper, cotton materials, and shoes; as well as in agriculture.

OLD MAN OF THE MOUNTAINS

Widely known for their rugged beauty, the White Mountains rise to their greatest height, 6,293 feet, in snow-capped Mount Washington. The itinerary of every traveler is sure to lead to the Great Stone Face, the unique wonder of the New England mountains, in which nature by wind and rain has carved out in stone the features of the "Old Man of the Mountains." The state's only seaport is Portmouth. Here on an island in the harbor is located a United States naval station. Concord, the capital city, was founded under the name of Penacook in 1725. Its State House is a beautiful structure of white granite taken from the nearby quarries which furnish the city's leading industry. At Newcastle, which resembles a lovely English fishing village, is a crumbling old fort, where the first blow for American independence was struck. The State University is at Durham, one of the oldest towns in the state.

MASSACHUSETTS: THE BAY STATE

From the language of the Algonquin Indians came the name of Massachusetts, meaning "place of big hills." Its first settlers, called the Pilgrim Fathers, landed in the *Mayflower* at Plymouth in 1620. Leading the colonies through early struggles, it became one of the original thirteen states. Most of the roads now entering its borders were once Indian trails. Whether the visitor arrives by the Old Post Road or by Mohawk Trail, both now splendid highways, the best advice he can be given is to "Get lost immediately!" It is fun to browse in Massachusetts, where every curve brings the observer to an interesting old landmark.

BOSTON—HOME OF BLUE-BLOODED AMERICANS

It has been said that Boston, capital and largest city of the state, has more historical spots to the square foot than any other town in the United States. This is not hard to believe. History has been made in and around Boston for over three hundred years. Practically every stone marks the spot of some vital incident in the early history of America. Here was staged the Boston

Courtesy Boston Chamber of Commerce

PAUL REVERE'S HOUSE IN BOSTON, NOW A MUSEUM

Courtesy Boston Chamber of Commerce

OLD NORTH CHURCH (CHRIST CHURCH), BOSTON
A Lantern in the belfry of this church warned Paul Revere that British troops were marching to Lexington and Concord.

Tea Party; here one may follow the course of Paul Revere's famous ride; or one may still stand in the Old North Church, in whose tower the fateful lantern was hung. Loyal devotion has preserved the house of Paul Revere, oldest dwelling in the city, supposed to have been built about 1650. Revere bought the house some 120 years later and lived in it for thirty years. Here the visitor learns that this famous character had forty varied accomplishments to his credit. The homes of many prominent writers and religious leaders are open to the public. The Museum of Fine Arts contains some of America's greatest art treasures.

The Old State House, with its beautiful colonial staircase, exemplifies early American architecture. Faneuil Hall, called the "Cradle of Liberty," is now the scene of a bustling city market; and the old assembly hall on the second floor, once used by pre-Revolutionary patriots, is open to visitors.

Otherwise known as the Good Ship, *Constitution*, this famous old hulk floats in her last resing place, the Charlestown Navy Yard. Bunker Hill Monument, also at Charlestown, is a spot at which every true American pauses in grateful memory. Harvard University, founded in 1636, is the oldest institution of higher learning in the United States and has one of the finest libraries in the country.

COMMERCIAL AND INDUSTRIAL

In addition to holding historical, cultural, and educational prominence, Boston is the greatest wool market in the United States. It serves as New England's chief port to the sea; and ranks second in the volume of imports. Its leather goods, cotton, and rubber manufacturies find markets throughout the states.

In Old Granary Burying Ground one can locate the graves of Revere, Hancock, and many other patriots. Along the waterfront at the end of Atlantic Avenue is Copp's Hill Burying Ground. At East Boston, then called Noodle Island, Donald Mackay built his far-famed clipper ships.

Boston Common—most uncommon anywhere—was purchased from a hermit three hundred years ago by the state's governor, to be used by the Puritans as "a trayning field and for feeding cattell." The British pitched their tents here a century and a half later; in another half-century Emerson's mother pastured her cows here; and still later Oliver Wendell Holmes walked over its historic ground.

INVITING CAPE COD

Next to Boston, Cape Cod attracts the greatest number of visitors to Massachusetts. Especially does Provincetown, artistic literary colony, attract a host each summer. Marblehead, Gloucester, and New Bedford offer the sight-seer a wealth of interests and varied opportunities for relaxation.

Courtesy Boston Chamber of Commerce

PUBLIC GARDEN OF MORE THAN 25 ACRES IN THE HEART OF BOSTON

Black Star photo

CAPE COD, MASSACHUSETTS

Black Star photo
THE PILGRIM MEMORIAL, PROVINCETOWN, MASS.

WITCHCRAFT

At Salem is the House of the Seven Gables, made famous in Hawthorne's tale. Also found here are the Witches' Jail and the Dungeon, grim reminders of the witchcraft persecution in Puritan New England.

Rockport, a sea town, is fascinating with its rocks, inviting cottages, and shady lanes. Glimpses of the sea through tree-framed glades make the ocean drive around Cape Ann a beautiful experience. At Lexington one finds old taverns and historic tablets. South Sudbury is the locale of Longfellow's tales of the "Wayside Inn," and of the first "the little red schoolhouse."

"THE SHOT HEARD ROUND THE WORLD"

At Concord is the far-famed Concord Bridge. Doubly interesting is this little town; both as the first scene of the Revolutionary War and as the nineteenth-century home of such outstanding American authors as Emerson, Thoreau, Hawthorne, and the Alcotts; together with such places to see as Orchard House, Old Manse, the Milldam, Thoreau's Cairn, and the Wright Tavern.

CONNECTICUT: "NUTMEG STATE"

Land of rolling hills, where in season the dogwood and laurel bloom riotously, where rivers and lakes hold in their names echoes of their Indian past, Connecticut is the southernmost state in New England. From the low sea coast on the south, with miles of fine beaches and friendly harbors, the land gently rises to an elevation of a thousand feet at the northern boundary. The state is watered by several rivers, of which only the Thames and Connecticut are navigable for any distance. Shipping and manufactures constitute the most important industries of the state. Connecticut is temperate in climate, having less severe changes of weather than has the rest of New England. Her name, derived from the Indian word *connecticut,* means "long river."

LEADER IN EDUCATION

As early as 1650 a statute was passed requiring every community of fifty householders or more to support a school teacher. Today Connecticut's public-school system is of highest rank; and there are hundreds of private schools and excellent colleges. Yale University, founded in 1701, has from the beginning maintained one of the foremost places in higher learning. Yale "Bowl," with a seating capacity of nearly 80,000, has witnessed many an exciting spectacle. Harkness Memorial Quadrangle is admired by many visitors to New Haven each year.

For those who like to pursue the early history of the state, there is an abundance of material in the New Haven Colony Historical Society Building. In Grove Street Cemetery are buried such well-known Americans as Eli Whitney, Charles Goodyear, Noah Webster, and Roger Sherman. Lighthouse Point Park presents one of New England's most beautiful waterfronts.

Newgate Prison is at East Granby; once a copper mine, it was used during the Revolution for imprisoning Tories. At Greenwich is "Put's Hill" Monument, marking the scene of General Israel Putnam's historical ride. Hartford has preserved the former homes of many eminent men and women, such as Mark Twain, Harriet Beecher Stowe, and Charles Dudley Warner; and the old State House is visited by many tourists every summer. Hartford, noted for its fine capitol, has beautiful residential and business sections, and an unusual park system. The city is known as the insurance center of the United States.

RHODE ISLAND: "CRADLE OF SOUL LIBERTY"

Smallest state in the Union, Rhode Island is also the most densely populated state, with ninety-seven per cent of the people living in its cities. Rhode Island colony was founded by Roger Williams in 1636, as a haven for religious refugees, and was called Providence Plantation. When Rhode Island became one of the thirteen original states of the Union, Providence was made the capital. Having played an important role in the development of the nation, this New England state is rich in historic lore.

As a summer playground the beautiful shore along Narragansett Bay is unequaled. Sun-warmed beaches, mild water for bathing, and excellent fishing attract vacationists from states far and near. Manufacturing is of primary importance in Rhode Island, textiles comprising about half of the total production.

Providence, largest city in the state, became a natural center for all kinds of manufacturing. Built on seven hills, with both water and forest near, the advantageous situation early attracted shipyards, factories, and mills. Many fine old mansions, the ivy-covered walls of Brown University, and the civic center enhance the city's charm.

Pawtucket, a few miles north of Providence, was established in 1790 by one Samuel Slater, who built here the first cotton factory in the United States. From this beginning, Pawtucket became the leader in the manufacturing of other products.

NEWPORT—SOCIAL LEADER

Newport, situated in Rhode Island on Narragansett Bay, justly boasts one of the most beautiful ocean drives ever built. Here in costly estates reside many persons of prominence; and as a whole the city is one of America's most fashionable resorts.

MIDDLE ATLANTIC STATES

If one wishes to feel the strong, steady pulse of that intangible something which is American, nowhere can one feel its beat more sharply than in the Middle Atlantic area. From the District of Columbia on the south to the northernmost tip of New York, the student of early American history may revel in patriotic shrines. He may visit the cradle of American independence; and, standing on the soil of Valley Forge, Harper's Ferry, and Gettysburg, he may view with his mind's eye the scenes long ago enacted there.

To the lover of nature a continuous panorama unfolds. For sheer mountain beauty one has the Adirondacks, the Catskills, the Alleghenies, and the Cumberlands. The hospitable and delightfully rolling countryside of Maryland, Pennsylvania, and New York states brings one to the sandy level shores of the ever-moving, ever-restless Atlantic, with its blue and sparkling days and in turn its ominous, pounding, gray days.

The industrialist will center his interests in the busy cities of Pittsburgh, Philadelphia, Baltimore, and New York. And no tour is complete for any traveler in the East which does not include Washington, the city beautiful. To sit in the Senate galleries, to see the President, and to take the inevitable trip to Mount Vernon are the ambitions of every boy and girl, as well as every foot-loose grown-up.

In New York City, most of all, one feels the heartbeat of America. What variety is here! Piers, at which are docked the queens of the sea; Wall Street, long the financial center of the nation; theaters, art galleries, museums, parks, universities, picturesque foreign neighborhoods, slums, subways, tunnels, magnificent bridges, towering modern architecture—all present a perpetually changing and inspiring experience for both the newcomer and the resident New Yorker.

NEW YORK: EMPIRE STATE

On an initial tour of New York State the average visitor is surprised to find more of livestock than of stockbrokers. Familiar with the name of Herkimer County, home of the far-famed cheese, the tourist is nevertheless surprised to discover the extent of dairying in this state; likewise, the importance of fruit-growing in the Hudson Valley and of farming throughout the state. Manufacturing is, however, the chief industry, of which New York City claims credit for more than half the total production. Two Great Lakes, Ontario and Erie, form parts of the northwestern boundary of the state; and within her borders, lie some two thousand smaller lakes. At the northeast corner, dividing New York from Vermont, is Lake Champlain, forming the necessary link for continuous navigation from Quebec to New York City. Niagara Falls, the Hudson River and the Catskill and Adirondack Mountains, with their countless attractions make this state indeed a popular resort the year around. Rich in legends of the old Dutch settlements are the little towns and all the countryside of the great Hudson Valley. Typical of these is Tarrytown, whose neighborhood is the locale for Cooper's novel, *The Spy*. It is also the town described in Irving's *Sketchbook*. Irving is buried here in the old Sleepy Hollow cemetery; and many an imaginative visitor looks expectantly for a sign of the ghost of Ichabod Crane, the long, thin schoolmaster of Irving's story.

Early in the seventeenth century Henry Hudson sailed up the river which came to bear his name and opened the region to the Dutch. Manhattan Island, now the fabulously rich central borough of New York City, was purchased from the Indians in 1626 for approximately twenty-five dollars of colored beads and trinkets. Although the Indians were generally friendly to the enterprising, thrifty Dutch, there is scarcely a town in the state without its familiar tale of at least one bloody massacre in the early days of settlement.

Black Star photo. By Dr. Paul Wolff.

SKYSCRAPERS OF NEW YORK, FROM THE EMPIRE STATE BUILDING

Courtesy American Airlines, Inc.

UNUSUAL VIEW OF NIAGARA FALLS TAKEN FROM THE AIR

The New York colonists played an important part in the French and Indian Wars, the Stamp Act Congress, and the Revolutionary War. After the opening of the Erie Canal New York State gradually took the lead in manufacturing, financial enterprises, and education. Public schools offer free and compulsory education. The regents of the University of the State of New York determine the state education policy. They, however, are subordinate to the state legislature. There are hundreds of colleges and private schools, of which the best-known are Columbia, New York, and Fordham Universities, and City College at New York City; Rochester, Syracuse, and Buffalo Universities; Vassar and Wells Colleges; and, of course, the United States Military Academy at West Point.

NEW YORK CITY

The largest city in the United States, and in all the world second only to London, New York City possesses sufficient points of interest to detain the traveler for many a day. It is the most cosmopolitan city in the country and one of its oldest. Innumerable historical sites rest under the shadow of towering skyscrapers and perpetuate the lives of those whose deeds made possible the present metropolis. The general view that first greets the visitor to New York City, whether he approaches by air, land, or water, surpasses the most unrestrained imagination—the skyline, a panorama with which there is none to be compared on all the earth. Towering monsters of stone and steel rise from the solid rock of Manhattan Island. The city as a whole consists of five boroughs: *Manhattan*, composed of the islands of Manhattan, Governor's, Welfare, Randall's and Ward's; the *Bronx,* north and east of the Harlem River, between the Hudson River and Long Island Sound, including City Island, North Brother, Hart, and Riker's Islands; *Brooklyn*, the former city of Brooklyn and all of Kings County; *Queens*, the county of Queens; and *Richmond*, Staten Island.

Almost the first choice of sight-seers is the Statue of Liberty, standing on Bedloe Island in New York Harbor. From Battery Park at the extreme south end of Manhattan Island, ferries make frequent trips to the statue. A climb up the circular stairs of this colossal figure is rewarded by the marvelous view of both the harbor and the city. While at the Battery it is interesting to see the Aquarium, where specimens of fish from various parts of the world have been assembled. Following the shore up along both sides of Manhattan Island are piers, at which dock ocean liners from all parts of the world. On certain days the newest and largest boats are open for public inspection.

Only a few blocks north of the Battery is Wall Street, the financial center of the nation. The Treasury building fronted by Washington's statue is nearby. The famed East Side with its characteristic streets, such as Hester and Delancey, lends its share of life to the city. Trinity Churchyard, almost in the middle of the financial district, still holds its century-old gravestones. Near here famous Brooklyn Bridge spans the East River. And a short distance north is Chinatown, with its representative Mott and Pell streets. Farther uptown on the west side of the island is Greenwich Village, once the home of many famous artists and writers. The house in which Mark Twain once lived and where Washington Irving was a resident guest, MacDougal Alley, Minetta Fountain, the narrowest house in New York, Waverly Place (where Poe wrote *The Fall of the House of Usher*), and Grace

Black Star photo. By Victor De Palma.

SECTION OF FAMOUS TRINITY CEMETERY IN THE WALL STREET DISTRICT

Church with its lacelike spires are all within a ten minutes' walk. Washington Square, where Fifth Avenue begins, is marked by its splendid arch, which was designed for the hundredth anniversary of Washington's inauguration.

Union Square, one of New York's open forum spots, is a colorful place to visit and is flanked by commercial shops catering to those who desire cheap but good merchandise. North on Fifth Avenue, at Forty-second Street, is the New York Public Library, containing one of the most complete collections of books in all the world, as well as world-famous works of art. West on Forty-second Street is Times Square, the entertainment center, where at night enormous electric signs blink over the heads of thousands of people strolling along Broadway. The Metropolitan Opera House during the opera season presents world-renowned artists. A number of blocks north is Central Park with its beautiful little lakes and reservoir, and a menagerie. Within the park also is the great Metropolitan Museum of Art, containing finest examples of painting, sculpture, medieval armor, American furniture and other works of art, rivaling the treasures of the Louvre in Paris and the British Museum in London.

To the north along the west shore of Manhattan runs beautiful Riverside Drive, on the banks of the Hudson. Overlooking the Palisades it affords a splendid view of the river and, on a clear day, of New Jersey on the opposite side. The Drive leads by Grant's Tomb and close by Columbia University. North of Central Park is the district of Harlem, the largest Negro quarter in New York.

The subway systems in New York City enable the sight-seer to cover within a few minutes the distances between points of interest; and a ride on the subway is an experience in itself. Other places of interest include the Bronx Zoölogical Gardens and the Bronx and Brooklyn Botanical Gardens. Coney Island, world-famous as an amusement center is on the southernmost part of Long Island.

TRAFFIC

Splendid streets and boulevards for motorists, elevated railways, busses, street cars, and ferries, as well as the subway systems having over five hundred miles of track, transport the unparalleled throngs of people living in and frequenting greater New York City. Communication between the five boroughs of New York City is necessarily facilitated by a number of bridges, among which the most important are the Brooklyn, Williamsburgh, Manhattan, Queensborough, Triborough, and George Washington Bridges.

Broadway is probably known, at least in name, to more people than is any other street in the world. It is one of the longest unbroken streets in the world, running for sixteen miles through central Manhattan, from the Battery to Yonkers. Along Fifth Avenue, which runs north from Washington Square, are many smart shops, offering exclusive merchandise from every corner of the globe. Parallel to this is Park Avenue, lined with the fashionable residences of prominent New Yorkers. Visits to the tops of such skyscrapers as the Empire State and Chrysler Buildings and those of Radio City give the sight-seer a lasting impression of the greatness of metropolitan New York.

BUFFALO

Buffalo is the second-largest city in New York. It is located at the east end of Lake Erie at the head of the Niagara River, twenty miles above Niagara Falls. Buffalo is an important port in the Lakes-to-Gulf shipping route; it is one of the largest ports in the United States.

The industries in Buffalo are greatly diversified. It is an important airplane manufacturing city. It leads in the production of analine, rubber products, flour, and meat products. It is also important in the manufacture of iron, steel, and copper. Lake ships bring Buffalo raw materials to be processed. Hydroelectric power from Niagara Falls is its chief source of power and largely responsible for its industrial growth. Buffalo has an extensive park system. There are many buildings and monuments of interest for the visitor to see.

ROCHESTER

Rochester is the county seat of Monroe County, New York, on the Genesee River and connected with the state barge canal. It lies in the midst of the most fertile truck garden sections in the entire country. The Genesee Gorge is perhaps, the loveliest of all spots in the city; its two sparkling waterfalls are in the very heart of Rochester. An important commercial and industrial center, the city manufactures machinery, wearing apparel, and photographic and optical supplies, foundry and machine shop products, boots and shoes, canned goods, nursery products, and office supplies.

Here are the University of Rochester, Nazareth College for Women, a Baptist theological seminary, a school of optometry, the Eastman School of Music and the Eastman Theater, and the Rochester Athenaeum and Mechanics' Institute.

SYRACUSE

Syracuse developed as a result of the discovery of salt in that region and the building of the Erie and Oswego canals. It is located about midway between Buffalo and Albany. Because of its large salt interests it is known as Salina City, and because of its geographical situation in the state as Central City. Important industries are the manufacture of salt products, iron furnaces, agricultural implements, and automobiles. There are six large parks and many small parks and playgrounds throughout the city. Located here is Syracuse University.

ALBANY

Albany is the capital city of New York. It is an important center of transportation because it is situated on the Hudson River, the Erie and Champlain Canals, and several important railroads. It has also the advantage of being located about 150 miles north of New York City. Its manufactures are stoves, shoes, auto accessories, and paper products.

Albany is one of the very oldest settlements in the United States. There were a few very early attempts at settlement, but the real settlement of it dates from the arrival of Walloon families who, in 1624, established Fort Orange. Albany has since that time been a center of political activity. There are many interesting buildings to visit when in Albany; amongst them are the State Capitol, State Normal School, State Arsenal, the old State House, Medical College, and the old Schuyler House.

OTHER CITIES

Jamestown is located at the foot of Lake Chautauqua. It has a population of about 45,155. Jamestown is especially noted for its manufacture of wood and metal furniture, also of textiles, paints, automobile parts, and washing machines.

Oyster Bay, situated on the north shore of Long Island, has great oyster fisheries, but it is more famous as a residential suburb of New York City. The tomb of Theodore Roosevelt is in Young's Memorial Cemetery. The Theodore Roosevelt estate, Sagamore Hill, is here in Oyster Bay.

Lockport, with a population of 23,160, is located at the locks of the Erie Canal. This city was situated here before the canal was opened. The sixty-foot fall in the canal provides the necessary water-power for its industries of paper, textile, and cotton batting mills, and iron foundries. The city is surrounded by a beautiful fruit-growing section.

Ithaca, at the south end of Cayuga Lake, is one of the most interesting American cities. It has a population of (1930) 20,708. It is justly famous for Cornell University, often called the most beautiful college campus in the country. Three creeks have cut deep gorges within the city limits, where waterfalls, cascades, and rapids play in resplendent abandon. Coal and dairy products are shipped from Ithaca. Salt products, electric clocks, and advertising signs are made in her own factories.

Corning, with a population of 15,777, is located near the junction of the Chemung and Cohocton Rivers. It is called the "Crystal City" because it is important in the manufacture of glass. Montauk Village is a shipping point of great quantities of seafood. A lighthouse, life-saving station, and a summer resort are located here.

NEW JERSEY: GARDEN STATE

New Jersey is a composite of enterprising cities, seaside resorts, cranberry bogs, snow-white doorsteps on red-brick farmhouses, and gemlike lakes in the woods, and prairies.

Each year some fifteen million vacationists trek across the state to Atlantic City, to stroll up and down the colorful boardwalk with its thousands of attractions and beautiful pier. Each year this resort draws the attention of the country to its playground activities with the traditional bathing beauty contest to find "Miss America."

Courtesy City Press Headquarters, Atlantic City. Photo by Fred Hess & Son.

ATLANTIC CITY SKYLINE AND BEACH

Courtesy Princeton University. Photo by Fairchild Aerial Surveys.

THE UNIVERSITY STADIUM AT PRINCETON, NEW JERSEY

Newark is the largest and most important city in New Jersey, a port of entry in the state, and one of the most outstanding manufacturing cities in the world. Highways, constructed to meet the inevitable congestion of such an area, are the finest and most up to date. Newark Airport Center is the nation's leader in airway travel lines. Museums, parks, a well-equipped public library, colleges, and a charming residential section with lovely drives winding through its spacious boulevards, enhance the city.

Jersey City is another great industrial center in the state of New Jersey. The largest practical clock in the world, the dial measuring 38 feet in diameter and the minute hand weighing almost a third of a ton, is located on top of one of the factories here. Paterson, where the first Colt revolver was made, where the first American silk mill was established, and where Alexander Hamilton hoped to use a seventy-foot cataract for water-power a century and a half ago, is the site of America's largest aeronautical plant.

Trenton, New Jersey's capital since 1790, was founded by a Quaker who erected a grist mill on the site. The town was proposed as the seat of federal government and was thus used by the Continental Congress. Trenton is replete with historic relics and old, old buildings. Three miles out of the city is a quaint Quaker village.

Princeton is the seat of Princeton University, which was founded nearly two centuries ago. Camden is a shipbuilding and radio-manufacturing center. At Elizabeth one may see the largest sewing-machine factory in the country; also the old Boudinet Mansion, and a number of historical landmarks.

DELAWARE: BLUE HEN STATE

Delaware's nickname came out of a Revolutionary War legend that no cock would fight unless its mother was a blue hen. The state's real name of Delaware was taken from that of Lord De la Warr, who, according to records handed down, shortly after 1600 entered the bay that bears his name. First settled by the Dutch, Delaware was later sold to the Swedes colonizing the region, and its ownership was changed a number of times before 1776.

One of the smallest states in the Union, Delaware nevertheless annually attracts thousands of visitors. At Wilmington chemicals are extensively manufactured, ships are built, and trade for the near-lying agricultural section is carried on. The city offers an imposing list of interesting places for tourists to see. The estate of Pierre du Pont, called Longwood Gardens, is located here. Dover, capital city of the state since 1777, was laid out by order of William Penn. It contains many colonial homes and buildings.

MARYLAND: OLD LINE STATE

Captain John Smith, whose name history links with Pocahontas, was the first white man who, with his little band, laid eyes on what is now Maryland. Then began a romantic and lively history in this little territory. Fort Henry, which inspired Francis Scott Key to write the "Star Spangled Banner" in 1814, still stands on a promontory jutting out into Baltimore Harbor. There the first monument was erected to honor George Washington. In the old Presbyterian graveyard is a literary shrine for poetry lovers the world over—the grave of Edgar Allan Poe, who died in Baltimore in 1849.

Courtesy Baltimore Association of Commerce
MT. VERNON PLACE WITH THE FIRST WASHINGTON MONUMENT, BALTIMORE, MARYLAND

COLONIAL "ATHENS"

Early recognized as an unusual center of culture and society, the beautiful old city of Annapolis has lost none of its charm today. It has been the capital of Maryland since 1649. There are many lovely old colonial buildings still in excellent repair. The town is most famous, of course, for the United States Naval Academy located here. Midshipmen in colorful uniforms create an atmosphere duplicated nowhere else.

Other things to be seen in Maryland include the world-renowned Johns Hopkins University and Hospital, Antietam Battlefield, National Military Park, and Conowingo Dam in the Susquehanna River.

PENNSYLVANIA: KEYSTONE STATE

Called "The Keystone" because of its position among the original thirteen states, Pennsylvania is one of the largest and most important Atlantic states. Familiar to every American is the origin of Pennsylvania's name, "Penn," in honor of the founder's father, Admiral Penn, and "sylvania," meaning woodlands.

COAL AND STEEL

The representative Pennsylvanian might well be pictured as a huge, dauntless, soot-blackened coal-miner or a hefty, sweating steel-worker. Pennsylvania owns the only extensive anthracite coal fields in the country and extremely rich bituminous deposits. Reverberations of the mighty iron and steel industries of the state are heard throughout the world. The tourist knowing these facts is pleasantly surprised to discover the great natural beauty of the state, which lies untouched by industry's "grimy hands."

SIGHTS GALORE

Steeped in a thousand tales of the country's early history, Pennsylvania is a delight to the story-minded traveler. Not only does he find excellent roads built over the most scenic routes, but

AERIAL VIEW OF HORSESHOE CURVE NEAR ALTOONA IN THE ALLEGHENIES

Courtesy Pennsylvania Railroad

PHILADELPHIA'S IMPRESSIVE SKYLINE
Looking from the Art Museum down the famous Parkway which leads from Fairmount Park, one of the largest municipal parks in the world, to the heart of the city.

also countless markers along these roads pointing out the things to see. There are days and weeks of pleasure to be found in this mighty state. Dozens of cities, each with distinct character and unique landmarks, vie with each other for the visitor's attention. Beautiful highways lead to national and state parks and memorials, and to many quaint spots of legendary interest.

QUAKER TOWN

Foremost of Pennsylvania's cities is Philadelphia, whose historic importance is perpetuated in many forms. It is an important American port, and is also one of the leading industrial cities of the world. The city holds an enviable reputation as a center of education, science, and the arts. Among the higher institutions of learning are the University of Pennsylvania and Temple University, the Pennsylvania Academy of Fine Arts, Drexel Institute, and Girard College. The Public Library, the Franklin Institute, and the State Historical Society offer the visitor ample reward for time spent in seeing their valuable collections.

Unsurpassed in historical background, the city furnishes an extensive field of study for enthusiasts of American history. Independence Square, Carpenter Hall, Betsy Ross House, the Liberty Bell in Independence Hall, Christ Church, Congress Hall, William Penn's House, and Old Swedes Church are but a few of the subjects that can be profitably and enjoyably studied in and around Philadelphia.

Nearby Valley Forge and Gettysburg, scenes of action in the Revolutionary War and the Civil War, respectively, are now beautiful parks, honoring the memory of the men who made history there. Washington Crossing State Park on the west bank of the Delaware commemorates Washington's famous Christmas Eve crossing of the icy river. Beautiful lakes among mountains of rocky grandeur throughout the western part of the state dot this varied vacation land.

SMOKE-BLACKENED STEEL CENTER

Once a colonial outpost of civilization, Pittsburgh ranks as the second city of the state, a great steel center, and an important river port. Famous for its smoke-blackened buildings in its early manufacturing days, Pittsburgh nevertheless has many beautiful sections. Carnegie Institute in Schenley Park, which holds a high rank among higher schools for technical training, Pittsburgh University, the modern Civic Center, the Historical Society's Museum, and the Zoölogical Gardens, should all be allotted a generous amount of time by the sight-seer. Unusual treats for the city's guests are a ride on the inclined planes, a view of the mighty city from Mount Washington Roadway, and a trip over Liberty Bridge and through Liberty Tubes.

NETWORK OF THRIVING CITIES

Scranton, third-largest city in the state, is the center of the American anthracite coal region. A model coal mine here is open to the public. The city is rich in sights that are interesting historically, culturally, and industrially. Reading is also vitally important in Pennsylvania's industrial output and has led in iron production for nearly a century.

On the picturesque banks of the Susquehanna River is the state's capital. The State Building is magnificent. East of the city is Indian Echo cave, affording an hour of fascinating surprises for the stranger. Hershey is a thriving industrial community. Co-

WASHINGTON: THE CAPITOL DOME AT NIGHT

Black Star photo. By Fritz Henle

lumbia centers an important tobacco section. Johnstown, now a steel center, is remembered as the scene of the disastrous flood of 1889. The old Quaker Meeting House at York makes its historic contribution.

DISTRICT OF COLUMBIA

WASHINGTON: THE NATION'S CAPITAL!

Belonging neither to the north nor to the south, the east nor the west—to every state and yet to no one state—thus was Washington, seat of the federal government, planned and established. Unique among world cities for its marble beauty, distinguished for its perfection of arrangement as a national capital, Washington may well be the pride and joy of every American.

Standing on Capitol Hill, approximately in the center of the city, is the Capitol itself. Its stately columns, massive dome, and broad grounds are a fitting site for the center of the national government. In the magnificent rotunda and Statuary Hall will be found many beautiful works of art. Here are the work chambers of the two powerful legislative bodies—the Senate and the House of Representatives.

THE WHITE HOUSE

The Executive Mansion is the Washington residence of the President of the United States. It was first occupied by President John Adams. It was burned by the British in 1814. During the restoration of the building, the stone was painted white to hide the marks of fire; hence, the popular name, "The White House." Part of the building is open to the public on week days, and thousands of tourists each year take advantage of the privilege of seeing it.

FOUR MILLION BOOKS

East of the Capitol is the Library of Congress, largest and most beautiful library building in the world. Four million books, besides many large collections of art and valuable manuscripts, are housed within its walls. Among the more important buildings of

THE LIBRARY OF CONGRESS VIEWED FROM THE CAPITOL

beautiful architecture are the Treasury, the Pan-American Building, the Smithsonian Institution, the New National Museum, the Freer Art Gallery, the Lincoln Memorial, the Supreme Court Building, and all of the new government buildings in what is known as the Triangle.

CHERRY BLOSSOMS EVERY SPRING

Americans should be indeed grateful to L'Enfant and Ellicott and the other far-seeing men, who not only planned the general pattern of the city, but created the lovely landscape as a background for the white marble of its buildings. The city's parks and driveways are unusually well laid out. Particularly beautiful is the Mall, sloping away from the Capitol to the grounds of the Washington Monument, and to the Lincoln Memorial. On the south slope of these monument grounds is the Sylvan Theater, a large outdoor stage where summer concerts, light opera, and interpretive dancing is presented. Encircling the Tidal Basin, an inlet of the Potomac River, are hundreds of Japanese cherry trees which become every spring a fairyland of pink and white, attracting thousands of visitors.

On the high slopes across the Potomac, reached by the new Arlington Memorial Bridge, are Arlington Cemetery and the great white marble Tomb of the Unknown Soldier. A military guard always on duty before the tomb, preserves the dignity of this simple but impressive monument to the heroes of the World War.

Six miles south of Washington is the historic old town of Alexandria, Virginia. Here George Washington and his family attended old Christ Church, which is still in use. In its graveyard are tombstones gray with age, which bear their tribute to the dead.

NORTH CENTRAL STATES

GREAT LAKES REGION

One of the geographical curiosities of the world is the chain of five Great Lakes, four of them forming part of the international boundary between the United States and Canada. These lakes—Superior, Michigan, Huron, Erie, and Ontario—have a combined length of nearly thirteen hundred miles.

Courtesy Cleveland Convention & Visitors' Bureau

ORE UNLOADERS IN CLEVELAND, OHIO

Their value is not measurable. Surely the history of the United States would have been much different without them. Six of the seven states in the North Central region border the Great Lakes. All six may attribute their tremendous industrial development and extensive wealth to their commercially strategic positions.

In addition, the Great Lakes form one of the nation's most popular and most enjoyable playgrounds. Scenically beautiful and ideally extended over the central and eastern portions of the United States, the five lakes afford fun and recreation for Americans the year around.

FATHER OF WATERS

Likewise in this North Central group is found the source of America's mightiest of rivers, the Mississippi. Navigable for thousands of miles soon after it finds its beginning in tiny Lake Itasca, Minnesota, the Mississippi has been a dominant factor in the history of the United States. For a long time this almost straight line was the western edge of American civilization. It forms the boundary line for the states lying on either side. A fascinating story could be written of the nineteenth-century history of this old "Father of Waters," as the Indians called it. Crossings of weary exploring parties, boundary disputes, Indian canoes replaced by river barges, the first steamboats, showboat entertainment, slave trade, and other stages of its history too numerous to mention here, make the Mississippi an integral part of American history.

OHIO: BUCKEYE STATE

The state of Ohio took its name from the Iroquois name for its chief river. Rugged hills and swamps in the south and southeast give way to broad prairies and plains in the north. The frontage on Lake Erie, extending for more than two hundred miles, has furnished the state with fifteen valuable ports; in addition, there are five hundred miles of navigable rivers.

Marietta, the oldest permanent settlement in Ohio, was established in 1788 at the mouth of the Muskingum River. Cincinnati was settled the next year. Ohio, like Indiana, was the scene of many of Mad Anthony Wayne's exploits with the Indians.

Manufacturing industries far outweigh the agricultural interests of the state, important as they are. Ohio is a state of large commercially-minded cities—Cleveland, Cincinnati, Toledo, Columbus, Akron, and Dayton, to list a few in order of their respective sizes. No matter what road the tourist takes, he is bound to come upon several booming, hustling business centers. He will find, too, at almost every turn of the road, famous old landmarks, historical buildings, and scenes of stirring early combats.

OHIO'S COMMERCIAL BEEHIVES

First among Ohio cities is Cleveland, the home of the Great Lakes Exposition in 1936 and 1937. Its history dates back to 1796, when it was a trading base at the mouth of the Cuyahoga River. With one of the largest and busiest airports in the world, and the Union Terminal Tower Building, often called a city in itself because of its tremendous capacity, Cleveland ranks among the leading cities of the United States. Educational leadership is evidenced in public schools of the highest standard, a number of private schools, Western Reserve University, Case School of Applied Science, and the Cleveland School of Art. The Museums of Art and of Natural History have valuable collections, which merit prolonged visits. The Cleveland Symphony Orchestra, one of few to have a permanent home, is given high rank by music critics.

Courtesy Cincinnati Chamber of Commerce. Photo by Longley.

CINCINNATI'S IMPOSING SKYLINE

Cincinnati, called by Longfellow the "Queen City of the West," is one of the most attractive large cities in the country. Now a hundred and fifty years old, Cincinnati ranks among art and cultural centers of the nation as a leader. The Conservatory of Music, College of Music, Art Academy, and the Cincinnati Symphony Orchestra are largely responsible for this reputation. The Zoölogical Gardens and Eden Park should not be missed by any visitor.

Located on the harbor of the Maumee River, Toledo, like Cleveland, is also on Lake Erie's shoreline. This city boasts more than a thousand manufacturing companies, and the importance of its industrial wheels is challenged only by the tremendous tonnage of iron and coal passing through its docks. Probably its proudest possession is the well-known Museum of Art. From Toledo one drives into the Maumee Valley to see several beautiful state parks.

Near the geographical center of Ohio is the capital city, Columbus. Important as to both commerce and immigration, Columbus has been a silent witness to the long trek westward during the past century. Here is located Ohio State University.

Akron, making thirty thousand varieties of rubber articles, has been called the rubber city. The airship factory here welcomes visitors, as do the manufacturers of tires. The city of Dayton is called "The Cradle of Aviation" because the Wright brothers, airplane inventors, got their start in this, their home town. The original laboratory of these men is on display here. Chief among Dayton's manufactures, of which there are eight hundred varieties, is the cash register. Zoar was settled in 1817 by a group of Separatists, who had been disbanded in Germany and emigrated to the United States. They were called Bimmelers, from the name of their leader, Joseph Bimmeler. At Kirtland stands the original Mormon church, which was built in 1831 as the headquarters of the religious body.

INDIANA: HOOSIER STATE

For five decades the center of population of the United States has been in Indiana, gradually moving westward. It is interesting that this region of such diversified terrain, with its shifting sands along white-beached shores on Lake Michigan, its fragrant fruit

Courtesy Elkhart Chamber of Commerce

GREENLEAF BOULEVARD ALONG THE ST. JOSEPH RIVER, ELKHART, INDIANA

lands, rolling prairies, forests and plains, rivers and lakes, fantastic dunes, and miles of underground passage, should for so long be distinguished as the population center of the nation.

"MAD ANTHONY," AN EARLY FIGURE

The first white men to visit Indiana's prairies were probably the Jesuit missionaries. Although a trading post was in existence in 1672, not until early in the next century was the first permanent settlement made at Vincennes. The first American settlement known to have been made was at Clarksville in 1784. Indian wars, following the Revolutionary War, were the occasion for the daring exploits of "Mad Anthony" Wayne in this region.

RICH IN "THINGS TO SEE"

Besides the state's lovely lake-shore parks, state preserves, wonderful caves, and towns rich in Indian lore and relics, Indiana has scattered over her wide area hundreds of interesting places to visit. Among these are the Indian mounds at Anderson, the birthplace of James Whitcomb Riley at Greenfield, circus winter quarters at Peru, old buildings in Vincennes, one of the largest electrical engineering schools in the world at Purdue University in Lafayette, the Seven Dolors Shrine maintained by the Franciscan Order southeast of Gary, and the largest broad-leaved tree in the United States at Worthington.

HOOSIER CITIES

The capital city of the Hoosiers is Indianapolis. Some of the state's finest architectural work is found here. The State Capitol is a splendid example of Corinthian style, and took ten years to complete. The Plaza of the Indiana World War Memorial occupies five city blocks, and the Soldiers' and Sailors' Memorial is the classic center of this interesting group. The city is famous, of course, for its great speedway.

Within fifty miles of Fort Wayne, second city of Indiana, are about a hundred lovely lakes and nearly as many summer resorts. The city is an interesting center for these resorts.

Notre Dame, the largest Catholic school for boys and men in America, is located in South Bend, which began about a century ago as a little trading post. Primarily a manufacturing town, nevertheless this little city has thirty-four parks and a number of historical landmarks to interest the visitor.

Courtesy Indianapolis Chamber of Commerce

THE SCOTTISH RITE CATHEDRAL, INDIANAPOLIS

ILLINOIS

Beautifully expressive of scenic Illinois are the poetic words of her state song, "By thy rivers gently flowing, Illinois, Illinois." What a picture land lies between the Wabash and the Mississippi Rivers and between Lake Michigan and the Ohio River! Hills, woodlands, streams, cliffs, prairies, and lakes are sprinkled generously throughout the state. Her fine roads, too, lead to many historic shrines, among which are those associated with Abraham Lincoln in Springfield and Ulysses S. Grant in Galena.

STARVED ROCK

Most spectacular of Illinois's state parks is Starved Rock. Here Indian legends abound. Rock formations bear weird names. The

Courtesy J. Ray Beffel, Ottawa, Ill.

WHERE MANY INDIANS DIED
Starved Rock, on the Illinois River. The Illinois Indians, trapped here by a hostile tribe, died of starvation.

beautiful Illinois River, meandering between rock-covered slopes, is one of the most scenic and picturesque paths imaginable for the little excursion steamer which winds its way up and down the stream. Here nine hundred acres of primitive woodland stretch into a popular summer playground.

Tourists and natives of Illinois alike will find it interesting to visit the only tract of White Pine in Illinois at Pines State Park; Mooseheart, "City of Children"; the Lincoln relics at Mattoon; site of the early Mormon settlement at Nauvoo; and the old State Capitol Building at Vandalia.

WINDY CITY

Outstanding of all Illinois's attractions is, of course, Chicago, the "Windy City." Geographically restricted to a long narrow strip skirting the southwestern corner of Lake Michigan, Chicago reaches to the far corners of the earth economically, industrially, and culturally.

Her tremendous booming industries are headed by the stockyards and meat-packing center. Her "Loop" shopping center is one of the greatest retail markets in the world. Among her better-known buildings, some of them young cities in themselves, are the Merchandise Mart, housing twenty thousand persons at one time; the Furniture Mart; Marshall Field's; the Stevens Hotel; the majestic Tribune Tower; the Wrigley Building; the Daily News Building; and the Civic Opera Building.

LEIF ERICKSON DRIVE

Only recently completed, this beautiful drive along the greater extent of the lake shore of the city has been constructed and landscaped on "made", or filled-in, land almost entirely. Capable of handling tremendous burdens of traffic smoothly and speedily, the Outer Drive is a great boon to Chicagoans and a delight to the city's guests.

Miles of beautiful parks, forest preserves, beaches, and numerous city playgrounds make Chicago a true summer resort. The

Courtesy Illinois Chamber of Commerce

CHICAGO'S MAGNIFICENT MICHIGAN AVENUE

Field Museum, Adler Planetarium, Shedd Aquarium, Museum of Science and Industry, and the Art Institute include a wealth of research material and valuable art and scientific collections.

Early faced with the problem of sanitation in such a concentrated and crowded area, Chicago solved that problem by constructing the Chicago Drainage Canal, so as to reverse the direction of flow of the Chicago River. Instead of flowing out into the lake to contaminate water used for Chicago's drinking supply, the river now flows in the opposite direction, carrying the city's sewage and emptying finally into the Des Plaines and Illinois Rivers. Changing the course of this river is considered a remarkable engineering feat.

Beautiful suburban areas, separately incorporated, surround the city. The famous North Shore, comprised of a number of small and exclusive villages and towns, boasts many palatial estates and a wooded section with unusual mansions, the like of which can be found in few other places in the world.

Two of the country's greatest universities and several smaller colleges and private schools are located here. The rich Gothic beauty and dignity of its gray stone buildings make the University of Chicago campus outstandingly impressive. To the north, in suburban Evanston, lies the romantically casual Northwestern campus with its shaded walks, bordering the sandy beaches of blue Lake Michigan. Both universities have "downtown campuses," with large enrollments of part-time students from the business and teaching worlds.

Springfield, the capital of the state, is situated in the midst of a vast prairie and one of the greatest corn-producing areas in the world. Here Abraham Lincoln practiced law in his early

FIELD MUSEUM OF NATURAL HISTORY, CHICAGO

Photo by Raeburn Rohrbach

SHEDD AQUARIUM, CHICAGO

manhood and made his home at the time of his election as President of the United States. Every year many persons travel to Springfield purposely to visit his former home and his stately tomb.

One of the state's important manufacturing cities is Peoria, located halfway between Chicago and St. Louis. In the southern part of the state, at the junction of the Mississippi and Ohio Rivers, is Cairo, a small city in the section of the state known as "Little Egypt." Protected from annual floods by a system of levees on both rivers, Cairo is surrounded on three sides by water. During the Civil War it was from here that General Grant led his first troops to victory. The second industrial city in Illinois is Rockford, now over a hundred years old. It has beautiful homes and a fine park system. At Elgin is the great watch and clock manufacturing company.

MICHIGAN: WOLVERINE STATE

Taking its name from the Indian's word for Lake Michigan, "big sea," Michigan has an extraordinary mileage of lake shore, in fact, is largely surrounded by water. The state is divided into two peninsulas by the Strait of Mackinac. A perfect vacationland, Michigan offers mountains and forests to her northern guests and rolling prairies interspersed with marshy lowland in the southern regions.

Courtesy The Detroit Institute of Arts

SYMBOLIC OF THE AUTOMOBILE INDUSTRY—ONE OF THE NOTED RIVERA MURALS IN THE DETROIT INSTITUTE OF ARTS

AUTO CENTER

Most famous for its great automobile industry, Michigan has lent the names of her former tribes of red men, their leaders, and the early pioneers to the many types of streamlined motor cars speeding over the highways. For example, there is Pontiac, chief of the Ottawas; Marquette, the French explorer; Cadillac, who founded Detroit; and LaSalle, who built a fort at the mouth of the St. Joseph. All these and more have become immortalized by Michigan's car industry.

Being on a main route from the East to the West, Detroit is visited annually by many hundreds of people. It is the largest of Michigan's cities. Belle Isle, incomparable city park, covers over seven hundred acres. With sixteen miles of river frontage, a beautiful residential section, and imposing public buildings, Detroit has much to attract the traveler, the business man, and the prospective resident. Its importance is increased by its position as a port of entry from Canada. In nearby Dearborn is an airport and one of the largest automobile factories. From Detroit leads the famous Pontiac Trail of Indian History winding up to Mackinaw City.

Grand Rapids, Flint, Saginaw, and Lansing, the state capital, have expanded tremendously in the last several decades, due to their great commercial and industrial activities. Michigan's large cities are her pride.

Among the spots most worth visiting in the lower peninsula are the Kellogg Bird Sanctuary at Wintergreen Lake; the University of Michigan at Ann Arbor, with its beautiful campus; the House of David colony at Benton Harbor; Saugatuck art colony; Interlochen, site of the National High School Orchestra Camp; and Battle Creek, the "pure food" city.

LAND OF PAUL BUNYAN

Eleven hundred miles of shore line along the Great Lakes, more than a thousand lakes inland, and dense forests everywhere,

Courtesy Jackson Board of Commerce

WORLD-FAMOUS ILLUMINATED CASCADES AT JACKSON, MICHIGAN

are found in the upper peninsula. This is the region where the famous Paul Bunyan Camp in Blaney Park is located. Moose herds are supported on Isle Royale. Twelve state parks beautify the landscape and make camping easier for the tourist. Near Amasa is the only dude ranch found east of the Mississippi. More important than these things, however, are the copper and iron mines of the region and the heavy lake shipping which passes in a steady stream through the government locks at Sault Ste. Marie throughout the open season.

This state is unusual in its number of areas set aside for recreation and fishing. State parks number sixty-five; state forests, twelve; and national forests, four. Fine highways penetrate into the forest areas. Camping and picnicking sites are plentiful. Public hunting and fishing grounds are generously scattered. The visitor finds a never-ending joy in Michigan's playgrounds, whether on the shore or inland.

WISCONSIN: BADGER STATE

Wisconsin is famous for her thousands of glacial lakes, providing beauty spots for city-weary eyes and minds, for the rich cheeses made on her dairy lands, and for the clouds of cherry blossoms in Door County each spring. Near Madison, capital of the state and home of the state university, are countless Indian mounds which delight the experienced eye of the anthropologist.

HAUNT OF THE GREAT SPIRIT MANITOU

As rich, if not richer, than any state in the Union in Indian lore, Wisconsin parks, forests, and reservations commemorate the age of the red man in the thousands of colorful names by which they are known. As popular for its excellent fishing in the country resorts as for its excellent beer in the city gathering places, Wisconsin presents to both its natives and its guests the utmost in good living.

Milwaukee has the distinction of being not only the greatest city of Wisconsin, but the twelfth most populous city in the country. And yet, a little less than two hundred years ago the territory in which the metropolitan area now stands was an Indian council ground. Its mighty list of industries are indicative of its financial leadership; its art galleries, museums, conservator-

Courtesy Milwaukee Association of Commerce

BEAUTIFULLY PARKED SECTION OF WISCONSIN AVENUE, MILWAUKEE, WISCONSIN

ies, and theaters are a strong reminder of its cultural importance in the Middle West. Milwaukee has likewise many scenic woodlands and ravines in her fine park system.

Madison, fair capital of Wisconsin, is enhanced by four charming lakes which surround the city. Her State Capitol with its splendid collection of Indian relics, her large and important university, and her resort facilities bring many visitors to the city each summer.

Racine, second largest city of the state, has discovered the presence of a prehistoric earthwork which has excited considerable interest. The city is primarily a manufacturing center.

Kenosha is a thriving industrial center. Superior is a shipping metropolis, whose large harbor accepts the largest lake boats with room to spare. Giant grain elevators are located here. The city connects with Duluth, Minnesota, by a gigantic new toll bridge.

From the bluffs of LaCrosse one gets a never-to-be-forgotten panoramic view of the winding Mississippi below. Oddly enough this region shows no traces of the glacial action which swept so completely over the rest of Wisconsin. Sheboygan is well known for the mineral water bottled and shipped from her artesian springs. The city is a most strategic shipping center. Green Bay is the center of a popular resort country. It has a museum holding a large and valuable collection of relics. Oshkosh, known to most small American boys as the place where their overalls come from, is one of Wisconsin's leading manufacturing cities.

MINNESOTA: LAND OF TEN THOUSAND LAKES

A never-ending, circuitous chain of blue-water lakes, vast tractless virgin timber, and some of the loveliest natural settings in the world draw large crowds to Minnesota each summer. Particularly is it a paradise for campers and fishermen who love to rough it. Meanwhile, Minnesota grows a large share of the

Courtesy Duluth Chamber of Commerce

DULUTH AND ITS HARBOR, SHOWING UNIQUE AERIAL LIFT BRIDGE, LEFT BACKGROUND

Paul's Photos, Chicago

DUCKS, BEWARE!
Minnesota's lakes are a paradise for hunters.

country's wheat, mines tremendous quantities of iron ore from open pits on the great Mesabi Range to the north, and manufactures countless forest products from the vast timber resources in the state.

The famous twin cities of the northwest, Minneapolis and St. Paul, offer a wide variety of entertainment. Six beautiful lakes within the city of Minneapolis provide an exquisite frame the year around for unusually beautiful residential sections. The great flour mills here are supplied with power from the Falls of St. Anthony. Longfellow's *Hiawatha* immortalizes the cascading Minnehaha Falls here. At St. Paul is the State Capitol, set on an elevation above the surrounding city. The Twin Cities have enough places of interest to keep a tourist busy for days.

PAUL BUNYAN'S PLAYGROUND

America's only legendary hero, Paul Bunyan, is hero of the great northern section of Minnesota used as a playground each summer. Here the motorist finds Duluth, strangely set against the steep bluffs rising almost sharply from the shipping docks on the Lake Superior shores below. Gateway to the vacationland to the north, Duluth, strange city of smoke and hills and bustle of ore shipping, is likewise the gateway to the industrial sections south and east.

Winona is set in a scenic region of bluffs, waterfalls, and lakes. St. Cloud has wonderful shaded motor roads and excellent fishing. At Hibbing is the scene of the world's largest open-pit iron-ore mine. Virginia is a quaint little mining town almost on the edge of the wilderness.

IOWA: "WHERE THE TALL CORN GROWS"

A leading agricultural state, Iowa has long been famous for her tall, waving rows of corn and the healthy, well-fed look of her farm boys and girls. Although her cities are few in number, as with other agricultural states, Iowa does considerable manufacturing, particularly of meat and dairy products.

FARMYARD SCENE IN IOWA
Agriculture is Iowa's chief source of wealth.

Paul's Photos, Chicago

Part of the great stretch of territory included in the Louisiana Purchase of 1803, Iowa did not come into the union until nearly half a century later. The Indians called Iowa the "Beautiful Land." Along the rocky bluffs of the Mississippi are picturesque ravines and bold cliffs of the palisades. And on the western side of the state are the lovely blue-water lakes, representative of which is Lake Okoboji. Forty state parks provide a welcome relief from cornfields for Iowa and her many guests.

Famous among her places to see is the tiny church at Festina, said to be the smallest in the world. It seats only eight people, but has been visited literally by hundreds of thousands in the past few years.

ICE CAVES

Very curious are the caves at Decorah. In the Ice Cave can be found a great deal of ice as late as August and September of each year. By January, the interior of the cave is 40 to 50 degrees warmer than the outside and the ice is, of course, gone. Freakish rock formations in this territory furnish beautiful scenery for the tourist.

One of the few bodies of water on a hillside is found near Forest City. Called "Dead Man's Lake" by the natives, it has come to be a stopping-off place for many tourists.

DES MOINES

The State Capitol at Des Moines is said to be to Iowa what Paris is to France. The beautiful capitol building is located in an eighty-six acre park and contains many historical and artistic items. Des Moines leads Iowa industrially; also culturally and educationally. Drake University is located here. Iowa State Fair, recognized as one of the country's greatest agricultural shows, draws great throngs here annually.

Davenport has an enormous roller dam across the Mississippi, which is a part of a flood control and navigation project. The dam is the largest of its kind in the world.

Clinton during Civil War days was part of the great "underground railway" which smuggled negroes north to freedom. Beautiful scenery along the Mississippi here thrills the tourist, no matter how many times he has already seen and enjoyed the "Father of Waters." At Iowa City, where the State Capitol was once located, is the university.

Commercially and industrially very important, Sioux City offers an imposing array of scenery on both sides of the Missouri and Big Sioux Rivers. An unusual view of three states is obtained from the summit of Mount Lucia.

SOUTH ATLANTIC STATES

SOUTHEASTERN SEABOARD

The South Atlantic states, the Virginias, the Carolinas, Georgia, and Florida, comprise an area in which romance, history, and memories of military strife are concentrated. These six states with the exception of West Virginia, which lies inland, form the south Atlantic seaboard, and one of the oldest settled regions in the United States. Gracious to the traveler and eager to make his stay enjoyable, the Old South proudly maintains its reputation for hospitality. In scarcely any other section of the entire country does life display more charm, more loveliness than here.

VIRGINIA: MOTHER OF PRESIDENTS

No state in the Union has been more outstanding in the production of great Americans than dignified old Virginia. Every generation, every field of achievement, and every degree of success are represented among her honored sons. Likewise the state contains countless numbers of landmarks which perpetuate the memory of her heroes. Thousands of markers have been placed along the Virginia highways to point out spots of interest to travelers, and even these cannot include all the places where there is a story to be told.

First among items of interest to visitors is beautiful old Williamsburg, for nearly a century the state capital, which, through the generosity of John D. Rockefeller Jr. is being restored to its pristine colonial appearance. Rescued from decay and ruin, many originals delight the visitor: old Raleigh Tavern, where Phi Beta Kappa, the first college fraternity, was organized; Martha Washington's Town House; the first theater in America; the House of

RESTORED COLONIAL GATE IN HISTORIC WILLIAMSBURG

Black Star photo

Burgesses, where, because he stuttered, Washington failed to make a speech; and William and Mary College, the second oldest in the country.

Always a favorite among tourists is Mount Vernon, George Washington's beautiful, rambling old mansion. Overlooking broad terraces sloping to the Potomac River below, Mount Vernon appeals to even the most unsentimental of visitors as an ideal home for Washington and Martha Custis, his bride. The estate is excellently preserved and furnished with many original pieces.

"OR GIVE ME DEATH"

Founded by Colonel William Evelyn Byrd, member of one of the leading families of Virginia, Richmond, the state capital, is a busy metropolis on the great James River. The capital of the

Confederacy during the Civil War, Richmond was the objective of repeated drives by the Northern troops. Here, in St. John's Episcopal Church, Patrick Henry delivered his great oration which ended with the famous challenge, "Give me liberty, or give me death."

Between tempting interludes of "Virginny baked ham and shortnin' bread," one visits the White House of the Confederacy at Richmond; Monticello, Jefferson's home; the Confederate tunnels in Petersburg; the "trail of the lonesome pine" in the extremely picturesque mountain region; the famous natural bridge in Rockbridge county, and dozens of other equally fascinating spots in the surrounding territory.

Arlington National Cemetery, near the District of Columbia, is a striking memorial. Like the national military parks, the towns of Petersburg, Fredericksburg, and Spottsylvania are visited by many tourists every year.

Norfolk and Newport News are the two leading ports. Norfolk's maritime importance is partially due to its distinction as an ice-free port. The Norfolk Navy Yard is the second largest in America and ranks high among the naval dockyards of the world. Newport News is located on the broad James River close to its estuary and Hampton Roads, one of the greatest roadsteads in the world; and the city claims that the Roads could house all the ships afloat without crowding.

Jamestown, the oldest permanent English settlement in America, is now a ghost town. Decaying walls and sorrowful reminders of vanished scenes stir the imagination of the tourist. Harper's Ferry tucked away among the hills of the Blue Ridge, has likewise a peaceful group of interesting ruins which recall its rôle as a storm center in the Civil War.

WEST VIRGINIA: "SWITZERLAND OF AMERICA"

This rugged inland state owes its origin to the Civil War. In spite of the fact that there had been from the beginning a division of interests and a difference in nationalities between eastern and western Virginia, no actual break came until 1863, when they joined the opposing parties of the South and North in the strife which split the nation, and West Virginia became a legal actuality. Greatly resembling Pennsylvania in the composition of its population, the little state is also like Pennsylvania a leader in the production of iron and steel goods, in coal mining, and in

Courtesy B. & O. R. R., Baltimore

HARPER'S FERRY, WEST VIRGINIA, SCENE OF JOHN BROWN'S RAID
Three states meet here at the conjunction of the Potomac and Shenandoah rivers.

railroad construction. West Virginia is believed to be capable of supplying the entire world with coal for a hundred thousand years.

Called the "Switzerland of America" because of her beautiful back-country scenery, West Virginia apart from her manufacturing centers, is indeed a land of inspiring mountain sights. Northeast of Beckley, in Raleigh County, is Grand View, one of the most magnificent panoramas in the state. In eastern Hampshire County is Ice Mountain, a freakish strip of ice six hundred by thirty-five feet, a natural refrigerator on even the hottest days of the year. New River Gorge is another outstanding scenic attraction of the state, and on Trace Mountain is probably the world's largest oak tree.

Huntington, the largest city in the state, is an important manufacturing area. In Wheeling, which has twice served as the state capital, is the largest patent medicine plant in the world, as well as the great steel mills, which are everywhere present in West Virginia. One of the most impressive sights in the state is the Ohio Suspension Bridge, an engineering masterpiece with a span of more than a thousand feet.

Charleston is the home of the magnificent new State Capitol Building. Situated near the scenic Kanawha River against a background of towering hills, the building and grounds cover about fourteen acres.

One of the last strongholds of mountain feudalism in the entire country is Smoke Hole in Pendleton county. This region is widely known for its narrow, deep gorges and its roaring mountain streams.

NORTH CAROLINA: OLD NORTH STATE

Often referred to as the "valley of humility between two peaks of arrogance," North Carolina has indeed played a social rôle which is insignificant by comparison with her industrial development. The state is among the world leaders in her production of tobacco. Her chief claim to historical distinction is lodged in the fact that Virginia Dare, first white child born in America, belonged to North Carolina's first colony.

AMERICA'S HANGING GARDENS

The Carolina mountains, in the heart of the Southern Appalachians, have been called a vast natural garden. Beautiful fern-banked terraces, hillsides bright with riotously tinted rhododendron blossoms, overhanging cliffs, unexpected waterfalls, and granite-floored gorges form one of the loveliest spots in all America. Little known before travel by motor became common, these Carolina mountain beauties are becoming popular vacation spots. Asheville, situated in the Appalachian highlands is a popular pleasure and health resort.

North Carolina's capital is the active industrial city of Raleigh, located near the east coast. The city is a trade center for the great cotton and tobacco industries of the state. Nearby, on the borders of the Piedmont Plateau, are two of the great educational institutions of the South: the University of North Carolina, beautifully situated at Chapel Hill; and Duke University, a rich and respected center of learning. A remarkable experimental school is Black Mountain, located in the mountains of the western part of the state.

Courtesy Winston-Salem Chamber of Commerce

MORAVIAN BROTHERS' HOUSE, WINSTON-SALEM, N. C.
Erected in 1769, this is the oldest building in the community.

MORAVIAN TRADITION

What the Puritans were to New England in colonial days, the Moravians were to this region. Also the victims of religious persecution, this little group built so sturdy a foundation for their settlements that their names and their old landmarks are revered by Carolinians. At Winston-Salem, one of the oldest and largest industrial centers of the Piedmont, stands the Moravian Brothers' House, erected in 1769. Although the historic buildings of North Carolina are in good repair, and most of them still in use, they lack none of the pleasing qualities of more decayed landmarks.

SOUTH CAROLINA: THE PALMETTO STATE

South Carolina's fine thriving cities and ever expanding commerce are splendid examples of the progress of the New South. Rich in agricultural products, well stocked with dairy farms,

Courtesy Charleston Chamber of Commerce

"WHERE THE SWEET MAGNOLIAS BLOOM"
Charleston's Magnolia beds are probably the oldest landscaped gardens in America.

owning her share of fishing villages, South Carolina is nevertheless a leading southern state in manufacturing.

Her cities are among the cultural centers of the old South, as they were before the Civil War, and her society counts among its members sons of the oldest families in the entire country. Likewise her beauty spots, especially the indescribably lovely magnolia gardens, are legion.

HISTORIC CHARLESTON

A city of historical importance in the United States, colonial old Charleston has been a world port for more than two hundred and fifty years. Her famous magnolia beds are probably the oldest landscape gardens in America. Long a cultural and social leader, this lovely city is interesting to the traveler and most gracious to the guest. One of the principal points of interest is the Powder Magazine, built in 1703.

On Sullivan's Island is Fort Moultrie, where the British were repulsed in 1776 in one of the first decisive victories of the American Revolution. The first shots of the Civil War were fired at the island stronghold of Fort Sumter in Charleston Bay.

Built on a bluff above the River Congaree and noted for its beauty, Columbia is surrounded by a rich agricultural and lumber territory. The University is located here, as are a number of other state institutions. Not far from the city is the famous Murray Dam in the Saluda River.

GEORGIA: CRACKER STATE

Georgia is so called because of its population of small farmers, who are termed "Crackers." The state claims distinction for its diversified climate; its territory extends into seven of the climatic zones into which the United States is divided. Last settled of the thirteen original colonies, Georgia nevertheless played an important part in the history of the South even before the Revolutionary War.

Georgia is chiefly an agricultural area, with cotton as the chief crop, but since the Civil War a new industrial empire has risen to vie with agriculture.

Indian burial mounds are found in almost every Georgia county, as well as fortifications made by the early Spanish settlers.

CENTURY-OLD ATLANTA

The state capital, Atlanta, has grown from a crossroads settlement of a century ago to a metropolis numbering almost a third of a million people. All the more remarkable is her history when one considers that after Sherman's famous and destructive march to the sea, Atlanta lay almost entirely in ashes.

This popular cry of the huckster, in romantic old Savannah, is said to have originated from the word *gratis,* meaning something *free.* Spoken by the white masters of a century ago, it was adopted by the slaves, who called it *bradus.* It has been transformed to *broadus,* and means giving a little extra with every purchase—a charming custom in a pleasant old city, which invariably gives more than is asked, whether commercially or socially.

Savannah is the site on which James Oglethorpe, founder of the colony of Georgia, landed and settled. Like Washington, D.

C., this is one of the few cities completely planned and laid out before it was built. From here sailed the first steamship to cross the Atlantic.

The "firsts" in Savannah's history began when the English originally landed and started their settlement; Georgia was founded without a shot being fired or blood lost by either Indians or white men. Interesting to the tourist are the paving blocks in Bay Street along the water's edge, which were brought from Europe as ballast in the sailing vessels which carried the colonists. At ivy-walled Old Christ Church, John Wesley, the founder of Methodism, preached his stirring sermons, and it was here that he founded the first Sunday school in America. In the old manse of the Independent Presbyterian Church, Woodrow Wilson was first married; and Lowell Mason, the famous hymn composer, began his career as organist and choir director in Savannah.

AUGUSTA AND MACON

Augusta, a fort in its early days, is the second oldest city in Georgia. Another old community, Macon, was a settlement four hundred years ago; but it has developed into a manufacturing center. The boyhood home of the poet Sydney Lanier is here, as is the site of Wesleyan, the oldest woman's college in the United States.

FLORIDA: LAND OF FLOWERS

The name of Florida is derived from the Spanish words for Palm Sunday; it was so called by that romantic explorer, Ponce de Leon, either in honor of the day he landed or because of the wealth of flowers he found. Best known as a fashionable winter resort, Florida maintains throughout the year the holiday spirit which its name implies. A tropical climate, waving palms above moonlit beaches, brilliantly colored blossoms on wide green lawns, all attract visitors from the colder zones.

Most valuable of all Florida's crops is its orange harvest, although agriculturally it has perhaps as great a variety of products as any other state.

St. Augustine is a charming remnant of Old World colonization, founded in 1565 and still an important city. Pensacola, meaning City of Sorrows, has undergone thirteen various periods of control, and flags of five different captors have flown over

Courtesy Tampa Chamber of Commerce. Photo by Burger Bros.

UNIVERSITY OF TAMPA, FLORIDA

the city. The Everglades contain the last remaining members of the Seminole Indian tribe, which is theoretically still at war with the United States, since it has never made any treaty with the government. Actually, they are peaceful people, whom most of the world has forgotten, since the days of the disastrous Seminole Wars.

MAGIC OF EVERGLADES

Scarcely fifty miles away from the sophisticated world of Miami lies the rich land of the Everglades, where a fertile agricultural region is being worked today. New highways make for an alluring exploration of this little known region, which for years was only a beautiful wilderness of useless swampland. Oddly garbed Seminole women selling their beads and other handiwork welcome the traveler, although he does not receive as gracious hospitality from the occasional wildcats and alligators.

SOUTHERN HOSPITALITY

Around no other section in all the country does there linger an atmosphere so sentimentally romantic as that which clings to the deep South. Rich in historic lore, spotted with glamorous century-old cities, and haloed with the misty fragrance of the snowy magnolia, the Old South bows invitingly to its northern and western neighbors.

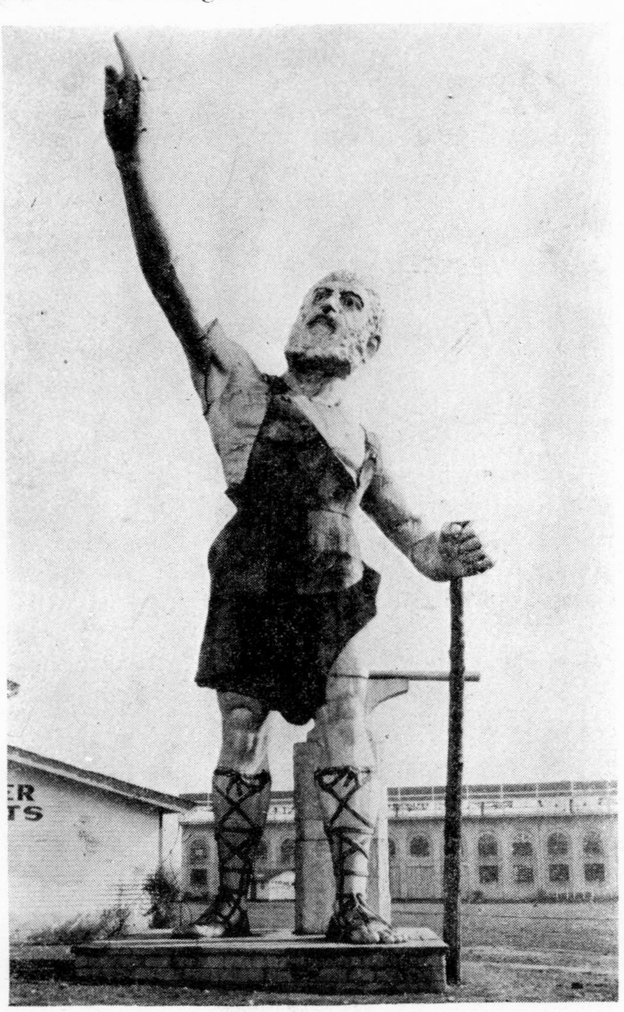

"VULCAN," IRON MAN TYPIFYING BIRMINGHAM

Weighing forty tons, this huge statue overlooks the city from its one-hundred-and-twenty-foot pedestal atop Red Mountain.

Courtesy Birmingham Chamber of Commerce

ALABAMA: "KING COTTON"

With a climate for the most part mildly temperate, but semi-tropical along the coast, Alabama is the home of magnificent cotton fields, stretching like great white sheets of the snow which is seldom seen in reality there.

Although the state can boast only a single seaport, she is proud of her splendid harbor at Mobile. To visitors she can offer in addition a wide variety of scenery presented by her mountains and valleys and seacoast, enhanced by invitingly languid climate.

Belying the leisurely atmosphere for which the South is famous, Birmingham maintains activity and production amazing to the visitor. It is indeed the "Pittsburgh of the South," so called because of its tremendous pig-iron trade.

Montgomery, second in size though first in political importance, is a charming site for the state capitol. At once industrial, cultural, and a civic center, Montgomery possesses sufficient historic color in its environs to be both an "old" and a "new" city.

MISSISSIPPI: HEART OF THE SOUTH

BATTLEFIELDS AND SOUTHERN BELLES

Vicksburg, beautiful site of National Military Park, has a flavor of southern romance. Widest known of all southern cities for its important location in the Civil War, today it has become the mecca for the tourist and student alike. Each spring, when the magnolias fill the air with their heavy fragrance, the Vicksburg Garden Club bids the traveler come and enjoy the friendly hospitality of beautiful old southern mansions, pre-war crinolines on lovely southern belles, the glamour of showboat days revived by pageants on the levee, and the soft melodies of Negro spirituals by torchlight.

FIVE FLAGS OVER BILOXI

More than two centuries old, the quaint old city of Biloxi has lived under five flags—French, Spanish, English, the Confederate States, and the United States. Shrimp and oyster fishing and canning form an important industry. Its delightfully mild climate has made Biloxi one of the most charming winter resorts on the Gulf Coast.

Courtesy Biloxi Chamber of Commerce. Photo by Ragusin.

"BEAUVOIR," LAST HOME OF JEFFERSON DAVIS, BILOXI, MISS.

Jackson, capital and largest city in the state, is surrounded by natural oil fields. Its many beautiful parks and picturesque old buildings, shaded by the lacy network of great sheltering trees, delight both the vacationer and sight-seer.

MAGNOLIA FESTIVAL

Although every town in Mississippi has its share of the exquisite magnolia blossoms, when the magnolias are in bloom, no other spot is as lovely as picturesque Natchez, to which every spring thousands of persons make a pilgrimage for the incomparable magnolia festival—one of the most unique celebrations in the world.

Not to be slighted by the tourist are three other active and sizable cities, Meridian, Hattiesburg, and Laurel. Their welcome is warm and their scenery lovely.

LOUISIANA: LAVENDER AND OLD LACE

Named for a once vastly larger area, and acquired by the United States under the title of Louisiana Purchase at the beginning of the nineteenth century, Louisiana is the home of the famous Creoles, whose picturesque quality has no equal in the imagination of the great American public. It is the home also of the world-renowned Mardi Gras, that annual carnival which fills the streets of New Orleans to overflowing with its color and joyous uproar.

If cities can have a personality, New Orleans is the grandest example of them all. From the beautiful iron scrolls on her romantic old balconies to the very scent in the air of the Old French Quarter, New Orleans is steeped in romance—tales of Spanish pirates, dark-eyed Creole coquettes, pedigreed gentry of faultless manners, daring intrigue, and lavish living.

There are many things to see: the most talked-about haunted house in America; a blacksmith shop that once belonged to two bold pirates; the former home of the Swedish nightingale, Jenny Lind; a hotel now famous as the one-time rendezvous of swash-

"EMBROIDERED BALCONIES"
Graceful patterns in wrought and cast iron characterize the architecture of many homes in the French Quarter of New Orleans.

Courtesy New Orleans Association of Commerce

buckling buccaneers; and the house of Napoleon. Here also is located the oldest building in the Mississippi Valley—the Ursuline Convent.

BATON ROUGE

Although the turbulent, changing waters of the Mississippi swirl past the very doors of Baton Rouge, the city is secure from floods because it is located on the first highlands above the Gulf of Mexico. The old state capitol, with its turreted walls and stained-glass windows, forsaken now, stands like a mighty sentinel over the old Mississippi.

Like a breath of lavender and old lace, redolent with beautiful traditions, are the lovely old mansions of another day. Framed by heavy magnolias, festooned with moss, these add a richness and color to the city that nothing else could give it. Here also is the large, modern Louisiana State University.

SOUTH CENTRAL STATES

This little group of states located in the south central portion of the United States, although mainly agricultural in pursuits, has much more in common than its warm, mild climate. Each produces a great variety of farm products, possesses mines, does some manufacturing, and has a number of interesting, scenic, and historic spots to attract tourists.

ARKANSAS: WONDER STATE

So called by act of legislature in 1923 because of its unusual natural resources, Arkansas is typically southern territory and exceedingly healthful. Her important oil fields at El Dorado and Smackover, her Hot Springs National Park, only spa whose healing waters are owned and recommended by the United States government, and the largest fish hatchery in the world, located at Lonoke, are special features of this rich state. In addition, Arkansas boasts cotton as a principal crop, coal as an important mineral, and lumber as a large natural resource.

Little Rock, whose population has reached nearly the 100,000 mark, is the capital. Both the Old and New Capitols here are worth visiting. The Albert Pike Consistory is one of the finest Masonic structures in the South. Fort Smith and Pine Bluff are important cities commercially and industrially.

At Murfreesboro are the only diamond mine on the North American continent and the largest peach orchard in the world, consisting of one and a half million bearing trees. At Luxora is a national Migratory Bird Sanctuary, and at Brinkley an important button factory.

TENNESSEE: HOG-AND-HOMINY

How many Americans know or have read that Tennessee suffered a severe earthquake in 1811? Very few, no doubt. Reelfoot lake, surrounded by beautiful Tennessee mountain scenery is mute witness to the great upheaval of earth which left a large depression in its wake over a hundred years ago.

T. V. A. CENTER

As part of the great, publicized Tennessee Valley Authority development program, the United States government is actively at work on Chickamauga dam. This dam will cost about twenty-five millions of dollars when completed and is prophesied to be one of the greatest flood control projects in the world.

Famous in Tennessee is Lookout Mountain, towering with inspiring dignity over the city of Chattanooga below. From this

AIR VIEW OF NORRIS DAM ON THE CLINCH RIVER IN TENNESSEE

International News photo

mountain is obtained an incomparable view of Moccasin Bend in the Tennessee River far below. Chickamauga battlefield, Missionary Ridge, and Cameron Hill, the site of the "Battle above the Clouds," are all fascinating memorials to famous scenes of bloody struggle. An incline railway, one of the steepest and most scenic in the world, takes the visitor to the top of Lookout Mountain, if he chooses not to drive or walk to the heights. This incline trip, perfectly safe, is an unforgettable thrill in itself.

Other points of interest include the Mississippi cantilever bridge at Memphis with a span of 790 feet, the Great Smoky Mountains and their peaks, and the Meriwether Lewis National Monument.

One of the largest trade centers in the country for cotton, Memphis has a wealth of legend, situated as it is on the Mississippi River. Also a large manufacturing city, Memphis, is an important railway center.

HOME OF "OLD HICKORY"

At Nashville is the home of General Andrew Jackson, seventh President of the United States. This beautiful and historic home, called "The Hermitage" lies only a little way from the heart of the city. The rooms are furnished with pieces that Jackson and his family used; the grand stairway in the lower hall is extraordinarily fine. Many beautiful monuments and buildings are to be seen in this glorious old city called the "Athens of the South." One of the most striking of these is a reproduction of the Parthenon.

KENTUCKY: BLUE GRASS REGION

Home of fried chicken and hot biscuits, Kentucky colonels and mint julep, and finally, beautiful women and fast horses, Kentucky is the tourist's paradise. Both Abraham Lincoln, President of the Union, and Jefferson Davis, President of the Confederacy, are native sons of this interesting old state.

Famous are the caves, particularly Mammoth, where Floyd Collins met his tragic end a number of years ago. At Bardstown is the scene of "My Old Kentucky Home." Near Louisville is Churchill Downs, where the famous Derby is run. "Man o' War" still lives in the beautiful blue grass region around Lexington, where breeding of famous horses is traditional.

DAIRY BARN AND SILOS NEAR LEXINGTON, KY.

Paul's Photos, Chicago

HORSE RACING AND TOBACCO

Louisville, largest city in the state, is pre-eminent for its hospitality. Here George Rogers Clark established his base of supplies when he started out on the mission that won the Great Northwest for the United States. His body lies in the city in Cave Hill cemetery.

Covington, second city in the state, has steamer connections with all river ports, and is the farming, livestock, and whiskey trade center of central Kentucky. More than a hundred years old, this interesting city has much to show the visitor. Latonia racing park is located here.

DARK AND BLOODY GROUND

Legendary hero of this state is Daniel Boone, who came over the mountains about the time of the American Revolution and founded Boonesboro. His companions were courageous and hardy pioneers from Virginia. Only the brave would venture into such an Indian-infested wilderness; and only the strong reached their destination.

This state has many beautiful parks; among them Cumberland Falls, where a beautiful moon-bow may be seen at full moon. At only one other place in the world may this phenomenon be seen—in South Africa. Pioneer Memorial State Park has replicas of the first settlers' log cabins, the first school house in Kentucky, collections of pioneer furniture, and the oldest cemetery in the state. The log cabin in which Thomas Lincoln and Nancy Hanks, parents of Abraham Lincoln, began housekeeping is near the entrance of the park.

Other parks include the Jefferson Davis Memorial Monument, Kentucky Natural Bridge State Park, the Audubon Memorial, and many other interesting resorts.

MISSOURI: "SHOW ME" STATE

Deriving its name from an old Indian name meaning "muddy waters," Missouri was set aside after the Louisiana Purchase of 1803 as Indian Territory. A scant two decades later, the state was admitted to the Union under the famous Missouri Compromise. With the Ozarks in the southwest and the Mississippi flowing along its eastern boundary for 500 miles, Missouri has its share of rugged hills and picturesque valleys, rocky ranges, and mysterious caverns. The region of the Ozarks is one of constant delight to the traveler. Miles of scenic wonderlands are covered by the state parks of Missouri.

MISSOURI'S METROPOLITAN CENTERS

Bustling cities and old towns of historical interest are scattered throughout Missouri. At St. Louis, one of the oldest cities in the state, are a famous art museum and Shaw's Garden, one of the finest botanical gardens in North America. The city also boasts the second largest municipal park and zoological garden in the country. Situated at the junction of the Mississippi and Missouri Rivers, St. Louis is a nationwide commercial center, and for a time threatened Chicago's supremacy as a meat packing center and stockyard leader.

Kansas City, not to be confused with Kansas City, Kansas, has a rich cultural background, evidences of which are to be found in its art gallery and symphony orchestra. Its beautiful parks and residential sections are renowned; its map is dotted with points of interest. Cliff Drive, carved out of limestone bluffs overlooking the Missouri River, is one of the loveliest drives imaginable.

St. Joseph, stepping-off point to the West in pioneer days, was called Black Snake Hills until the middle of the last century. The original Robedeoux Cabin of the founder is now standing in one of the public parks. Reminiscent of old Pony Express days, St. Joseph is also the former home of the notorious bandits, the James brothers.

Jefferson City, situated on the Missouri River, about one hundred miles from St. Louis, is the state capital. The capitol, the State Library, and Lincoln University (for colored students) merit recognition by the traveler.

Courtesy Kansas City Chamber of Commerce

THE PIONEER MOTHER
Impressive group of statuary in Penn Valley Park, Kansas City, Mo.

Hannibal, situated on the Mississippi River, about 125 miles from St. Louis, is known chiefly as the early home of Samuel Clemens, whose pen name was Mark Twain. Near the town one may visit the scenes of the exciting adventures related in *Huckleberry Finn* and *Tom Sawyer*.

"HEART OF THE WEST"

Scarcely half a century ago, savage bands of Indians roamed freely over a wild and woolly West. The great block of rolling plains now known as North Dakota, South Dakota, Nebraska, and Kansas was repeatedly the fierce scene of many scalpings of lonely white adventurers. Fleets of "prairie schooners," whose "skippers" were frequently in deadly terror of roving Indians, crossed this treasure chest of natural resources, little dreaming of its underground riches as they crawled slowly and laboriously on toward that distant paradise called California. Few white men remained, or cared to remain, where life was such a hazard, where only fierce prairie winds and hostile Indians seemed to survive.

GOLD!

Then came the miracle—gold was discovered on historic French Creek in the Black Hills in the summer of 1874, and overnight began an amazing bustle of activity. Men, women, and children by tens of thousands swarmed into Custer and the territory surrounding, often with no more than a frying pan and the clothes on their backs. Indeed, here is the origin of the term "panhandler," meaning beggar; for, when the hysterical and empty-handed prospector arrived at the scene, he soon discovered that polite begging was his only hope of surviving. There were no stores. There was no organized society. Those who had thought to bring supplies were expected to share with those who had not. Only a man's frying pan was sacred to his own use, since he not only cooked in it and ate from it, but also used it for panning the precious gold. Those who must borrow even the frying pan of a neighbor became known as "panhandlers," truly a scornful epithet, if the remaining old-timers are to be believed.

What an amazing scene it must have been! Every man a law unto himself! Cities were evolving from trading posts. Indian trails gave way to wide, irregular wagon roads, of which some of the deep-rutted grooves can be traced even today by the interested motorist.

THE PRIMITIVE SURRENDERS

The rich soil of the great plains yielded more than gold ore. Soon appeared seemingly unending stretches of golden wheat waving in the prairie winds. Other grains ripening on rolling hillocks made a vast checkerboard of the once barren plains. Herds of cattle, often thousands in number, roamed the land wrested from the Indians in a bloody struggle. The heart of the West had sprung to life!

RIDE 'EM COWBOY!

Dear to the American heart are the tales and the landmarks of the Old West. What person has escaped a thrilling hour with a western fiction magazine, overflowing with the colorful escapades of brave-hearted cowboys, scar-faced rustlers, and sturdy pioneers. Dear to every schoolboy—and to some schoolgirls—are the names of Buffalo Bill, General Custer, Deadwood Dick, Calamity Jane, and Potato Creek Johnny. Likewise, nothing stirs the imagination of the traveler today so much as the realistic enactments of the old roundups and the rodeos, held in frontier towns during the summer months.

In spite of the fact that cities have expanded into national metropolises, and dirt roads have become four-lane speedways, changing days to minutes in traveling time, there still lingers the glamour of adventurous days for the tourist, who, roaming leisurely through the old haunts of his western heroes, can live in fancy the roaring time when hearts were big and trigger fingers capricious.

NORTH DAKOTA: FLICKERTAIL STATE

North Dakota, of the North Plains states, probably the least touched by civilization, got its nickname from the little ground squirrel on which a bounty had been placed to help rid the state of its presence. A story is told of a native, who, knowing that only the tail of the little pest need be produced in evidence at the state office in order to collect the bounty, kept a large pen of the creatures, which he mated after cutting off their tails, thereby actually farming tails, on which (according to the story told) he collected enough bounties to grow rich. The almost total lack of any woodlands and the presence of salty lakes are interesting evidences of glacial action in North Dakota many thousands of years ago. The largest of these salt lakes is Devil's Lake, about four hundred square miles in area.

A sparse population scattered over a wide area has resulted in an absence of any large cities. One of the most interesting little towns in North Dakota is, perhaps, Mandan, which retains the atmosphere and freedom of the northern outposts. Bismarck, the capital, is exceeded in population by Fargo, Grand Forks, and Minot, each of which is an important trading center for large surrounding agricultural areas. These little cities are true metropolises to the people who make periodic shopping trips to them.

SOUTH DAKOTA: BAD LANDS

LAND OF OPPORTUNITY

South Dakota has altered little since the exciting days when high adventure rode the crooked trails. Here, perhaps as in no other state in the Union, are so many contrasts in scenic wonder that the traveler is never satiated. Rich, too, is its historical and legendary lore. In few places in the world will the traveler find scenery so weirdly fantastic, with the history of all time written so plainly, as in the big Bad Lands of western South Dakota, between the White and Cheyenne Rivers. Pinnacles, towers, spires, domes, castles of unbelievable size and variety, colored with every hue in the rainbow, show high and clear above the sky line. As the

Courtesy Northern Pacific Railway. Photo by Brown

SOUTH DAKOTA'S FAMOUS BAD LANDS

wide-eyed tourist rides smoothly over a broad, fine highway, and views these eroded formations, bare, and solid-looking as rock, he finds it very hard to believe he has not been transported to another world. Prehistoric fossils, available to anyone willing to walk fifty feet from the road, are mute evidences that this region was once an ocean bed. The visitor shakes his head and rubs his eyes; it can't be true! But it is!

BEAUTIFUL BLACK HILLS

Without doubt the most famous section of this state is in the Black Hills, so called because of the vast forest of blue spruce which covers them. There are to be found a region of romantic history, magnificent drives, beautiful canyons and gorges, quiet camping spots, dude ranches, splendid fishing, and, above all, colors of trees, rocks, and sky in such unusual contrast that rarely does a visitor leave without regret. The Black Hills are divided into two natural and distinct sections: the southern or scenic; the northern or historical.

Adjudged one of the most beautiful ten-mile drives in the West, Needles Highway, a marvelous engineering feat passes between needle-like granite spires, through tunnels cut from solid red granite, near sheer drops of hundreds of feet on either side of the road, and among tremendous mountain ranges that rise abruptly on all sides. What a breathtaking experience to drive secure and comfortable through this historic wonderland!

The traveler leaving Needles Highway, going east, turns on to Iron Mountain Road, a curious twisting ascent through dense forests of blue spruce. A unique solution for climbing to the greater heights over jagged mountainsides by car is the use of "pig-tail" bridges, which carry the motorist over a bridge in the shape of the figure "8," forming a loop, and then crossing at a higher level the road he has just traversed. A curious sensation is experienced, reminding one of an amusement park whirligig.

RUSHMORE MEMORIAL

One experiences a thrill on approaching the first long, dark tunnel cut from a wall of solid, bright-hued granite on Iron Mountain Road. It takes a moment to accustom one's eyes to the heavy darkness in the tunnel. Then the tiny circle of light at the far end gradually enlarges. Suddenly, with startling clearness,

Black Star photo

THE GREAT STONE FACES OF MT. RUSHMORE, SOUTH DAKOTA
These gigantic Heads of Washington and Jefferson have been carved in the solid rock of the mountain.

one sees the cameo-like sculpture of the beautiful and impressive Rushmore Memorial, framed in the ever increasing circle of light as one leaves the tunnel. What an unforgettable introduction to the great stone faces of Washington, Jefferson, Lincoln, and Roosevelt; cut from the enduring granite of Mt. Rushmore. One of the most monumental feats of sculpturing ever known, it is being done under the direction of world-famous Gutzon Borglum, and under the supervision of the national government. When completed, each stone figure will measure 230 feet from waist to brow. According to geologists, these stupendous giants have a good chance of remaining as they are for a million years! What a thought! The spectator is momentarily lost in space as he tries to conceive of so much time.

SMOOTH ROADS BY SILVERY STREAMS

Dozens of places in the Hills have a magic all their own. Tiny Sylvan Lake nestles like a sparkling sapphire at the foot of Harney

Peak and looks up on all sides at towering mountain walls. One contrasts its placid, sheltered beauty with the point where Spearfish Creek tumbles noisily out of mountain crevices to find its way to the prairies, its waters teeming with tantalizing game fish. Again, in upper Spearfish Canyon, west of Lead, is one of the most gloriously colored canyons in the Hills.

The great natural bowl located near Rapid City is a constant source of pleasure to visitors. It was here in 1935 that Stevens and Anderson ascended in their balloon to a height of over thirteen miles above the earth.

BLACK HILLS MAGIC

No vacation is more delightful than the first trip to one of the underground palaces, such as the three famous caves in the Black Hills—Crystal, Jewel, and Wonderland. Many miles of paths and literally hundreds of natural rooms have been explored in these underground fairylands. Here every conceivable formation of crystal beauty, myriad lakes, and pools of limpid water reflecting thousands of colored gems formed by the action of water during countless ages, delight the imagination of the visitor and the ever enthusiastic guides who conduct groups every hour of the day and night.

In what has been called the Picture City of the Southern Hills, hot springs rise from the earth to cure and heal with their waters. Here is found the largest warm-water plunge in the world. The curious traveler bathes in a spring where Indians were supposed to have taken the "cure."

A far cry from the almost uninhabited, sylvan beauty of the Southern Hills is the cluster of delightful little western towns in the northern portion. These towns are overflowing with legends of pioneer days. Without doubt the most satisfying of these pioneer towns is Deadwood, near the famous gold deposits. Lying narrow and deep in crooked Deadwood Gulch, this vigorous little town is actually only one street in width, the sides of the mountains rising sharply like the arms of the letter "V."

Here is the home of that notorious character, "Deadwood Dick," and his "lively, picturesque, rough-riding, gun-totin' lady friend, Calamity Jane." Many are the anecdotes in Deadwood re-

EXAMINING A PETRIFIED LOG IN S. DAKOTA BAD LANDS

Courtesy Northern Pacific Ry.

garding these two. Half a dozen real old-timers are still there, now gracious and patient with the eager questions of the thousands of visitors who pass through the town each summer.

A KEY TO THE ROMANTIC PAST

While in Deadwood no one should think of missing the Adam Memorial Hall Museum, which contains one of the richest and most fascinating collections of its kind. The visitor needs at least several hours to stand in fond reminiscence over the last reminders of the famous pioneers of Deadwood—the shirts they wore, the guns they used, the dice they fondled so lovingly, the axes with which they built their cabins, and the handkerchiefs now more than half a century old, many of which show the stains from some wound.

At Mt. Moriah Cemetery, many of the old characters are buried. Their graves are marked with curious and crude monuments, sentimental tributes to well-loved personalities. The history of the early gold-rush days is reenacted annually by the descendants of the pioneers in one glorious week of pageantry and festive celebration.

MILE HIGH CITY

Several miles southwest of Deadwood is Lead, home of the largest gold mine in North America—the famous Homestake, which in its sixtieth year of operation has already turned out over 300 million dollars in gold. Visitors delight in trying their hand at "panning" gold, in nearby mountain streams, but, although the fun is great, the returns are small.

Dinosaur Park, located in Rapid City, is the eastern gateway to the Black Hills; the mighty, lifelike figures of these prehistoric beasts stand out in bold relief. The School of Mines, also at Rapid City, has housed in its museum a priceless collection of fossil remains.

THE NATION'S BIGGEST LITTLE CITY

Largest city in the Dakotas, Sioux Falls has the decided distinction of a population 88 per cent American-born. Besides a number of important state institutions and public buildings, Sioux Falls has four beautiful parks. Loveliest of many features are the Japanese gardens in Terrace Park, where unusual plants and beautiful landscaping combine to produce one of the quaintest man-decorated corners in the West.

NEBRASKA: CORNHUSKER STATE

The old-timer in southwestern Nebraska points with pride to the wheel ruts in some long-since discarded road. Here, as a wind-blistered youth, he counted in but a single day as many as three thousand lumbering wagons creaking past the sod hut of his parents. The huts as well as the roads have been replaced today, and in their stead now stand luxurious ranches, beautiful homes, and well-built roads and highways.

The peace now enfolding the wide sagebrush country makes it hard for the traveler to picture the fierce Indian warfare once violently breaking the monotone of the wind. Today, the district, the nucleuses of which are Trenton and Benkleman, is famous as a prosperous livestock and farming country.

Scottsbluff National Monument, jutting from the plains to an altitude of almost 5,000 feet, is the commemorative landmark of the pathetic fate of a fur trapper named Hiram Scott, who, weak from the dreaded typhoid fever, was finally deserted by his two companions and left to die alone in the wilderness. Knowing the entire scouting party was destined to meet at the then unnamed bluff, the fever-ravished man almost miraculously dragged himself along and crawled over hills, sagebrush, and gullies the entire hundred miles to the foot of the bluff. There he died—too late to reach his party. His skeleton was found the next year.

BUFFALO BILL'S REST HOME

Mecca of thousands of visitors each year is the old ranch of "Buffalo Bill" Cody, established sometime about 1878, and located three miles northwest of North Platte. Here the interested spectator renews his tales of the famous scout and recalls the amazing story of the 4,280 buffaloes which Cody shot and killed for food for the railroad construction gang in one eighteen months' period.

Farther east is Kearney, the site of historic old Fort Kearney, famed in pioneer days as a military outpost. Earthworks and parade grounds are still visible.

THE SYMBOL OF INHERENT POWER

Nebraska's new State Capitol at Lincoln, which, compared with other cities of like population, is still in its swaddling clothes, represents the most vivid and original conception ever thought out in the field of American art. Unlike any other capitol building in the United States, it is not only a creation; it is an expression of Nebraska's purposes and ideals.

The base, in the form of a rectangle over 400 feet square and only two stories high, typifies the wide-spread fertile Nebraska plains. The central tower, serving as the chief architectural feature of the building and rising triumphantly to a height of 400 feet, expresses the aspirations and ideals of the citizens. As richly decorative and unique on the interior as it is classically simple and artistic on the exterior, this governmental monument is the most important single spot worth contemplating in all of Nebraska!

Courtesy Omaha Chamber of Commerce. Photo by Bostwick

NEW JOSLYN MEMORIAL ART BUILDING, OMAHA, NEB.
Built of Georgia pink marble, this majestic structure houses ten art galleries and a concert hall.

AK-SAR-BEN

Ranking first among the butter producing cities of the world and second in livestock and meat packing, Omaha has been jested the world over as the home of one of America's popular stock characters—the "big butter and egg man." Six thousand business men are responsible for Ak-Sar-Ben, an organization whose annual stock show is a nation-wide event.

KANSAS: THE PRAIRIE SUNFLOWER STATE

Enormous herds of buffalo once roamed the vast sun-baked prairie now known as the greatest wheat-producing state in the entire country. Although the buffalo and the hostile Indians are no longer a menace to the Kansas farmer, he still struggles painfully with his hazards of fire, drought, floods, and grasshoppers.

Second in fame only to Kansas' enviable annual crop of wheat is its output of petroleum—or "black gold," as fiction writers have romantically dubbed it. Twelve miles north of Hutchinson is located the veteran producer of the state. Although this well has been on the pump constantly for nine years, it is still producing 195 barrels of oil a day.

SALT CELLARS

Hard on the heels of agricultural and drilling pursuits comes the seemingly inexhaustible supply of salt beneath the Kansas grasses. Discovered accidentally about sixty years ago, three mines near Hutchinson are worked constantly for an output of over fifteen thousand carloads a year. The sight-seer looks at his guide in amazement when he hears these figures. Fifteen thousand carloads a year! But where does it come from? As a matter of fact, the deposits originate more than six hundred feet—the height of a skyscraper—below the earth's surface, where actual "rooms," more than seventy-five in one mine, have been cut from a solid vein of salt. Geologists and engineers claim that the supply is well-nigh inexhaustible. The soil may deteriorate, oil wells may gush and go dry, but Hutchinson, in all probability, will always be a "salt cellar."

Claiming the unique distinction of being the exact geographical center of the United States, Fort Riley has erected Ogden Monument as a marker to designate the exact point.

GREAT OPEN SPACES

It was a weird land that attracted the first settlers west of the Mississippi River, along the endless stretch of territory bordering old Mexico. In its great open spaces the land is still as awe-compelling as it was when white men first saw it. Far-flung deserts stretch into remote horizons. Purple-bordered mountains rise majestically. Canyons and caves belie the even serenity of arid wastes.

PAGEANT-LIKE HISTORY

As in a long and colorful parade, first the cliff-dwelling Indians, followed in turn by the old Spanish missionaries, roaming Mexicans, mining prospectors, and finally ranchmen have moved into the territory, all leaving their marks.

Guest ranches abound in this Mexican borderland. The desire to gain health, rest, and recreation brings thousands yearly to the region of the old Spanish missions and towering mountains. Adobe houses on the edge of the desert prove a delightful haven of rest. A visitor is delighted at the sight of wide green lawns, shady pepper trees, orange groves, date palms, olive trees, and the desert cactus.

The four states in this group, each including a large expanse of territory, comprise one of the largest natural divisions in the United States and one of the least populated regions.

OKLAHOMA: "SOONER" STATE

Oklahoma was set aside by the government early in the nineteenth century as Indian Territory. Repeated pressure on the part of whites to have it opened up to settlers finally resulted in the setting of a day and an hour for the beginning of staking claims in this territory. Thousands of men, women, and children—their covered wagons loaded as lightly as possible for the sake of speed—waited behind the starting line until the word was given. At that moment began one of the greatest races in history. Horses galloped with wagons careening behind them. Men ran, women and children at their heels. It was not long, however, before everyone discovered the best land had been taken. A large group of shrewd hustlers had got past the guards and taken the choicest spots. They had come in before the day of official opening of the territory. In scorn, the law-abiding persons who had waited called these hustlers "sooners." This was the origin of Oklahoma's nickname.

OIL WELLS NEAR CENTER OF OKLAHOMA CITY

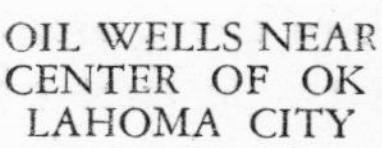

The state's capital has become an important oil-producing center, with hundreds of derricks adjoining business houses and factories.

Oklahoma is the only one of the states in the south plains not bordering on the Gulf or on Mexico. It is located in the very heart of the section where great wheat and cotton areas overlap. This state is very near the top of the list in annual production of both these crops.

OSAGE MILLIONAIRES

Most curious and interesting of all Oklahoma natives are the comparatively small group of Osage Indians, who have become enormously rich by leasing their land to large oil companies. These companies have discovered phenomenally productive oil pools and have vied bitterly with each other for use of the Indians' property. The white people in the territory tell many amusing and often pathetic stories about the Indians and their new-found money.

The state capital of Oklahoma is her far-famed Oklahoma City. This modern, industrial metropolis, numbering 185,389 people, a mere forty-five years ago consisted of only prairie land and tall, waving grasses. Home of the well-known Oklahoma University, a fine State Historical and Indian Museum, a beautiful residential district, and a stately capitol building, the city offers much worth seeing. One may also visit stockyards and oil fields. About one hundred miles from Oklahoma City is a fine national park—Platt, a health and pleasure resort.

Tulsa, second city in Oklahoma, is the center of large oil fields. It is situated in a region of coal, limestone, natural gas, and hardwood. There are many beautiful, modern buildings and lovely parks here. Like Oklahoma City, Tulsa is a "brand new" metropolis.

TEXAS: LONE STAR STATE

Texas, it has been humorously remarked, occupies all of the continent of North America, except the small part set aside for the United States, Mexico, and Canada. Actually, the state is 825 miles wide, and 740 miles long, easily the largest state in the Union. By strange contrast, Texas' population is less than twice that of the city of Chicago.

Texas is still known as the "Lone Star" state. It is the only state in the Union that has been an independent republic with its own president and constitution. Texas is also unique in having changed her capital thirteen times.

Courtesy Corpus Christi Chamber of Commerce, Texas

PRIZE STEERS ON A TEXAS RANCH

Three counties in southern Texas have a live stock "population" of over 300,000 head.

Austin, the present capital, had a most unusual beginning. In 1839, while Texas was still a republic, a commission was appointed to select "the prettiest spot in all the state" for the capital. The site of Austin was chosen. Immediately the city began to develop, although there were a number of changes before the Texas legislature finally made Austin the permanent location of the State House.

Texas covers so much territory that it is hard to generalize about its climate. After all, there is almost as much distance from any one of the four boundaries of the state to an opposite side as there is from Chicago to New York. Generally, the climate is sunny, dry, and very healthful. In the southern extremes snow is almost unknown and the climate nearly tropical. In the northern parts snow and cold weather appear but not in great amounts. Large irrigation projects are gradually relieving the excessive dryness of the land.

Photo by H. L. Summerville

THE ALAMO, SAN ANTONIO, TEXAS

"HOWDY STRANGER!"

The Texas visitor may ride the great plains and see vast herds of cattle trailing to the roundup. Or he may visit the oil fields where throbbing pumps gush forth a wealth of "flowing gold." He may even stop for a time in San Angelo, center of the wool and mohair industry. Texas is unusually eager to please her guests. When the great Texas Centennial Exposition was held in 1936, every city put on its holiday attire, although the main celebration was held at Dallas. Many of the attractions for this world's fair have since been made permanent features of the city of Dallas.

Houston, situated on Buffalo Bayou, was named in honor of the Texas soldier and statesman, one-time president of the Texas republic, later senator, and finally governor. The city is a railroad terminal. Its important buildings include the Carnegie Library, the Union Station, the United States Government Building, the City Hall, and the Cotton Exchange and Market. It is now the largest metropolis in the state, having direct connection with the Gulf of Mexico through a long canal which makes the city an important shipping port.

Dallas, home of the 1936 Fair, was just one log cabin in a vast prairie a hundred years ago when the lone-star flag was lowered and the stars and stripes raised. From then on a great city was in the process of development. Today Dallas is the largest inland cotton market in the world.

"REMEMBER THE ALAMO"

San Antonio, where "sunshine spends the winter," is the home of the historical and sacred Alamo, a mission erected by Franciscan monks in 1760. In 1836 the Texans fighting for independence used the church building for a fort and for two weeks withstood the Mexican troops under Santa Ana. But the struggle ended in defeat with the massacre of all but one of the Texans. Today the Alamo stands an ivy-clad monument to a glorious sacrifice for liberty.

Forth Worth is called the capital of cattle kings. Once an army post, seventy-five years ago a tramping ground for Indian hunters, the city is now one of the four greatest oil centers of the world and the leading grain market of the United States. The famous Botanic Gardens, the Coliseum, and the Auditorium are especially enjoyable to visitors.

The Sun Carnival is held in glamorous El Paso each year during those months when northern states are sloshing through winter mud and shivering through blizzards. El Paso is a well-known health resort. There are other Texan cities not to be missed by the visitor, Galveston, where a mighty breakwater protects a justly famous harbor; and Corpus Christi, where Texas meets the sea in a splash of beauty. On the whole, Texas cities make it well worth the visitor's while to ride across the long, lonesome Texas plains.

NEW MEXICO: SUNSHINE STATE

New Mexico derives its name from the title of the Aztec war-god, Mexitli. Valiant but weary Spanish adventurers were the first white men to set eyes on the state's magnificent distances, marked contrasts, and romantic beauty.

Imagine the wonder, delight, and the unbelief of the first white men who came upon the Carlsbad Caverns. Pictures and words cannot tell the story of such wonderful underground beauty. More than thirty miles of these caves on three distinct levels have been explored. How far they really extend horizontally and vertically man may never know.

AZTEC RUINS IN NEW MEXICO

Courtesy Aztec Chamber of Commerce
Photo by Hammock

SIXTY MILLION YEARS OLD

There is an icy splendor to the stalagmites and stalactites in these dome-roofed underground palaces. Nowhere else in the world can the vacationist-explorer travel for five and a half consecutive hours through such fairyland. Lunch is served in the chilly recesses 750 feet underground. Lights are extinguished and the hollow, solemn chords of an organ thrill the tourist through and through. Suddenly he feels very much "buried alive" down in the inky depths. It would be difficult, indeed, to forget the experience at Carlsbad Caverns.

Santa Fe is one of the oldest cities in the country. Colorful, with low, broad Spanish patios, the little town enchants the visitor. Weird Hopi snake dances, Indian pueblos, massive white missions, prehistoric ruins furnish abundant entertainment. Caves, canyons, and petrified forests make fascinating side tours. A point of interest to the visitor is the old Palace of Governors, erected before the Pilgrims landed in America.

THE VANISHING AMERICAN

Old ruins are everywhere and constitute a region of forgotten cities of the Aztec, existing for how many thousands of years no one knows. Gallup, the center of an Indian empire, is representative of a number of Indian towns in this territory. Its inhabitants, peaceful, sober-faced Navahos, own millions of sheep, ride like Cossacks, make exquisite silver jewelry and colorful rugs, and perform ceremonial dances in all the seriousness of their customs.

Albuquerque has been described as nestling like an emerald between the river and mountain. Largest city in New Mexico, this old town is the commercial center of the state. It is a scene of strange contrasts, cosmopolitan because of its reputation as a health resort, yet colorful with cowboys and Mexicans. Small Taos has been made famous the world over by writers and artists. No visitor to New Mexico permits himself to overlook this charming little spot.

ARIZONA: EGYPT IN AMERICA

Arizona resembles southern Egypt in that it is a region of intense heat during the summer months. Both desert and oasis areas in Arizona bear a strong resemblance to that seat of ancient history. This state is, like Egypt, a haven of recuperation where thousands seek its health-giving climate each year.

Courtesy C. & N. W. Ry. Co.

NORTH RIM, GRAND CANYON OF ARIZONA
At this point the canyon is fourteen miles wide and more than a mile deep.

NATURE'S WORK OF ART

Greatest of all Arizona's attractions is that indescribable wonder, the Grand Canyon. From its north rim the canyon is thirteen miles across. Its depth is seven thousand feet. Like a slender thread the Colorado River winds through the bottom of it. Hundreds of thousands of jagged rocks and cliffs line the brilliantly colored walls. Descents may be made to the bottom of the Canyon with the aid of guides. The less venturesome prefer to climb to Indian Tower and look toward the Painted Desert, which lies some sixty miles away. The Grand Canyon National Park offers the most remarkable example of erosion.

Phoenix, the state capital, has streets and parks which are adorned every month of the year with lovely palms and bright-colored flowers. The city has been called a green island in a sea of topaz sand, situated as it is in Salt River Valley. It is surrounded by olive, orange, and grapefruit groves. Nearby is Apache Trail with seventy-six miles of splendid scenery and historic appeal. Roosevelt Dam can be seen from this trail.

Tucson is the only other Arizona city of commercial importance. It has been the home of desert inhabitants for four hundred years. Here are located the state university and several beautiful public buildings. According to the weather reports, this is the only region in the United States having more than eighty per cent of the possible amount of sunshine.

THE ROCKY MOUNTAIN REGION

Least affected by the touch of man, and likely to always remain untamed, the mighty Rocky Mountains stand in defiant ruggedness and primitive majesty. Splendid are the white-capped, precipitous peaks of the Big Horns, the Grand Tetons, and the Snowy Range. Spreading over millions of acres is the forest wilderness. Age-old glaciers feed exquisite, gem-like lakes. Throughout the region is heard a never ending symphony: the staccato notes of cool waters rushing over jagged rocks, the high crescendo of the wind in the trees, a constant chatter of lesser waterfalls, and the gentle swish of shallow, ever curving streams. Cities are few and scattered; they, too, seem to exist in a free, un-

Courtesy Idaho Chamber of Commerce

PAYETTE LAKE, NEAR McCALL, IDAHO

trammeled state. Men are active, alert, and self-reliant. The stories of the fearless Westerners who battled the elements, the impassable country, and the stampedes of wild animal herds, supply a large part of American tradition.

IDAHO: THE GEM STATE

The name of Idaho originated from a morning rallying cry of the Shoshone Indians—"*Ee-dah-how*," which means "see the sun coming down the mountains." One marvels at the appropriateness of the name for a region so full of towering peaks, cascading rivers washed in sunshine, and fresh mountain air. One short glimpse of Idaho, and the traveler sees far grander possibilities of the state than being merely the best producer of baking potatoes.

Boise, the capital, is fortunate to have a perfect natural supply of pure hot water, which is taken from a flowing, boiling spring.

The city rose from an early trading post of the Hudson's Bay Company. Pocatello, established as a stage station about seventy-five years ago, is known as the "Gate City" and ranks second only to Boise in population. A great portion of all the trade and travel in the northern Rockies still passes through its great crossing. Idaho Falls, the state's third largest city, is situated among rich irrigated lands from which are harvested wheat and sugar beets, as well as the famous potatoes. The falls, for which the city is named, are on the Snake River, a tributary of the Columbia. Farther west in the course of the Snake River are two cataracts, both of which are higher than Niagara: Shoshone Falls drop 210 feet, and Twin Falls drop 180 feet. Arrowrock Dam in the Boise River, Lava Hot Springs, Lo Lo Trail (traveled by Lewis and Clark), and Craters of the Moon National Monument are of special interest among the wonders of Idaho.

UTAH: THE MORMON STATE

Six times as salty as the ocean, Great Salt Lake is undoubtedly Utah's major attraction. There is a powerful and inexplicable fascination in swimming in water in which one cannot sink. The average depth of the lake is only about twenty feet, its length is seventy-five miles, and its width is thirty miles; although both the depth and the dimensions are subject to considerable variations. Saltair, a beautiful resort, offers special attractions to bathers and dancers.

A GARDEN IN THE DESERT

Rivaling the wonder of Great Salt Lake is the heroic story of the Mormons, the religious group driven west by persecutions in the east. Brigham Young brought the first group into Salt Lake Valley almost a hundred years ago, and the record of their achievements is a tribute to his ability. A monument stands at the place where the venerated leader is supposed to have said, "This is the place." For nearly half a century Utah was prohibited from entering the Union because of polygamy practiced by the Mormons. Finally the practice was abolished by the Mormon Church in 1890, and six years later the state was admitted, not as "Deseret," as it was first to be called, but as Utah, after the Ute Indians.

Courtesy Salt Lake City Chamber of Commerce

NIGHT VIEW OF FAMOUS MORMON TEMPLE, SALT LAKE CITY

The Mormon Tabernacle with its remarkable acoustics turn a whisper into a shout, is internationally known for its size, beauty, and unusual construction. The district Federal Reserve Bank is also located in Salt Lake City, financial center of the intermountain territory; and the University of Utah, situated here, is one of the oldest colleges west of the Mississippi.

Strategically located at the mouth of Weber Canyon, Ogden is an important gateway. One of the city's interesting features is an apparently inexhaustible supply of sparkling, pure artesian water, spouted at the rate of eight million gallons a day from wells a few miles up the canyon.

NEVADA: SILVER STATE

The state of Nevada is an important producer of gold, silver, copper, and semiprecious stones. It is less densely populated than any other state in the Union. Boulder Dam is one of the greatest triumphs of modern engineering. The dam controls the water of

BOULDER DAM FROM THE FRONT, WITH ALL OUTLETS OPEN

Courtesy Union Pacific Railroad

the Colorado River in the reach of its course where it forms the Nevada-Arizona state boundary. The dam, which tapers from the unbelievable thickness of 650 feet at the base to forty-five feet at the top has created the world's most extensive artificial lake, spreading its surface over 227 square miles. Four and a half million cubic yards of concrete were poured in the making of the mighty dam which will provide electric power and irrigating water for millions of people in the southwest.

CITIES OF UTAH

Las Vegas, near the great dam, is the center of a charmed circle of mountain and desert splendor. Still a frontier town, this little city is both picturesque and hospitable. Reno is interesting almost as much for the prominence of her temporary citizens as for her garish and exciting personality. Carson City, named for Kit Carson, the famous frontiersman, is the capital of Nevada. Located about thirty miles southeast of Reno, it is the heart of a busy mining district and the seat of a branch of the United States mint.

The city is a popular summer resort on account of the beautiful scenery of the Sierra Nevadas. Other scenic spots in the state are the famous "Lost City of Nevada," the "Valley of Fire," and many wonderful caverns.

COLORADO: LAND OF MOUNTAINS

Ample evidence remains today of the prehistoric cliff dwellers who once lived in the mountains of southern and southwestern Colorado. The stirring old ruins of their homes have been the scene of much enthusiastic digging by modern research workers, and they have shed no little light on America's past. The Ute Indian Reservation holds the living remnant of the great, roving bands of Indians who once occupied the northern section. The first Europeans to arrive were the Spanish, who named the region Colorado, for the red color of the great river flowing through it. Colorado's eventful history never fails to thrill its students, and the traveler cannot go far in the state without finding the opportunity to learn much of it.

MOUNTAIN PLAYGROUNDS

Famous for its national parks, which encompass most of the scenic areas of the state, Colorado furnishes a summer vacation home for many Americans each year.

The circle tour of the Rocky Mountain National Park, includes Big Thompson Canyon, Estes Park, Horseshoe Park, Hidden Valley, Fall River Pass, Milner Pass, Grand Lake, Berthoud Pass, and Idaho Springs. This is one of the wildest and most rugged sections of the Rocky Mountains. Through it runs the Continental Divide, sometimes called the spinal column of North America. It is a region where tarrying is delightful, where leave-taking is reluctant.

AT THE TIMBERLINE

Timberline is a fascinating sight. At about ten thousand feet above sea-level the thick forests of the valleys, the aspens, oaks and maples disappear. Pines, too, become scarce and scrawny. The altitude, cold, and wind have made gnarled old dwarfs from what might have been tall, straight pines on a lower level. At eleven thousand feet may be found a last tree, sprawled along the uneven ground like a mighty vine, scarred by the struggle with bleak gales and heavy snows. Yet at this height the eager climber is amazed to find the tiniest and the most intensely colored blossoms, exquisite daintiness in the midst of a massive rugged landscape.

"PIKE'S PEAK OR BUST!"

Near Colorado Springs, the third largest of Colorado's cities, is Pike's Peak, which soars fourteen thousand feet into the air and is one of the most frequently climbed mountains in the world. An excellently engineered highway leads with security and comfort to the summit, through the most scenic area of the mountain ascent, making the climb by motor a far cry from the first scalings of the steep slopes and crags. The traveler may choose, however, to ride the famous cog railway: hauled by a powerful cable, the line holds the amazing record of never having had an accident. Or you may drive to the very top in an automobile.

Nearby is the picturesque spot termed "The Garden of the Gods." Here huge masses of vivid red sandstone form such imaginative figures as the Seal, the Kissing Camels, the Cathedral

Courtesy Union Pacific Railroad

PIKE'S PEAK, COLORADO

Courtesy C. & N. W. Ry. Co.

GATEWAY TO THE GARDEN OF THE GODS

Spires, and others, all dramatically set against a verdant backdrop. Another geological wonder is the "Cave of the Winds," where the sight-seer may roam through long underground passageways and find everchanging forms and color.

FOREST WILDERNESS

Beautiful and primeval, in spite of their great popularity as vacation spots, are Roosevelt, Medicine Bow, San Isabel, and Mesa Verde National Forests, all within the boundaries of Colorado. Cliff-dwelling ruins in Mesa Verde have the ghostly splendor of discarded palaces, standing in villages deserted yet well preserved.

CAPITAL CITY

Denver, the largest of Colorado's very interesting cities, is ideally located in the foothills of the Rockies. It is famed as a leading recreational center and health resort and has thirty-eight beautiful parks in its environs; but it is also known as the center of a large agricultural and stock-raising section. Her civic center includes a five-million-dollar municipal building, a Greek theater, and a beautiful public library. The massive, gray granite walls of the State Capitol are a fitting symbol of the importance of the state's mineral wealth. A United States mint is located here.

Second largest community in the state, Pueblo takes its name from the old Indian word meaning village, and is noted for its important iron and steel smelting and stockyards. About thirty miles northwest of Denver is Boulder, home of the State University of Colorado, whose campus commands a view of magnificent mountains. This is a popular starting point for trips to glaciers and to peaks in the Rocky Mountain National Park.

"GO WEST YOUNG MAN"

Horace Greeley about 1870 gave this famous advice, "Go west young man"; and it was followed by a group of New England colonists, sponsored by him, and resulted in the settlement of Greeley in northeast Colorado. This settlement was named in honor of the famous eastern newspaper editor. In 1930 Greeley had a population of 12,200. It is a distribution point for the surrounding rich agricultural and mining regions. Colorado Springs is seventy-five miles south of Denver. It has become a famous health resort because of the nearby mineral springs.

WYOMING: LAND OF INDIAN PAINTBRUSH

Cowboys, fully as colorful as any yarn in fiction ever painted them, whoop over the endless sagebrush prairies of Wyoming. Plaintive howls of coyotes still sound across the desolate, flat wastes at night. When the moon is rising, the distant peaks of the Big Horns appear like the brawny shoulders of a gigantic herd of buffalo crouched in the darkness. Little wonder that the Indians here left a rich store of legend behind them.

The region abounds in beauties: color-splashed canyons, rocky towers, mysterious hot springs whose healing waters flow from some unknown underground source, frequent patches of velvety, fertile green lying long and low between surrounding bluffs, and finally the thousand and one mysteries of the incomparable Yellowstone Park in the northwestern corner of the state.

Courtesy United States Department of the Interior

"OLD FAITHFUL" GEYSER IN ACTION,
YELLOWSTONE NATIONAL PARK

REGION OF SUPERLATIVES

When Jim Bridger, energetic old frontiersman, returned from an exploration of Yellowstone territory over a hundred years ago, his stories were received with jeers and his enthusiasm with stones. Little wonder! Even today's traveler finds lifted eyebrows and amused skepticism in response to his enthusiastic reports to the folks at home.

Yellowstone is indeed a wonderland almost as difficult to comprehend with the eye and ear as with the imagination. This famous park contains many geysers; more than three thousand are said to be in one area of about two square miles. Here, too, are found boiling springs, petrified forests, and mud volcanoes. Yellowstone Canyon has beautiful scenery and shelters thousands of wild animals.

The tourist gets his first thrill before entering the actual limits of the park. Approach is made either by famous old Cody Road, past the magnificence of Shoshone Dam's granite walls of almost rosy pink, or by the newer and equally scenic route of Red Lodge Highway, where one may stop at the side of the road to make a snowball in mid-August. The first acquaintance with the park is by a long, sylvan drive through dense growth of lodgepole pine and spruce.

One may make his first night's stop at any of the half dozen main camps, each of which is located near some major attraction of the park—Mammoth Hot Springs, Canyon, Tower Falls, Fishing Bridge, Thumb, and Old Faithful. These camps maintain luxurious and yet rustic accommodations for every class of visitor. Housekeeping cabins are well built and equipped. To the visitor's surprise, he finds no sign of man's encroachment on the wilderness except for these few places set aside for campers.

Imagine sitting, as Yellowstone guests do, in a huge cage outside the bear-feeding pit at Canyon, while grizzlies roam at will on the outside. Imagine the warmth thrown from the blazing logs of a huge campfire, where an alert young ranger naturalist holds his nightly audience enthralled with tales of the park wild life. The museums in each camp, the superb guide service to be had by tourists merely for the asking, and the ever watchful care and protection of guests (over 400,000 in 1937) go far to make the park the excellent recreational and instructive wonderland that it is.

BEARS AND HOT WATER

Three of the greatest attractions in Yellowstone are the bears, Old Faithful Geyser, and the Canyon. The bears have learned to beg and to rob most cleverly. Often a huge, clumsy old black bear walks into a cabin to get the bacon that she has smelled, or climbs into the back seat of a car to find the grocery box. However, tourists are warned and should follow the rules conspicuously posted, to save them from such ravages. Though dangerous if tantalized, the bears are a source of constant amusement and enjoyment to the discreet person, who finds it wise always to obey the rule of the park, "Hands off the bears."

Old Faithful Geyser, not the highest nor yet the most spectacular of its three thousand brothers and sisters, is nevertheless by far the most popular. It has received its name from its punctual and frequent eruptions, shooting a silvery fountain of boiling water and steam some one hundred and fifty feet into the air every sixty-five minutes. The beauty of this mighty eruption, as colored flood-lights from the Old Faithful Inn play on it each night, challenges the imagination.

Courtesy C. & N. W. Ry. Co. Photo by Haynes

CLEOPATRA TERRACE, MAMMOTH HOT SPRINGS, YELLOWSTONE NATIONAL PARK

YELLOWSTONE CANYON

From Artist's Point one looks down on the great chasm of the Yellowstone Canyon to see every color in the rainbow along the rocky walls. Far, far below drops a waterfall 308 feet, splashing to a greater depth than the famed Niagara. From such great height the turbulent waters of the Yellowstone River appear like a flat, twisted ribbon. Hundreds of artists and a greater number of photographers have tried to reproduce the grandeur of this natural phenomenon. Few experts have been even partially satisfied with their results. Nature seems to defy duplication of her supreme efforts in majesty.

Nowhere else in the entire country can the average American see huge herds of ragged buffalo grazing at large on the grassy slopes. Nowhere else can he approach so closely to moose, elk, and deer. Mountain sheep, with their queer, curved horns, run lithely up a steep mountainside in full view of the autoist and his party. Smaller animals scurry across the road and then stop to gaze back curiously at the human intruder. Unafraid, seeking the shelter of the dense forest only when some unusual alarm drives them, the animals of Yellowstone are perfectly willing to be watched, photographed, even sketched. For nearly half a century there has been a law against harming them in any way, and they have lost their fear of man.

Two hundred miles east of Yellowstone, Thermopolis has the largest hot spring in the world. Here medicinal springs attract many visitors, and the state has made this area into a state park. Famous as a health center, this little city is rivaled only by Saratoga. South of Thermopolis is the entrance to Wind River Canyon, where from solid granite a twelve-mile road has been blasted. There is no more stirring automobile drive to be had in all the west than this trip at sundown.

"FRONTIER DAYS"

Cheyenne is the capital of Wyoming and the largest city. The environment of Cheyenne is so reminiscent of its hurly-burly past that it is hard not to imagine one's self in the frontier days of several decades ago. Here each year is held one of the greatest rodeos and roundups in the country, "Frontier Days."

Casper, second largest city in east central Wyoming, has a bustle and an activity which belies its moderate-sized population, (1930) 16,619. The town gives the impression of being considerably larger than it is; this is due, no doubt, to the prominence of the three huge oil refineries which have enriched the city. Scenic Casper Mountain towers above the city and provides excellent views of the river below. Just west of Casper is Hell's Half Acre, a vast natural bowl filled with highly tinted and grotesque formations originating from wind and water erosion.

Independence Rock is a large granite rock which was a landmark on the old Oregon Trail.

Laramie, location of the large and prosperous University of Wyoming, is surrounded by one of the world's largest and richest natural mineral basins. The region has coal, iron, gold, and silver mines. Old Fort Sanders (a frontier post on the Overland Trail), the oil fields, and the large stockyards are of special interest to the visitor.

Sheridan is the railroad station for the many "dude" ranches of the Big Horns. Rock Springs is in the center of a coal-mining region. This city of 8,400 is located in the mountains west of Laramie. Rawlins, in southern Wyoming, is in a livestock and oil-producing region. Cody, a tourist center east of Yellowstone National Park, was named after Colonel William F. Cody (Buffalo Bill).

MONTANA: THE BONANZA STATE

The adventure of new frontiers challenges the Montana visitor. The eastern three-fifths of this state lies in the Great Plains. The Missouri River is the chief means of drainage for this area. Irrigation is necessary throughout most of the state because of the semi-arid condition. This state is rich in minerals, lumber, and water-power. Montana also has some very interesting cities. Helena, charming capital, but not the largest town, is the site of far-famed Last Chance Gulch, where rich gold was uncovered at about the time of the end of the Civil War. The State Capitol here, in which is preserved the collection of the State Historical Society, is interesting to visitors. Called Montana's Garden City, Missoula lies snugly at the base of majestic mountains. Here are located the University of Montana, founded in 1893, and a giant sugar plant. Billings is situated on the Yellowstone River in southern Montana. One of the largest beet-sugar factories in the world has been established in this city. The extensive irrigation system has made this district very productive. It is also a trading and shipping point.

Butte is the largest mining city in the world. The most important ores mined in this region include copper, silver, manganese, and zinc. Gold, arsenic, and lead are mined in smaller quantities. The State School of Mines is located at Butte. This city has today the greatest population in Montana (1930), 39,532.

Photo courtesy C. M. Oehler, Chicago

MT. ROCKWELL, GLACIER NATIONAL PARK, MONTANA

Near Butte are four valuable hot springs. Situated on the Vigilante and Yellowstone Trails, Butte offers a wide variety of scenic, historic, and recreational activities for the visitor.

THE PACIFIC COAST

The three states comprising the Pacific group completely border the west coast of the United States. They form a large and fascinating area for a vacation trip. Their varied scenery, extremes in climate, and widely differing features seem to shorten the trip for the traveler. Here are mountains, glaciers, deserts, fruitful valleys, arid wastes of cactus, extinct volcanoes, hundreds of miles of virgin forests, and big cities, rivaling those in the East in many respects and surpassing them in beauty.

Early Spanish explorers, fur traders, the Lewis and Clark expedition, American control under the name of Oregon Territory, Indian fights, and boundary disputes make up the early history. Finally came the great gold rush, which stimulated settlement and intensified interest in probably the greatest area of natural resources in the country. Washington, Oregon, and California are now three of the richest and most progressive states in the Union.

WASHINGTON: THE EVERGREEN STATE

Transition from a frontier trading post to an outstanding industrial and agricultural state in less than half a century is Washington's remarkable record. Although white men were near this territory as early as 1543, trappers and a few missionaries still made up the only white population for the next three centuries. England and America occupied the country jointly from the beginning of the nineteenth century until 1846, when England relinquished her hold on it, and it was made part of the Oregon Territory. In 1853 Washington Territory, with its own governor, was organized, and thirty-six years later this state was admitted into the Union. From that year on, the state developed rapidly.

"THE MOUNTAIN THAT WAS 'GOD'"

Thus described in a book title because of the intense nature-worship given to this superlative peak, Mount Rainier comprises about one fourth of the immense national park bearing its name. More impressive than the other two American peaks which surpass it in actual height, Rainier rises not from adjoining tablelands, but directly from its base to a snow-capped skyline. The crater of an extinct volcano, Mt. Rainier contains no less than forty-eight square miles of glaciers. Its ice streams, cascading from the summit in all directions, have been compared to the arms of a great starfish. One of the most thrilling experiences America affords is the ascent of this vast mountain, in the care of an expert guide, whose service is furnished by the national government.

Other spectacular sights in Washington include Mount Olympus National Monument in Olympic National Forest; the Cascade Tunnel through the Cascade Mountains, eight miles in length; the San Juan Archipelago, in Puget Sound, and a Federal Irrigation Project on the Yakima River.

Courtesy Tacoma Chamber of Commerce

MOUNT RAINIER, WITH PARADISE VALLEY IN THE FOREGROUND

THE CHARMED CITY

Seattle is surrounded by so many differently shaped bodies of water that its setting is one of unusual beauty. Facing Puget Sound in the Pacific Ocean, this city's background is a huge mountain range. Two lakes within Seattle's limits and the beautiful, long Lake Washington behind it make an exquisite framework for the city. The many public parks, the waterfront campus of the state university, the aquarium, mammoth piers, and dozens of other attractions invariably tempt the visitor to tarry here longer than he had planned. Agriculture, timber, minerals, and fisheries have enriched the city and swelled its population almost to the half-million mark.

Spokane, the eastern gateway to national parks of the Pacific Northwest, has a wealth of beautiful natural scenery within its own confines. It is the nearest large city to the Grand Coulee Dam, one of the greatest engineering and construction undertakings of all time.

LUMBER CAPITAL OF THE WORLD

Tacoma, third city of importance in Washington, has a wonderful harbor. Here lies the entrance to Mount Rainier National Park, amid a district of rich berry farming, truck gardening, commercial bulb growing, and poultry raising. Tacoma is situated in one of the loveliest areas on Puget Sound.

Olympia is the state capital and smallest of the metropolitan districts of the state. Vancouver is the oldest city in the state. Walla Walla, meaning small rapid river, boasts that because it was liked so well, it was named twice. This beautiful little city is over a hundred years old.

OREGON: THE BEAVER STATE

Oregon, the ninth largest state in the Union, easily entertained her more than half-million automobile guests last year. Broad, cool highways flanked by some of the largest trees in the world, mountain lakes in forest settings, a paradise of wild flowers, large cities with every modern improvement—these comprise a few of the many reasons for visiting Oregon.

The Cascade Range divides Oregon into two distinct geographic and climatic regions. Along four hundred miles of coast are sandy beaches and many small bays; here the climate is humid and uniform. East of the Cascades are rugged tablelands with a dry and variable climate.

VOLCANIC JEWEL

Lying in the crater of an extinct volcano, where walls are a thousand feet high, is the beautiful blue Crater Lake. The national park located here is named for it. The traveler finds

Courtesy Portland Chamber of Commerce

BONNEVILLE DAM ON COLUMBIA RIVER
Forty-two miles east of Portland, Oregon

mountain-climbing, fishing, and sight-seeing of the finest kind in the world. Imagine mountain trails winding to the summit of the crater and, after crossing the rim, winding down a thousand feet to the shore of the great, silent indigo sea, five miles wide and two thousand feet deep. The effect is indescribable; the memory is lasting.

Oregon's miles of underground wonders have been preserved in Siskiyou Forest. Here the visitor finds beautiful limestone caverns to visit by day; and campfire entertainment provided for the evenings. Oregon's beaches, the Columbia River Highway, and the scenery and sports on Mt. Hood are also worth noting.

At Portland each year is held a rose festival, to which come people from all over the world. Portland, the largest city in the state, is beautifully and strategically located on the Columbia River. Her harbor accommodates ocean-going ships. Here is manufactured more lumber than anywhere else in the world. The

Pacific coast's beach resorts, always of interest to the traveler, especially if he comes from far inland, are within a day's journey to Portland.

In Salem, the capital city of Oregon, the well-known Oregon State Fair is held each year. Astoria, probably the oldest town settled by white people in the northwest, received its name from John Jacob Astor, by whom it was established in 1811 as a fur-trading post. Eugene, Corvallis, La Grande, and Medford are leading cities of the state.

CALIFORNIA: THE EL DORADO OF THE WEST

Southern California offers to the weather-weary her even, subtropical climate and exhibits a personality all her own, while northern California is cool and energizing. Unique features of the state are Death Valley, 276 feet below sea-level, and the Colorado desert, the hottest place in the United States, the temperature occasionally exceeding 130 degrees in the shade.

Courtesy Los Angeles County Chamber of Commerce

SNOW-CLAD PEAKS VIEWED FROM A CALIFORNIA ORANGE GROVE

From the time Sir Francis Drake put in at a California bay to repair his ships, about 1579, until the present day, the history of this state has been exciting, tempestuous, and record-breaking. Spain occupied the region with missions and bold adventurers in the eighteenth century. Spain's control, with Mexico as agent, continued until the state was ceded to the United States after the Mexican War in 1848. In the next year came that mighty flood of humanity across the desert in the gold rush. Cities sprang into being overnight. Roads grew as thousands of people poured over foot trails. As California settled into a more dignified and placid statehood late in the nineteenth century, she suddenly realized a new problem—one to be faced for the first time by an American state. Chinese and Japanese immigration to California was crowding the white population. With the solution of this problem scarcely under way, earthquakes and fire destroyed San Francisco. Today she has a new problem which is the most desirable yet. It is that of acting as gracious hostess to the countless numbers trekking across the continent from every direction to see her "sights," enjoy her climate, and otherwise spend their vacations.

A NATURAL WONDERLAND

California has a number of national parks. No traveler ever considers that he has really seen California until he has visited Yosemite National Park and enjoyed the beauty of Yosemite Falls.

The Sequoia National Park in eastern California is equally as famous. Situated on the western slopes of the Sierra Nevadas, this park was established to preserve the forests of California's big trees. Here are some of the oldest and largest trees in the world as well as many of other scenic attractions.

Lassen Volcanic Park contains Lassen Peak, the only active volcano in the United States. Here also are mud geysers and hot springs. The spectator is fascinated by the fantastic lava formations and multi-colored crags of this weird region.

The General Grant tree in General Grant National Park has the greatest base diameter and the largest diameter at two hundred feet from the ground of any known sequoia. This tree is 267 feet high. Wild flowers and shrubs abound in the giant forests.

MARIPOSA GROVE OF GIANT SEQUOIAS, YOSEMITE NATIONAL PARK, CALIFORNIA

THE QUEEN OF ANGELS

City of a million and a quarter people, Los Angeles has measured practically all her growth in the last seventy years. Ultra-modern shops and imposing buildings line the business streets. Beautiful homes, even to the tiniest cottage set in a wreath of flowers, delight visitors. Within the environs are sixty-seven parks, an unusually large number; museums of art and history; and Hollywood, a suburb. Los Angeles' greatest distinction is that of being the largest city in area in the United States, and it ranks fifth in population. This city is the seat of the University of Southern California and the southern branch of the University of California.

Hollywood, a part of Los Angeles, is the most visited of all the state's interesting spots. Famous as the center of the motion picture industry, it contributes the largest portion of the world's supply of moving pictures. The famous suburb is the home of many movie stars who maintain luxurious estates. Some of the notable sights in this city are the Hollywood Bowl, Griffith Park, the Japanese Gardens, the movie lots where pictures are made, famous theaters, and night clubs.

AMERICA'S MOST COLORFUL CITY

San Francisco is located on a peninsula between the Pacific Ocean and San Francisco Bay, which are connected by the strait of the Golden Gate. San Francisco calls herself the city of lights and laughter. The tourist calls her the city of courage and vision. Not only her recovery from the terrible earthquake tragedies in her history, but her program for the future justifies this more serious description. The great San Francisco-Oakland Bay Bridge was recently opened and the motorist may enter the heart of California's historic city by driving over the four-and-one-half-mile aerial highway of the Bay Bridge, two hundred feet above the blue waters of the bay.

San Francisco beckons her guest to her choicest sight-seeing spots—Golden Gate Park, University of San Francisco, and Telegraph Hill; the hill rises above the Latin Quarter, where the guest visits studios and bohemian restaurants, and breathes a piquant atmosphere. The city's opera and symphony buildings, and Chinatown, are world-famous. The great new Golden Gate

Courtesy Los Angeles Chamber of Commerce

ONE OF THE MANY GROUPS OF MOVING-PICTURE STUDIOS for which the suburbs of Los Angeles are famous.

Bridge is a point of interest to visitors as well as an item of pride to the native Californian. An American battle fleet at anchor, the taking off and alighting at the municipal airport, and ships of all nations passing in and out of the Golden Gate are never to be forgotten. No matter how old or large San Francisco grows, she will never quite lose the flavor of those first days when her hardy, boisterous, and undaunted spirit spread her reputation around the world.

OTHER CITIES

Oakland, which is almost directly opposite the Golden Gate and on the east side of San Francisco Bay, rises on hills above the business section below. Once a station of the famed Wells Fargo Express of gold rush days, Oakland is now the metropolis of the East Bay Empire. There are parks, museums, an art gallery, and various schools and colleges that serve the guests of Oakland as well as her own inhabitants.

Courtesy California Toll Bridge Authority. Photo by Hellings

AERIAL VIEW OF THE GREAT SAN FRANCISCO-OAKLAND BAY BRIDGE OPENED NOV. 12, 1936

A great cattle plain, with the city of Livermore as its hub, lies back of Oakland. Seat of the nation's largest state university, University of California, Berkeley is famed as a scientific, cultural and educational center. Sacramento, in the heart of a great fruit belt, is the capital of the state. Because this city is situated at the

Courtesy San José Chamber of Commerce

BLOSSOM TIME IN SANTA CLARA VALLEY

confluence of the American and Sacramento Rivers, it is an important distributing point for the surrounding agricultural and mining region. The Capitol is in a park well known for its flowers and trees.

San Diego has an excellent harbor. This city, located in southern California, is a distribution point for the large fruit-raising district that surrounds it. The California State College, the Naval Aviation Base (headquarters of the Eleventh Naval District), San Diego Bay, the beaches, the airport, and Lindbergh Field are some of the places and sights of interest.

Santa Barbara, in southwestern California, is beautifully located in a section famous for its flowers and fruits. Each year a fiesta is held here in celebration of the history of the city. Spanish and Mission are the chief styles of architecture used throughout Santa Barbara.

Long Beach, with a popular harbor and seven-mile beach, is located in the southwestern part of the state. This city is a year-round resort.

Palo Alto is best known as the seat of Stanford University. This city, thirty miles southeast of San Francisco, is the home of Herbert Hoover, former President of the United States.

Whether the tourist begins or ends his tour of the United States with beautiful and rich California, he will not want to miss it altogether. The dream of many Americans is to spend all the hours possible in this sunny, healthful climate, in this region of big trees, beautiful flowers, snowy mountain peaks, deep blue harbors and lakes, and fertile fruit farms. Americans have learned to explore it and to love it.

ALASKA FISHING BOATS

SITKA, ALASKA

COLUMBIA GLACIER

A solid ice wall four miles wide, reaching heights of nine hundred feet.

(Illustrations on this page courtesy Alaska Steamship Company)

Courtesy National Railways of Mexico

MARKET SCENE IN MEXICO SHOWING BEAUTIFUL FLOWERS

MEXICO: BANDITS AND REVOLUTIONS

THERE was a time when the word Mexico meant a country harassed by bandits and revolutions. That was because Mexico was going through a period of growing pains and, like a bad boy, was a little obstreperous. Ever since the Aztec empire was overthrown by the Spaniard Hernando Cortés, between 1519 and 1521, Mexico has been a seething volcano like its famous Popocatepetl. Mistreated by Spanish conquistadors, enslaved by Spanish plantation owners, drained of their resources by strangling taxation, tithe-bled by the regular and secular clergy, it was not surprising that the Mexicans revolted. After independence was won in 1821, Mexico entered upon a period of revolutions and internal disorder. International disputes led to foreign intervention and an invasion by a French army which seated Maximilian of Austria on the throne. The usurper was overthrown in 1867, but peace did not come to Mexico. A series of internal disorders engulfed the country until Díaz emerged as a dictator.

PYRAMID OF CHICHEN-ITZA, YUCATAN, MEXICO

Black Star photo
By Neofot

THE AZTEC CIVILIZATION

Before the conquest of Mexico by the Spaniards the country was far from uncivilized. In fact, the Aztec and Maya Indians were the most civilized people on the North American continent, and, when Cortés subjugated the Aztecs, they were at the peak of their civilization. For instance, of the entire Indian population of North America, only the Mayas and the Aztecs recorded a documented history of their nations. Using a rebus type of writing, in which pictures represented the various syllables, Aztec scribes made records of their laws, their poetry, their conquests, and even the movements of planets. Because they also included writings about their gods, whom the Spanish priests called pagan, these early records were burned in the public squares. Thus, with the exception of a few scattered fragments, was destroyed the history of the most civilized people in early North America.

HERNANDO CORTÉS — CONQUEROR OF MEXICO

Into this thriving Indian civilization came Hernando Cortés. Piqued by rumors of amazing quantities of gold and precious jewels to be found in the New World, the Spanish governor of Cuba sent this Spanish explorer to look into the matter. He found in Mexico an amazing group of people who built pyramids, miles of roads, lighthouses, magnificent temples, and palaces gorgeously decorated with gold and precious jewels. What the rapacious Spaniards did when they arrived makes an unpleasant story.

Their eyes bulging with viewing wealth in prodigious quantities, they stopped at nothing in an orgy of murdering, looting, betraying, and eventually almost destroying an entire civilization.

When the Spaniards under Cortés first arrived in Mexico, at Vera Cruz, the Indians thought they were gods because of their fair complexions. At Tabasco they fought a battle with the Indians, and with their superior horses and guns were victorious against the natives' arrows and spears. At Vera Cruz, Cortés began to negotiate with Montezuma II, the Aztec emperor. During this time, his men mutinied and he finally burned his ships to prevent their desertion. Then began a long trek into the interior, to Tenochtitlan, now Mexico City, which was the capital of the empire. Here, again, they were thought to be gods by many; but soon dissensions arose and Cortés seized the emperor as a hostage. Emperor was murdered while Cortés was away. When the conqueror returned, he found his men, under the leadership of Lieutenant Pedro de Alvarado, seriously threatened by the slain emperor's subjects. They managed to escape after a bloody battle was waged, and succeeded in returning to the coast, the scene of their first depredations. In 1521, they returned to Tenochtitlan, captured the city, and ransacked it of all its treasures. It was with the downfall of the capital that the dissolution of the Aztec civilization was begun.

SPANISH COLONIZATION

Then began the period of Spanish colonization of New Spain, as the Spaniards termed their acquisition. Cortés sent out a number of exploring expeditions. Later he was recalled and died in obscurity. But, following him in New Spain, in quick succession, came a series of representatives of the king: viceroys, sixty-one in number, who ruled over Mexico. Negroes were brought over to work as slaves. Under the *encomienda* system, which was intended to be the means of entrusting their welfare to Spanish conquerors who had been given grants of land, the Indians were supposed to be missionized, educated, and protected. But this benevolent paternalism deteriorated into vassalage, slavery of the most abject kind, which perhaps was worse than the slavery of the Negroes who, at least, could buy themselves out of slavery.

As a result of this influx of different peoples, the population became mixed. Although the Indians predominated, there arose new variations because few Spanish women cared to pioneer in New Spain. *Mestizos* were the children of Indians and Europeans; *sambos* resulted from the marriage of Negroes with Indians and *mulattoes* were born of white and Negro unions. Currently the largest three racial groups are the *mestizos*, the pure-blooded Indians, and the pure-blooded, white Spaniards. It is partly because of this volatile admixture of races, that the subsequent history of Mexico has been so tumultuous.

MEXICO AND THE CHURCH

The Franciscans were the first of the regular churchmen to come into Mexico. After them came the Augustinians, the Jesuits, and the Dominicans. In time, the Church became the most wealthy and, therefore, the most powerful faction in the country. In 1821, it owned more than half of the money and land. Its main purpose was to convert the pagans to Christianity and to educate them. A number of universities were erected, the most notable of which was the Royal and Pontifical University of Mexico, the oldest on the North American continent, established in 1553. Although this educational system purported to educate the masses, it served only to furnish religious and legal education to comparatively few. When Mexico had a population of 6,000,000, only 30,000 were able to read and write.

It should be noted to the Church's credit, however, that it continually warred with the state regarding the continuance of the enslaving *encomienda* system. It was Miguel Hidalgo y Costilla, a priest, who assembled an army of peons at his little church, the *grito de Dolores,* and revolted against the government in 1810. With the battle-cry of "Long Live Our Lady of Guadalupe!" he led his men into forays with government troops, defeating them a number of times. But, in the battle of Calderón Bridge, his army was routed and eventually Costilla was apprehended and executed.

WARS—INVASIONS—REVOLUTIONS

For 300 years, the Spaniards dominated Mexico. In 1808, when Napoleon conquered Spain, the first whispers of independence circulated among the Mexicans. The mother-country

Black Star photo. By Hugo Männer

THE CATHEDRAL IN MEXICO CITY

Black Star photo

RUINS OF AN OLD NUNNERY NEAR MEXICO CITY

was no more; therefore its rights to possession were automatically surrendered. The movement for Mexican independence developed rapidly and, paralleling it, the period of bloody, internal warfare that ushered in murder, rapine, guerrilla butchery, assassinations, and general disorder. In 1810, the aforementioned Hidalgo led the revolt against Spain and was shot near Chihuahua. Augustín de Iturbide decreed himself Emperor of Mexico after he had deserted to the patriot's cause. In 1823, General Antonio López de Santa Anna dislodged Iturbide from his shaky throne. This same Santa Anna annihilated the Texans at the Alamo in the next decade. Texas succeeded in winning its independence in 1836, and was annexed to the United States nine years later. The Mexican War followed, as a result of which additional areas were lost to the United States.

In 1858, Benito Juárez, Mexican national hero, became president and immediately ordered the property of the Church to be sold and returned to the people. Later, in 1861, he suspended payment on loans made by foreign powers. Occupation of Mexico by the French followed, because the United States, being involved in its Civil War, was incapable of enforcing its Monroe Doctrine. The Hapsburg, Maximilian, was made Emperor of Mexico; but in 1867, he was executed after the French support was withdrawn. Juárez then resumed the presidency.

In 1871, Porfirio Díaz led a revolt against Juárez which was unsuccessful. But, in 1877, after Juárez had died and Sebastian Lerdo de Tejada assumed the presidency, Díaz again revolted, exiled Tejada, and became president. Diaz ruled Mexico for more than thirty years, and the country began to emerge from its non-productive shell politically and economically. But, in 1911, Francisco Madero rebelled and overthrew Díaz. Two years later, in 1913, a Díaz lieutenant, Victoriano Huerta, deposed and murdered Madero. Then, Venustiano Carranza overthrew Huerta with the aid of Álvaro Obregón and Pancho Villa. The Carranza regime received its official stamp of approval when the United States recognized it as being the representative government of Mexico.

With the year 1917, when it adopted a new constitution, Mexico began the present period of industrial improvement and economic security which, under General Lázaro Cárdenas, made the Republic of Mexico a force to be reckoned with in the family of nations.

MAÑANA AND STILL MAÑANA

What impresses the newcomer to Mexico is, primarily, the presence of a splash of brilliant colors throughout. And, what is more, these colors are not thrown about heedlessly but shape themselves into definite forms and designs for which, somehow, the Mexican has developed intuitive tastes.

Another seeming wonder is the laziness of the average Mexican peon. Time to him is non-existent. He lives only from day to day. The past is gone, the present is glorious, and the future—*quién sabe?* To him it does not matter whether the job he must perform is completed today or tomorrow—or next week. He needs little to satisfy himself; therefore, he does not believe that he should work harder to obtain something which does not add to his satisfaction but which tires him tremendously. He works no

Courtesy National Railways of Mexico

PICTURESQUE GARB USED ON FESTIVE OCCASIONS BY NATIVES OF OAXACA, MEXICO

Courtesy Illinois Central System

NATIVE MEXICAN TYPES

harder than is necessary. Perhaps, to people who live in a time-mad world whose slogan is "do it now," this attitude savors of laziness. Perhaps the insistence of the Mexican in deserting all work at *siesta* time is simply being lazy. Perhaps his participating in an endless series of feast-days and festivals, instead of laboring in the fields, does not produce additional dollars. But, if more dollars mean nothing, if people are happy with little, if the line of least resistance taxes the muscles less, may it not be said that a leisurely life is to be praised?

Perhaps the most amazing thing about Mexico that startles the newcomer is that there are primitive conditions just a few miles from its large cities. In some sections of Mexico the natives continue the same primitive civilization that their ancestors developed hundreds of years ago. If we see them at church, we sense an underlying flare of paganism actuating their worship. If we see them at work, we feel that, somehow, we are peering through a magical time-machine that is taking us back through the ages. Time has been made to stand still.

The typical Mexican peon always wears a sombrero, a broad-brimmed hat with a conical top which keeps the intense Mexican sun from his eyes. His trousers are simply dirty-white cotton pajamas and his blouse is usually of the same material. Over his shoulder he wears a brilliantly-dyed *sarape* which he also uses as a blanket. His feet are usually bare, but when they are covered he walks on thong sandals. In the main, this typical peon subsists on maize and beans prepared with condiments so hot as to make them almost unpalatable to foreigners.

TRAVEL IN THE INTERIOR

As yet, the highway system of Mexico is undeveloped. Most of the towns distant from the larger cities are almost inaccessible except by burro, the Mexican's chief mode of transportation. Therefore, a large part of Mexico's 763,944 square miles basking lazily in an era that time seems to have forgotten must remain unknown to the traveler. But the government, through a vigorous program of road-building—if we are to accept vigorous only with its Mexican connotations—is constructing a network of highways that will bring even the remotest village closer to civilization. Its greatest achievement in this endeavor is the almost completed highway that leads from Nuevo Laredo, through Monterrey to Mexico City, a distance of 763 miles. With the exception of about thirty-two miles between Chapulhuacán and Jacala, which is in the process of being surfaced, the entire highway is fully paved—the only paved highway connecting the United States with the interior of Mexico. Railroads, however, connect most of the important cities with the United States.

MEXICO CITY

Since tourist activity centers around Mexico City, from which all of the main roadways and railroads radiate, thus making it the most important city in the Republic, it would be best, in dealing with the wonders of Mexico, to begin with the capital city. Situated in a verdant valley on a plateau a mile above sea-level, Mexico City's climate is ideal. Seldom does the temperature fall below 35 degrees; rarely does it rise above 79 degrees. A beneficent sun

Black Star photo. By Hugo Männer

NATIONAL SQUARE IN MEXICO CITY
The National Building is at the right, with the National Theater at left.

smiles down warmly the entire day. At night, it is delightfully cool.

Derived from one of the names of the old Aztec gods of war, Mexitli, the capital's name is truly symbolical of the wars and battles that have shaken it from time to time. Starting with the Spaniards, Mexico City was subjected to warfare in 1692, during the first revolt; in 1847, when the American general, Winfield Scott, occupied it; in 1863, when the French marshal, Forey, took possession; and at many other times when the various Mexican revolutionists, starting with Díaz and ending with Carranza, battled for its occupancy.

CHURCHES AND MUSEUMS

Mexico City now shows few signs of the warfare that has marred its history. Although tall buildings are nonexistent, because of the shifting marshy insecurity of the ground on which the city has been built, a number of imposing edifices still remain,

Black Star photo. By Pierre Verger

HISTORIC BELL TOWERS IN THE VILLAGE OF ACATEPEC, MEXICO

reminders of the Aztecs, the Spaniards, and the European-minded president, Díaz. Spanish architecture predominates, reflecting the Moorish influence, with its system of building around an inner court or *patio*. The Cathedral, begun in 1573 and completed in

1811, stands where an Aztec temple was razed by Cortés. It is one of the largest churches on the continent and contains some of the finest ecclesiastical art to be found in the world, including two Murillo paintings, carvings, and statuary. The National Palace, official home of the President and many of the government offices, is an immense edifice on the site of which was once the palace of Montezuma. Outstanding here are the mural history of Mexico by Diego Rivera and the Liberty Bell, which was always tolled when the peons revolted, and this perhaps accounts for its worn appearance!

The National Museum, fronting the Plaza, present in every Mexican city, town, and village, is a storehouse of antiquity. Here can be seen the "calendar," supposedly dating back to the Toltecs, and the "sacrificial stone" of the Aztecs. The government pawnshop, Monte de Piedad, was first a vice-regal palace and was erected in colonial style. The National Library building was formerly an Augustinian monastery built in 1692, and has in its vaults copies of books written by the Indians.

There are numberless churches in this country, where religion is so ingrained and where almost every mountain top is crowned with a carved crucifix. Palaces, built by the old Spanish grandees, are still to be seen at scattered places. The National Theater, the Castle of Chapultepec in which is now a military school, the Iturbide Palace, the Jockey Club, and the Palace of Justice are all architectural sights well worth viewing.

NATIVE MARKETS

Trips to the native quarters are replete with delightful surprises. The markets, for instance, are resplendent with the color of Mexico, particularly the Flower Market on Avenida Hidalgo, aflame with gorgeously colored tropical plants and blooms interspersed with cages of raucous tropical birds whose colors would shame the rainbow. Stores throughout the city feature displays of native handicraft and antiques, leather-work, silversmithery, glassware, pottery, tiling, fiber and straw wares, jewelry *sarapes,* baskets, rugs, lacquerware and ceremonial masks. And in them all is evidenced the same love of color and design that has been the Mexican's heritage for centuries. Nowhere in Mexico, however, will one from the United States, find the standards of cleanliness to which he is accustomed; nor as good service.

Courtesy National Railways of Mexico

ROMANTIC FLOATING GARDENS AT XOCHIMILCO

PARKS AND SUBURBS

Chapultepec Park is reached by traveling the magnificent Paseo de la Reforma, a boulevard that is lined with statues and eucalyptus trees. In the park itself is the Castle on Grasshopper Hill, built by a viceroy, used by Maximilian and the later presidents. The Fountain of Don Quixote, overhung with moss from a giant *ahuehuete* tree which is as old as Mexico's history, splashes merrily for the delight of the many black-eyed Mexican *señoritas* who use the park as a favorite trysting place.

It is impossible to tell of all the glorious sights that Mexico City has to offer. Surrounding it are dozens of other cities and towns which almost demand description. For instance, there is San Angel, a suburb, with its Carmelite Convent, in which are interred the mummies of early Spanish grandees and churchmen. The famous Pyramid, at Cuicuilco, is the largest relic of prehistoric Mexico that has weathered the ravages of time.

STRANGE SIGHTS

At Xochimilco are magnificent floating gardens built for the pleasure of Montezuma and which still blossom with hundreds of varieties of tropical flowers, eucalyptus trees, olive trees, moss, vines, and shrubs. The only way to see these gardens is to take a little boat which is poled through the various canals connecting a series of tiny lakes in which flower-bedecked islands float. Similar gardens are to be found at Santa Anita and Ixtacalco.

The Pyramid of Tempanzolco at Cuernavaca was thought to be a natural mound until cannon-fire disclosed that it was really a massively-built stone structure that had been used by the Aztecs as a temple. At Cuernavaca stands the Palacio de Cortés, capitol of the State of Morelos, begun in 1530 by Cortés. The Cathedral, begun in 1529 and used by Cortés as a place of worship, is still being used as a church.

For over 400 years, Mexicans have been going to Cuautla to take the warm sulphur baths in the springs that bubble in the vicinity. And if you want to receive a little shock, notice the red-headed Indians about, whose hair pigment has been changed by the chemical action of the water in the neighborhood.

From the plaza in Amecameca can be obtained a beautiful view of Popocatepetl, the famous active Mexican volcano, rearing ominously to the heavens and, beside it, Ixtaccihuatl, "The Sleeping Woman," as they call it, another volcano whose contours and whitened peak have given it the name it bears. Here, also, come the religious pilgrims to the tomb of Martín de Valencia and the statue of Santo Entierro.

IN THE CATACOMBS

Guanajuato, being built on the side of a mountain gorge, presents a most peculiar sight. The roofs of many of the houses are on a level with the streets of the houses above them. Much of the Mexican gold that the Spaniards seized came from this section. In fact, the Valenciana Cathedral, a beautiful example of the many churches which are here, was maintained by solid chunks of ore given by miners as their offerings. Here, also, are the famed underground catacombs filled with the mummies of those whose relatives were unable to continue payments on crypts in the Panteon, the cemetery of crypts built above the sparse topsoil of the vicinity. The Alhóndiga, formerly a fort and now a prison, and the Legislative Palace are two buildings of interest.

CITIES OF SILVER AND OIL

Another famous church, Nuestra Señora del Carmen, is to be found in the city of San Luís Potosí, with its brilliantly colored dome of blue, green, yellow, and white majolica. Calle Hidalgo harbors most of the shops; but the native markets, with their crowds of Indians selling fruits and pottery and other native-ware, are the most colorful. The largest silver mines in the country are centered around this city.

Because of the recent oil-field developments, Tampico has become one of the largest ports in Mexico. With the importation of American technicians and money came naturally an Americanization which is greater than in most Mexican cities. Ordinarily, the weather is delightful, the summers being cooled by seawinds and the winters seldom going below 45°. But June and July are the months to avoid when visiting Tampico. Tarpon fishing in the sea is an attraction that draws many to the city, as do the bathing resorts of Playa de Miramar and La Barra.

SALTILLO AND MONTERREY

Saltillo, the capital of the state of Coahuila, interests the tourist mainly for its brilliant *sarapes*, for which it is one of the centers of manufacture. The alameda, a beautiful park, contains a lagoon shaped like Mexico. The Cathedral of Santiago has a carved door that is amazing in its execution. At one time, Tampico was the capital of Mexican territory which included the states of Texas and Colorado.

The first important city on the stretch of road from Nuevo Laredo to Mexico City is Monterrey. Here the old and the new rub elbows, modern steel mills and flour mills standing adjacent to the houses of Indians who manufacture the same products by hand. The Plaza Zaragosa furnishes the foreigner with an insight into what is a typical Mexican institution. Here, every Sunday at nine in the evening, sloe-eyed Mexican *señoritas* walk arm in arm in one direction while their prospective beaux promenade in the other direction, under the overhanging orange and palm trees. Thus the young people view their likely partners, separate into couples, and soon walk together through the park and eventually through life.

The Obispado, an old fortress of massive proportions, squats on top of a western hill. Its battle-scarred walls have been stormed by Americans, French, and Mexican insurrectionists. The Topo Chico hot springs are four miles away and are a favorite summering place. The Garcia Caves nearby are labyrinths of underground tunnels, beautified with gleaming, hanging stalactites, with an underground lake as an added feature. Three miles east of Monterrey is Guadalupe where the bull-ring is located.

THE BULLFIGHTS

It might be well to make some mention here of Mexico's favorite sport, bullfighting. Adopted from their Spanish ancestors by the Mexicans, the sport became as popular as baseball is to the Americans, the "fans" gossiping of their favorite toreador as much as the Americans discuss their Babe Ruth. The fights at Guadalupe take place in the season that extends from November to March. In Mexico City, where the Plaza de Toros seats 20,000 people, the season is the same, and the best matadors of Spain and Mexico indulge in this brutal but colorful spectacle for the delight of the Mexicans and the tourists. Lately, however, bullfighting as a sport has given way to *pelota*, a form of handball, and the Fronton Mexico in Mexico City seats 4,000 spectators of the game. Cockfighting was another favorite sport of the Mexicans, but in the larger cities its popularity has waned. The main arena is to be found in the Patio de Gallos in Mexico City. Every village on market day sports a cockfight, which is hotly followed by its *afficionados*, as they call their "fans."

BULLFIGHTING IN MEXICO

Black Star photo. By Crosby.

AGUASCALIENTES AND GUADALAJARA

The city of Aguascalientes is a popular health resort, noted for its warm mineral springs. Honeycombed beneath it are labyrinths of old tunnels, the origin of which nobody knows. Horsehair hats, linen, and *serapes* are sold in the many streets branching out from the flower-filled plazas.

Somehow, Guadalajara, the capital of the state of Jalisco, reminds one of a city in southern Spain, because of its clean and orderly streets. In addition, the bustle of Mexico City, Tampico, and other large Mexican centers seems to be absent, although it is the second largest city in the republic. Its pottery works, especially those in Tlaquepaque, three miles from the city, are world-known. The university summer school has been attended by students and teachers from all over the world.

The government palace and the cathedral, facing the Plaza Mayor, are two interesting picture-spots, the latter with arcades on two sides housing shops that sell the usual Mexican handicraft. The San Francisco Church and Garden, with its roses and fountains, are quaint places that make a trip to Guadalajara worth while. But, as is the case with most Mexican cities, the native markets present the main interest, especially the *Mexicaltzingo*, grouped around an ancient church. Chapala, a few miles distant, offers one of the few interesting lakes in Mexico because it is the wintering home of thousands of many-colored tropical birds, and because of the picturesqueness of the natives who fish in its waters.

JALAPA AND VERA CRUZ

Flower lovers, in particular, will find Jalapa a paradise of tropical blooms that fill the city with their redolent odor throughout the year. In passing through the city on his march to Mexico City, Cortés founded the San Francisco Convent. The climate is cool during the summer, making Jalapa a haven for summer resorters. But there are times during the wet season when the rain falls sometimes for an entire week.

Another of Mexico's chief seaports is Vera Cruz on the Gulf coast, about 265 miles from Mexico City. Like the mother country, the city has been the scene of continuous warfare since the time that the Spaniards first set foot in the country. Since 1914, conditions have been improved considerably. Being easily accessible, Vera Cruz always received the initial attacks in warfare with the French, the Spaniards, the United States, and also from buccaneers who captured it a number of times. The castle of San Juan de Ulua in the bay has been cannonaded by enemies many times. The shark-infested waters surrounding the grim edifice have deterred the escape of prisoners incarcerated there when it was a prison fortress.

OAXACA AND ITS RUINS

The city of Oaxaca is an example of the insularity of many Mexican sections because of the lack of suitable roads. The only practical means of getting to it is by rail, the roads being simple dirt paths, dangerous for driving. The prime interest in Oaxaca is due to the recent archaeological finds made in the vicinity of the Mitla Ruins, where the ancient Indians worshiped the dead. Many tombs have been uncovered, and from the ruins are being disclosed some of the secrets surrounding Indian civilization which heretofore have gone unsolved. One mystery concerns itself with the oriental cast in the natives' faces. The buildings here have been built massively—to withstand earthquakes—of a green stone peculiar to the district. The Church of San Domingo is reputed to have cost more than $4,000,000 and, from the thickness of the gold leaf laid into its decorations, one can well believe it. The Municipal Building and the Federal Palaces are noteworthy edifices.

PUEBLA—CITY OF CHURCHES

One hundred churches have given the city of Puebla the title of "The City of Churches." El Carmen Church, built with the tiles for which the city is famous, gleams in the sun. The churches of Santo Domingo and La Companía have columns, domes, grills, and architectural details that entrance the eye. Casa de Alfenigue, housing the State Museum, is likewise covered with the city's glinting tiles. The famous Pyramid of Quetzalcoatl, identified as the sacrificial temple of the Aztecs, is at Cholula, eight miles from Puebla. The city is also a fine place to obtain a view of Popocatepetl, Ixtaccihuatl, and Citlaltepetl, hazy in the distance.

Altogether, the Republic of Mexico offers many pleasant days of travel to all who appreciate beauty. Color, much of it in true primitive style; scenery ranging from the arid deserts of Quintana Roo, in Yucatan, to the peak of Popocatepetl in Mexico; the floating gardens of Xochimilco; the modernity of Mexico City; the ancient splendors of Mitla Ruins; the beauty of cathedrals; the strange charm of the Pyramid of Quetzalcoatl; peons and haughty officials; bullfights and *pelota;* all of these combine to make Mexico one of the most attractive countries in the entire world.

Courtesy Illinois Central System

MT. POPOCATEPETL, MEXICO

Black Star photo. By Guss

RUINS OF SAN FRANCISCO CHURCH, ANTIGUA, GUATEMALA
Repeated earthquakes have failed to demolish this famous old edifice.

CENTRAL AMERICA

THE CENTRAL MARKET IN GUATEMALA CITY AND OTHERS

Black Star photo. By Palmer.

GUATEMALA

THE EARLY history of Guatemala, like that of its neighboring country, Mexico, is a story of conquest by the Spaniards. The Cortés of Guatemala, and, in fact, of most of Central America, was Pedro de Alvarado, who conquered this country in 1522. Thereafter, Guatemala was visited by a varied succession of catastrophes which included floods, volcanic eruptions, political eruptions, and earthquakes. Perhaps it is because of the varied mixture of its population—the aboriginal Indians with the volatile Latin temperaments of the Spaniards—that its history has been characterized by revolutions and assassinations, beginning with the revolt against Spain, in 1821, including the murders of a number of presidents, and ending with the coup d'état of General Manuel Orellana, in 1930. Foreign affairs have been enlivened by disputes with El Salvador and Honduras regarding boundaries.

About two-thirds of Guatemala is mountainous and volcanic. The northern part and coastal plains are covered with dense, jungle vegetation. The Indians who live in these hot, steaming morasses are the most numerous of the various elements of the population. The next larger group of the two million population are *mestizo*. Coffee, bananas, sugar, and maize are grown in the more arable portions of the country. The roads are few but con-

Black Star photo. By Guss

LAKE MANAGUA, NICARAGUA

nect the various large cities, as also do the railroads. Water traffic is confined to the two coasts, the Atlantic and the Pacific, and to a few navigable rivers and lakes. The capital is a station of the Pan-American Airways.

THE PHOENIX BIRD CITY

Guatemala City, the capital, has a population of about 200,000. It is the largest city in Central America. Founded in 1527 by Alvarado, it was destroyed in a flood in 1541, transferred as a result to the foot of Mount Agua, a volcano. There it was completely destroyed in the earthquake of 1773. Since then it has been rebuilt, like the mythological Phoenix bird, out of the fertile volcanic ash upon which it rests. It is the distribution point of most of the country's imports and exports, being connected by rail with Puerto Barrios on the Caribbean Sea, San José on the Pacific Ocean, Ayutla on the Mexican border, and San Salvador in the adjoining Central American republic of El Salvador.

San José is the country's chief Pacific port. Its population numbers only two thousand, and has little to interest the tourist. Puerto Barrios, on the Caribbean, is slightly larger. It is from here that sight-seers leave to climb the Rio Dulce to Lake Izabal to view the old Spanish fort of San Felipe. The scenic views from here are magnificent. Of interest, too, are the Mayan ruins at Quirigua, about sixty miles from Puerto Barrios. Ancient Zapotec Mayan and unidentified findings have been unearthed between San José and Guatemala City, and also at Baul and Pantaleon. The historic remains of Cotzumalguapa, Mitla, Utalan, and Tecpan are also worth a visit.

NICARAGUA

The history of Nicaragua reads very much like the histories of all the Central American republics. In 1522 Gil Gonzáles Dávila landed and claimed the country for the Spaniards. In 1821, it cut itself off from Spain, together with its sister colonies. A number of times Nicaragua has become involved with various nations. Because of supposed mistreatment of its citizens, Germany, Britain, and the United States frequently menaced the country with warships. When Nicaragua was not involved in a boundary dispute, it was in the throes of a new revolution. At one time the Nicaraguan route was considered by the United States as the one through which to run the proposed canal connecting the Atlantic with the Pacific; but, because of the unfeasibility of the plan, the change was made to Panama.

Two mountain chains run through Nicaragua. The elevated lands are livable and fertile; while the lowlands, especially those near the coasts, have swampy, malarial, and impenetrable jungle vegetation. Lake Nicaragua and Lake Managua are two important bodies of water, the former navigable and connected with the Atlantic Ocean by means of the San Juan River.

Most of the population of 675,000 live in the western half of Nicaragua. The balance, largely Negroes from the West Indies or mixed Negroes and Indians, work the banana plantations in the east. The western part has regular rainy and dry seasons, but the east is subjected to almost continual rainfall. Tropical fruits, coffee, sugar, and rubber are the most valuable exports of the country.

Managua, the capital city, was almost destroyed and depopulated by an earthquake in 1931. However, rebuilding work has advanced so rapidly that it is well on the way to completion. From the road that runs along the banks of Lake Managua there is obtained a beautiful view of Mototombo, an extinct volcano. Mototombito, another extinct volcanic crater which juts up out of the lake, and Mount Masaya are truly inspiring sights. Bluefields, Granada, Leon, with its beautiful cathedral, and Masaya are other important towns, the latter being close to the Santiago volcano.

COSTA RICA — PEACEFUL REPUBLIC!

Columbus is supposed to have landed in Costa Rica on his fourth voyage to the Americas in 1502, but the Spanish conquest was not completed until 1530. Costa Rican independence was won from the Spaniards in 1821. With the exception of two wars, in 1863 and 1885, when Costa Rica fought with Guatemala, the country has been exceptionally free from warfare, and particularly from internal revolts. Consequently, this little nation is more modern and prosperous than the other Central American republics.

Most of Costa Rica's inhabitants live on the fertile central plateau. Here, where the climate is ideal, the Costa Ricans of pure Spanish descent dwell in the towns of Cartago, Heredia, Alajuela, and San José, the capital. The Atlantic coastal plain area is tropically hot and is inhabited in the main by West Indian Negroes and overseers of the banana plantations. The port of

BELIZE, BRITISH HONDURAS, CENTRAL AMERICA

Homer Smith photo

A COSTA RICAN HOUSEWIFE

Courtesy Illinois Central System

Limón is the shipping center. Coffee, which has been cultivated for over a century, and bananas comprise the country's chief exports.

The architecture in the city of San José is a delightful combination of the modern and the traditional Spanish. The million-dollar national theater is the pride of the city; it is an architectural gem, one of the most beautiful in the entire world. The national congress building is impressive. Scattered about the city are dozens of well-kept parks, large and small. The finest are the Sabana and the Children's Park. The courting promenades of San José's young men and women frequently take place in Morázan Park. The metropolitan cathedral, the national museum, Bolívar Park, the zoölogical garden, and the market are all points of interest to the sight-seeing visitor. Scenic trips can be taken from here to view the Irazu and Poas volcanoes in rugged, mountainous country. From the crater of Irazu, on a clear day, it is possible to see both the Atlantic and the Pacific oceans.

The inhabitants of Limón are predominantly Negroes, brought across from the West Indies to toil on the banana plantations. The city is well laid out and presents a thriving business scene. Most of the country's passenger and freight traffic comes through this busy Atlantic port. Alajuela, the hub of the sugar industry, is also a favorite summer resort; and close by is Mount Poas, which boasts the largest volcanic crater in the world.

PANAMA

PIRATES AND PRODUCTS

The modern history of Panama begins with the completion of the Panama Canal in 1914. Before that, Panama had been a province of Colombia, and then a slow-moving Central American republic of little importance. Rodrigo Galván de Bastidas discovered it in 1501 for the Spaniards; and in the next year, during his fourth voyage, Columbus visited Port Bello on the coast. Balboa was beheaded there in 1519. Henry Morgan, the notorious pirate, attacked, looted, and burned the capital city of Panama in 1671, after having fought a superior army of Spaniards which used, in addition to men, wild bulls. In 1821, Panama declared its independence from Spain and united with Colombia, only to secede in 1903, the year it signed a treaty with the United States for the Panama Canal.

Only one fourth of its 32,380 square miles is inhabited. There live about 79,000 whites, 70,000 Negroes, 43,000 Indians, 4,000 Orientals, and 271,000 Mestizos, or persons of mixed descent. The principal agricultural and export products are bananas, coconuts, cocoa, and *cubé,* the last being a root used in making insecticides. The jungles are full of such tropical animals as alligators, tapirs,

Black Star photo. By Guss

STREET SCENE IN A PANAMA VILLAGE
Mud walls and thatched roofs still prevail.

hogs, and Mexican cats. There are also spider, night-howling, and capuchin monkeys.

Panama City, the capital, founded in 1519 by Pedrárias, is the oldest European city in the American continents. The chain of hills surrounding the city affords a fine scenic view. Panama, too, has a national theater building which is of magnificent proportions.

San José Cathedral possesses a mother-of-pearl dome and a solid gold altar. The City Hall, the churches of La Merced, Santa Ana, and Santo Domingo, and the post-office building are all splendid edifices.

THE PANAMA CANAL

The most important aspect of Panama, of course, is the Panama Canal. Contrary to popular opinion, the site of the canal was not chosen solely because of the narrowness of the isthmus at

Black Star photo. By J. B. Guss

GATUN LOCKS OF THE PANAMA CANAL

that point. The hills here are lower than at any other place on the isthmus, which made digging through them easier. The canal, from ocean to ocean, is a little more than fifty miles long and varies from three hundred to one thousand feet in width and from forty-two to eighty-five feet in depth. The canal route uses Gatun Lake, the Río Grande River on the Pacific side, and the Chagres River on the Atlantic. Culebra Cut was the most spectacular engineering feature, being gouged out of nine miles of solid land and rock.

The original idea of cutting a canal at this point, to save ships from making the tortuous trip around Cape Horn of South America, was long a dream. But not until Ferdinand de Lesseps arrived in Panama in 1881 were the preliminary surveys made. A French company was incorporated soon after for more than $250,000,000, and work was begun. But after nineteen miles had been completed, the money was all spent. The United States government took over the project after paying the French company $40,000,000, and completed the canal in 1914, at the total cost of $375,000,000. The Republic of Panama received $10,000,000 and a rental of $250,000 a year, together with absolute jurisdiction over the port cities of Panama and Colón. All other cities and territory in the Canal Zone are under the jurisdiction of the United States through the governor of the Panama Canal.

The failure of the French company to build the canal is attributed, in great part, to the fact that the Canal Zone was ridden with malaria and yellow-fever. But, through the vigorous work of Colonel Goethals, the Canal's first governor, these diseases have been permanently eradicated, appearing only occasionally in the interior.

Homer Smith photo, Chicago

THE ROAD TO BARILOCHE PEAK IN THE ARGENTINE ANDES, PROVINCE OF RIO NEGRO

Ewing Galloway photo, N. Y.

PICTURESQUE RIVER MARKETPLACE, BARANQUILLA, COLOMBIA
The rivers are practically the only roads in Baranquilla, and boats the only vehicles by which produce is marketed.

COLOMBIA: EARLY HISTORY

LITTLE did the Chibcha Indians realize, when they saw the sailboats of Alonso de Ojeda beaching on Cape Vela in 1499, that their country was soon to be taken over by the Spaniards and that they were to be almost completely eradicated. With the establishment of a settlement in Bogotá by Quesada in 1536, the actual acquisition of Colombia—then called New Granada—was begun. Growing discontent with the mother country resulted in open revolt in 1811 under the leadership of Simon Bolívar, the great South American liberator. After a series of insurrectionary movements, the Republic of New Granada was founded in 1832.

Its official name was changed to the United States of Colombia in 1863. Social unrest and political discontent have characterized Colombia's history since its independence from Spain. Before 1903, Panama belonged to Colombia, but in that year it seceded, due to difficulties over the isthmian canal project. Not until 1921, after the United States had paid Colombia $25,000,000 as compensation for the loss of Panama, did she recognize the tiny republic's independence. Boundary disputes with adjoining South American countries have been settled, and the country now is well on the way to economic advancement.

MILLIONS OF ORCHIDS

In Colombia's lowlands the weather is hot—torrid is the better word, for the country is in the north torrid zone. Here are the typical, steaming South American jungles, filled with unusual birds—the macaw and the toucan, and interesting tropical animals —the armadillo, lizards, and alligators. Mosquitoes and insects by the million plague the traveler. There is an abundance of lovely wild orchids to be found in every forest, together with numerous other examples of exotic, grotesque plant life. In the mountainous regions the climate is temperate; but at high elevations, cold, bleak, and ice-ridden, the country is far from comfortable. The vegetation here is of the usual temperate-climate variety. The seasons are divided into "wet" and "dry," each lasting about three months. In the northern and eastern sections, rains have been known to last six whole months. In Choco it is possible to tell the time by the rain which falls every day in the afternoon and evening.

COFFEE, PEARLS, AND PLATINUM

Coffee is Colombia's chief product, it being the second largest producer of the "delectable bean" in the world. Bananas, tobacco, sugar, and rubber follow in importance. Tagua, a vegetable ivory nut, from which buttons are made, grows in great quantities in the lowlands. Off the Goajira Peninsula and near Guapi are extensive pearl-fishing banks. Colombia possesses, in the Chivor and Muzo mines, the best emerald sources in the world. Platinum, gold, and silver are found in abundance, as is "liquid gold"—petroleum. Panama hats are manufactured in great quantities.

CULTURE CENTER—BOGOTÁ

The early Chibcha Indians, as well as the first Spaniards, found the plateau on which the city of Bogotá is situated an ideal spot for colonizing. In time, it became the cultural center not only of New Granada, but of the entire South American continent. The cathedral, national library, and university are indicative of this aspect. The Plaza Bolívar, in the center of the town, is overlooked by a large statue of Simon Bolívar, the national hero. A new observatory further carries out the city's cultural traditions. Although its public markets are not as colorful as those of Mexico, Indian costumes and types are sufficiently in evidence to give a good picture of native life.

The salt mines at Zipaquira, scintillant with rock-crystal gleams from the salt formations on the walls of the underground caves, are "musts" in a tourist's list of things to be seen in Bogotá. The Tequendama Falls, a short distance from the city, are likewise scenically interesting.

CARTAGENA

The city of Cartagena was an important port even before the Spaniards set foot on Colombia. Buccaneers and pirates have sacked it a number of times. When Bolívar was attempting to wrest independence from Spain, Cartagena sided with the loyalists and, although Bolívar succeeded in taking the city, the loyalist general, Morillo, regained it and kept it for the duration of the insurrection. After Colombia gained its independence, the port was snubbed by the rest of the country, which subsequently established the port of Baranquilla as its shipping center.

THROUGH THE MANGROVES

The approach to the city, through a narrow channel, leads through overhanging groves of ever-present mangroves, filled with the brooding stillness that permeates all of South America's tropical rivers. The shrill cries of macaws and other vividly colored birds, the whir of insects, and the screams of monkeys issue frequently from the swampy fastnesses. About seven miles inland is Cartagena, nestling at the foot of the hill, its white houses gleaming in the sun, all barred and balconied in typical Spanish fashion.

Of interest to the tourist are the cathedral, La Popa Castle, the San Felipe de Barajas fortress, the Muralla de las Bovedas, site of the old Spanish fortification wall, the palace of the Inquisition, the tombs, and the government buildings.

BARANQUILLA AND OTHER TOWNS

Baranquilla, seven miles from the mouth of the Magdalena River, has its port in Puerto Colombia, a small uninteresting collection of native huts. It has the usual cathedral fronting the usual plaza with the usual statue of Bolívar erected in its center.

Buenaventura, Bucaramanga, Cali, Medellín, Tumaco, Santa Maria, and Cúcuta, the last rebuilt after the earthquake of 1875, are other important Colombian cities.

VENEZUELA: "IN SEARCH OF EL DORADO"

The coast of Venezuela was the first glimpse that Columbus had of the New World mainland. He sailed along this coast in 1498 and a year later, Alonso de Ojeda landed on the Paria peninsula, accompanied by Amerigo Vespucci. Later, in his search for the mythical El Dorado, Sir Walter Raleigh sailed up the Orinoco River, into the interior regions. Federmann, a German explorer, was another who sought El Dorado, and found, instead, a country rich in natural resources. Strangely, two other expeditions landed in Bogotá in the same year, 1536, neither of which knew of the plans of the other. Because of the warlike nature of the native Carib Indians, the Spaniards had much more difficulty in conquering the country than they had encountered elsewhere.

Venezuela tried to break away from Spain much earlier than the other Spanish possessions. In 1797, España and Gual led an insurrection. In 1806, Francisco Miranda did likewise, unsuccessfully, dying in a Spanish dungeon because of a betrayal. In 1813, Simón Bolívar, the country's hero, led a series of battles which, with victories at Boyacá and Carabobo, eventually won separation from Spain. Independence naturally brought internal dissension.

In 1902, Great Britain, Italy, and Germany blockaded Venezuela's ports because of the non-payment of loans they had made, but President Roosevelt, invoking the Monroe Doctrine, warned the foreign powers that the United States would not tolerate European invasion of South America. Earlier, the United States had invoked the Monroe Doctrine in a boundary dispute between Venezuela and Great Britain.

THE WINE, BEER, AND COW-TREES

Venezuela experiences three varied types of climate—torrid, temperate, and cold—depending on the height of the land. The Orinoco River, one of the largest in South America, courses through it. Lake Maracaibo, 8,000 square miles in area, is navi-

A FARM IN THE MOUNTAINS OF VENEZUELA

The mountain people make a living despite primitive implements and unfavorable conditions.

Paul's Photos, Chicago

gable to ocean liners. The rainy sections of the country are webbed with impenetrable jungles and dense forests. The *moriche* tree is a most amazing source of raw material. For instance, the fruit of the tree is eaten as fruit, or the juice is squeezed out to ferment into beer. The sap furnishes an excellent wine. The pith is scraped out and baked into bread. The leaves are used to thatch roofs. The veins of the leaves are stripped off and make sturdy fiber twine out of which the natives weave hammocks, nets, and rope. The wood is hard and quite usable for lumber. Another amazing plant, the cow-tree, as it is called, furnishes a milkish sap which the natives drink.

Coffee, sugar cane, cotton, and cacao are the country's chief agricultural products. Chicle, used in the manufacture of chewing gum, is obtained from Venezuela's vast forests. Pearls are fished out of the waters near Margarita Island.

CARACAS, CIUDAD BOLIVAR, AND OTHER CITIES

The capital city, Caracas, has a temperate climate although it is in the torrid zone. This is because of its three-thousand-foot altitude. It has weathered the attacks of pirates and earthquakes. In its great Plaza Bolívar stands a statue to the Liberator. The churches, particularly the cathedral, are of definite interest. The university, founded in 1725, is architecturally harmonious. The house of Bolívar is an interesting museum of relics and mementoes of the country's savior. The buildings of La Pastora, the city hall, and the Holy Chapel are all worth the traveler's interest. A visit to the bull ring on Sunday gives a picture of the reaction of the fiery, Latin temperament to the popular South American sport of bullfighting.

Ciudad Bolívar, on the Orinoco River, is one of the chief ports in Venezuela although it is 270 miles from the mouth of the river delta. Its shipping interests employ most of the 20,000 inhabitants; gold, timber, hides, and the tonka bean are the most important items of export.

Puerto Cabello with its two forts; Valencia, embodying the beauties of old Spain in its spacious plaza and cathedral; San Cristobal and Coro, the trading centers for goatskins; and Aragua de Barcelona, are other important cities of interest.

MARACAIBO AND "LIQUID GOLD"

One of the fastest growing cities in Venezuela is Maracaibo, situated on the northwestern coast of the lake of that name. Although its ocean harbor is too shallow for steamships, it still is the largest coffee export city in the country. The discovery of oil in nearby Indian villages along the lake has brought an influx of foreigners and foreign trade that seems to go with the production of "liquid gold." A number of important buildings are to be seen here, particularly those of the government offices, the public library, the nautical school, and the national college. The grounds of the botanical garden are glorious with their vivid splashes of coloring.

THE GUIANAS

The Guianas alone of the huge European empires in South America remain as colonies. Divided among the British, French, and Dutch, their main value lies in their diamond fields, which rank second in supplying the world with these gems.

First sighted by Columbus, and later by Vespucci, they did not come in for particular notice until Sir Walter Raleigh heard of the legend of El Dorado, the "Gilded King" who was supposed to cover himself with gold and bathe in a sacred lake. Raleigh and many others searched for this fabulous king, expending much time and money. Apparently there is a hidden supply of gold in the inland portions of the country even today, for quantities are occasionally brought down to the settled portions by the natives from some source which no white prospector has ever been able to locate.

Homer Smith photo, Chicago

PARAMARIBO, CAPITAL OF DUTCH GUIANA
Airplane view, showing houses of Dutch type of architecture in this South American city.

Beyond a mangrove swamp-bordered coast are magnificent forests rich in valuable woods. Fortunes in orchids hang from the trees, all sorts of tropical fruits grow in abundance, and beautiful birds are plentiful. The most interesting of all is the bell-bird, a lovely creature whose voice is like the sounding of a silver chime. Lilies grow in profusion, especially the famous and exquisite *Victoria regia.*

The capital of British Guiana is the old port of Georgetown, which has changed hands frequently. Beyond the city is the forest-covered interior into which it is almost impossible to go any distance whatever except by water. An oddity noticed when using these water routes in British Guiana is the deep, rich brown, color of the rivers as they flow through the forests, and their milky whiteness while in the savannahs.

Dutch Guiana has as her capital and most important city Paramaribo, the center of the sugar cane industry. For this region of the New World, Holland was once forced to relinquish her colony in North America, which is now New York.

The French Guiana's claim to fame, or infamy, is its penal settlement. Since the middle of the last century France has been sending hardened criminals, who were condemned to more than

Paul's Photos. Chicago

CONVICTS AT WORK IN GOLD MINES, FRENCH GUIANA

eight years of labor, to the colony. The best-known part of this penal settlement is Devil's Island, where the most desperate criminals are sent—and from which few escape.

ECUADOR

Bartolomeo Ruíz, the first Spaniard to set foot on Ecuador, marveled as he saw the magnificent empire of the Incas at what is now Tumbes. The shadow that he cast was a grim symbol of the destruction which his countrymen, under Pizarro, were to cause in this land. With the execution of Atahualpa, the Incan emperor, in 1533, the Incan civilization began its rapid descent into oblivion. Pizarro established the city of Quito, the first Spanish town in Ecuador, the next year. From that date began the conquest of Ecuador by the ruthless Spaniards. Weathering various consolidations with Peru and Colombia, the Ecuadoreans finally achieved independence in 1831. Their wars, however, with these countries regarding boundary lines have continued until this day.

Because of its lack of transportation, Ecuador is one of the most backward of the South American republics. Travel is impeded mostly by the chain of the Andes mountains, their snow-capped peaks climaxed by Chimborazo and Cotopaxi, a volcano which erupted in 1877. The plain between the Andes and the Pacific Ocean is torrid and typically tropical. To the east, the valleys and plateaus of the Andes chain are temperate and are agriculturally productive.

QUITO, GUAYAQUIL, AND OTHER CITIES

Quito, the capital city, has undergone a great many disturbances. Originally an Incan capital, it was taken over by the Spaniards, who beautified it with their architecture. It was almost completely destroyed in the earthquake of 1797, and has suffered through a number of civil wars. Ruins of an Incan road, together with ancient forts and temples, are still extant. Hovering over Quito is Mount Pichincha, indeed a glorious sight in the early morning or late evening. Interesting to visit are a Jesuit church, buildings of monastic orders, the university, the Sucre, a state theater, and some excellent museums. Being only a few miles below the equator, after which the country of Ecuador is named, the city of Quito has all year days and nights of equal length, night falling regularly about 6 o'clock. Rain falls every day for an hour with clocklike precision.

The most important seaport and commercial city of Ecuador is Guayaquil on the Guayas River. Along this river front is a beautiful promenade. Small parks scattered about also serve to set off the city. An air view of the city would show a predominance of shiny tile roofs gleaming in the sun. At one time Guayaquil was a pesthole of yellow fever; but, thanks to the Rockefeller Foundation, the scourge has been eradicated and the city is healthful and livable. On a clear day the snowy cone of Mount Chimborazo can be seen in the hazy distance. The usual tropical exports pass through this port, as well as the famed Panama hat.

Ibarra, Riobamba, and Latacunga—a short distance from Cotopaxi, the volcano—are other cities worth seeing. Riobamba, in particular, is an excellent spot from which to obtain a view of

Courtesy Illinois Central System

INCA RUINS IN PERU

the Chimborazo volcano together with three other volcanoes in the vicinity. The Saturday market day is interesting and the objective of many sight-seers.

PERU

Three varied divisions can be made of Peru's land-levels, each of which has its own peculiar climate, soil, and agricultural products. The strip along the coast is sandy but contains many fertile valleys. The Andean region includes most of the large towns. The *montaña,* across the mountains, is a region of tropical rivers and dense vegetation. The coast is arid, a desert watered only by the rivers. The Andean area is temperate in climate and has moderate rainfall. The *montaña* district is tropically hot and wet.

The history of Peru is similar to that of its neighboring republic, Ecuador. After killing the Inca emperor, Atahualpa, in 1533, the Spaniards made a complete conquest of the country. Jealousy and greed among the Spanish leaders made of Peru an early model for fighting between the men who succeeded them. In 1821, San Martín declared Peru an independent nation. Various wars with Colombia, Chile, and the mother country, Spain, followed by insurrections, revolution, rebellions, revolts, and uprisings, made Peru a huge battlefield.

LIMA AND PIZARRO

Lima, the capital city, has been the seat of the government for over three hundred years. Founded in 1535 by Pizarro, who built the first cathedral, the entire city was destroyed in the earthquake of 1746. The cathedral that was erected again has on view in a glass casket a well-preserved mummy, supposed to be that of Pizarro.

Lima's important Plaza de Armas is faced by government buildings, formerly the residences of the Spanish viceroys. The portales, or arcades, are interesting sights on the plaza. A fine example of Spanish colonial architecture can be seen in the famous Torre Tagle. The Mercado de la Concepción, the congress building, Inquisition Plaza, the garden of the Barefooted Friars, and, of course, the bull ring must be visited to be appreciated. The streets are very narrow, with overhanging balconies which almost enclose the streets like a canopy in true Spanish style.

The University of San Marcos, built in 1551, is the oldest university in the Americas. The exposition palace, housing historical and anthropological relics, together with a zoo and a botanical garden, are places really requiring a week of a tourist's time. Almost within walking distance of the city are the foothills of the Andes Mountains, and the heights of the chain are scarcely fifty miles away.

YOUNG INDIAN WOMAN OF PERU IN NATIVE DRESS

FORTIFIED CALLAO

On the Pacific coast and acting as the port for Lima is the city of Callao. The city's inhabitants, mostly working people, have had brief time for city building; hence there is little of architectural importance to be seen.

Its history, however, is replete with excitement. It was Callao that Sir Francis Drake attacked and looted in the late 1500's. In 1866, the Spaniards bombarded it when the country declared war on Spain. Now, with a submarine and naval base in the harbor of San Lorenzo such attacks would be quickly and effectively repulsed.

THE MAGNIFICENT ANDES

The Andes Mountains in Peru have always been an attraction to tourists. They contain almost unsurpassable scenic spots. A trip to Arequipa, in southern Peru, brings the sight-seer to the base of El Misti, 19,967 feet high and snow-capped; Chachani, 19,970 feet high, its cone a perpetual white; and Pichu Pichu, 17,800; three mountains that are worth traveling the world around to see.

At Cuzco, high up in the Andes, can be viewed Incan and pre-Incan ruins, particularly the Fortress of Sacsahuaman. This wonder of antiquity was formerly the stronghold of the Incas. Built of stones, some of which are twenty-five feet long, twelve feet thick, and weighing thousands of pounds each, this wall has baffled archaeologists who cannot understand how the Indians were able to transport the immense blocks to the site and there fit them together exactly. Here also is the monastery of Santo Domingo, the foundation of which was part of the former Incan Temple of the Sun. The cathedral at Cuzco has a bell that can be heard twenty-five miles away.

LAKE TITICACA

Truly one of the world's most beautiful natural wonders, Lake Titicaca is the highest large body of water to be found anywhere. Its waters shimmer in the rare atmosphere 12,500 feet above sea level. One hundred and thirty-five miles long and sixty-six miles wide, the lake may be traversed by excursion boats for a truly unique experience. A morning view of it, at sunrise, presents a crystal-clear picture with myriads of colors, reflections from the green and brown hills and forests, and the deep blue of the lake. The native Quechua Indians sail their reed-constructed boats on the lake, the odd shapes of which against the sun form a scenic view that is exquisite. A number of large steamers ply the lake. Interesting is the fact that they were built in Scotland and were carried up in pieces to the lake where they were re-assembled.

Courtesy Pan-American Airways

AIR VIEW OF THE CITY AND HARBOR OF RIO DE JANEIRO, BRAZIL

BRAZIL: JUNGLE AND CIVILIZATION

Largest of the South American republics, and comprising over one-third of the whole continent, Brazil is also one of the most beautiful and interesting. Its irregular coast, providing many harbors, seems to breathe the word adventure, and to make one long to explore it and to dream of pirates. And inland there is the famous Amazon whose valley was, until recently, nothing but an unexplored expanse of tropical undergrowth and lurking death.

In contrast to this jungle is the broad plateau which rises so sharply behind Rio de Janeiro. There one finds thriving industry and agriculture, a civilization having little semblance to the Amazonian area. And then Rio itself—that glorious resort city! Possessing a harbor of the greatest natural beauty, her citizens have done everything to make the city of equal architectural loveliness. And to match such a city there is a sophisticated society of the highest order, which forms a part of the intelligent and modern population.

EXPLORERS, PIRATES, AND CONQUERORS

Brazil was claimed for Portugal in 1500 by Pedro Alvares Cabral when that explorer was on his way to India. First named "The Island of the True Cross," the new discovery was soon rechristened Brazil because of the dye-wood of that name with which the country was well supplied. The next year Amerigo Vespucci was sent to explore the new possession of Portugal, and it was he who was responsible for the many "saint" names along the coast, for he baptized each new point after the saint on whose own day it was discovered.

While Portugal, more interested in the Indies, neglected Brazil, other European nations practiced piracy there. The French were the most daring, not only using the land themselves, but even attacking Portuguese ships. When the Portuguese began fostering colonization under royal control, the Frenchmen, not frightened, seized and for a few years held the harbor of Rio de Janeiro. The Portuguese, however, managed to expel them and to block all future French attempts at colonization and exploitation of Brazil. The Dutch too were active there, and for a period of thirty years held Pernambuco, the most important city in the sugar section of the north. They were dispossessed by a rebellion of the plantation owners, and after 1661 made no further attempts to deprive Portugal of her rich colony.

In 1693 gold was discovered in the modern state known as Minas Geraes, and the rush which followed was equal to that of the Klondike or the California stampedes. Formerly well-populated sections were emptied as all who could migrated to the gold country, where new towns jumped up over night. A steady stream of gold flowed to the mother country for over a century, while in the eighteenth century diamonds were discovered to add to the value of the colony.

DOM JOÃO OF PORTUGAL

When, in its terror-spreading course, the Napoleonic menace threatened Portugal, Dom João VI fled for safety to Brazil. The colony immediately grew in importance, and as an indication of the reforms of every sort—political, social, and educational—which took place, a royal decree of 1815 declared that Brazil be included in the kingdom as "The United Kingdom of Portugal, Brazil, and Algarves." But in 1821 Dom João VI had to go back to his kingdom to prevent a revolutionary movement from becoming too strong. He left his son as regent, and sailed for Lisbon. The revolutionaries tried to force Pedro to return also, but with the backing of the people of Brazil he refused, and in 1822 proclaimed an independent empire of Brazil and was crowned emperor. By 1824 that independence was assured, though not recognized by the Portuguese government until 1825.

Although he realized that absolute power was a thing of the past, Dom Pedro would not act as though he had ever heard of the French Revolution. His whole policy was too much in the "I am the State" tradition, and after ten years of growing dissatisfaction on both sides, he finally abdicated as his subjects wished. Leaving a son five years of age as heir, he involved the country in the troubles of a regency which became too much for the governing body, and when Dom Pedro II was only fifteen he was proclaimed king. From 1840-1889 he reigned wisely and well, and it was then that Brazil took many of her forward steps, but his good deeds only served to overthrow him. The landowners whom his government had dispossessed of their slaves in 1888, the clergy whom he had angered by punishing when culpable, and the army officers whom he would not allow in politics, all gave their support and prestige to the republicans. An army revolt precipitated the revolution, and Dom Pedro II also abdicated. Since that time Brazil has been governed by a constitution based on that of the United States, although adjustment to that constitution has been difficult and at times marked by dictatorships and violence

Homer Smith photo, Chicago

BRAZILIAN HEAD HUNTERS

These natives of northern Brazil are expert in the use of the blowgun and poison darts, which cause almost instant death to their victims.

TROPICAL JUNGLES AND BLANKETS

Most people believe that Brazil is a tropical country, which though nice for a winter vacation, would be unbearably hot for a place of permanent residence. This popular belief is not true. Granting that the valley of the Amazon is a tropical section in which there is little change of temperature, one must realize that altitude, distance from the sea, rainfall, and winds make a difference in the conditions which one would normally expect in such a latitude. Consequently, there are parts of Brazil—especially the Plateau—where it is always cool at night, and where conditions are perfectly healthful. Nor is the disease question so pressing as it once was. Science has discovered that even the deadly Amazon Valley is safe for others than the native Indians by the use of the same methods that conquered fever in Panama.

THE EMERALD CITY

It was the use of these methods which made Rio safe as well as beautiful, and which has transformed that city into the delightful resort which it is. Its splendid harbor, with natural breakwaters of protruding fingers of land and islands, is one of the loveliest in the world. The city itself is well planned and clean, and its architecture is magnificent. Entering the harbor amidst a riot of islands which vie with one another to be proclaimed the loveliest, one is greeted by Sugar Loaf Mountain (its musical native name is Pão de Assucar) whose top is bathed and half-hidden in rolling mists, and crowned by a towering crucifix which gives the city a constant blessing. The mountains, which almost entirely surround the city on the land side, offer remarkable opportunities for sightseeing, and the government has built highways to facilitate driving up these mountains for the view.

Palm trees at the water's edge, gently waving their luxuriant green fronds over the emerald clear sea, and the foliage-covered mountains in the background, make a perfect setting for the brilliant whiteness of the buildings of Rio de Janeiro. Palatial marble buildings border palm-shaded avenues which curve along the coast; outdoor cafés group themselves beside the gay mosaic sidewalks; the formal gardens of the Quinta de Boa Vista are as lavishly beautiful as those of the Old World. At night the city is equally breath-taking as lights glow everywhere, and the gay populace throngs to the casinos of Urca, Copacabana, and Atlantico.

Rio de Janeiro has been called "The Voluptuous City" because of the character of its people. Temperamentally influenced by French culture, they are devoted to Woman as sovereign of the graceful life which is so much in evidence in this gracious South American capital. As another expression of this type of life, they are great lovers of literature. And that literature takes as its subject matter the glorification of the exquisite women of Brazil. Finding an earthly paradise in their city, the Brazilians in Rio live a life more or less aloof from materialism. Their whole experience is one tinged with romanticism and elegance, which has the swing and charm of a Viennese waltz.

For Rio has not forgotten that it was once the capital of the Portuguese kingdom, and that following the break with the mother country it was the capital of an empire. These facts have given Rio a tradition of elegance—the elegance which is a part of court life and a diplomatic center. Although the palace of Dom Pedro II at the Quinta de Boa Vista is now a museum of natural history and geology, it is still an impressive and memory-stirring sight. And there is another museum, full of relics of the imperial era. These tangible evidences of the glamour of royalty cannot but add a note of refinement and splendor to the life and atmosphere of the city.

THE AMAZON

Famous as one of the largest rivers in the world, the Amazon and its valley cover over a third of the total area of Brazil. Most of this section is heavily wooded with a dense tropical forest, commonly known as a deadly spot where explorers in search of ancient ruins and relics of former days have disappeared never to be heard of again except in fantastic rumors. This part of the valley is peopled largely by Indians who are accustomed to the extreme tropical heat and moisture, and who have not as yet been subjected to the influences of civilization. The government is exerting every effort to make the valley more habitable for the white races so that the tremendous resources, especially of valuable timber, may be developed.

The southern part of the Amazon lowlands is less damp and therefore more suited to the white race. Its center is São Paulo, the second largest city in the republic and important as a coffee center. Built on hills like old Rome, São Paulo is strictly modern with

Homer Smith photo, Chicago

COFFEE PLANTATION, SAO PAULO, BRAZIL

its bustling traffic and busy trade. The Avenida Paulista, making its way along the hills, is lined with the magnificent homes of the coffee magnates. Marble palaces rising from formal gardens possess their own marble swimming pools and well-kept tennis courts. And in keeping with such wealth, the shops carry the latest Paris gowns; jewelers prosper; and the town is the center for the finest schools in Brazil. In its suburbs, now marked by a splendid museum of natural history, is the spot where Brazilian independence was proclaimed in January, 1822.

"THE GILT-EDGED RAILWAY"

Leaving São Paulo through the world's most expensive station, one must take what has been called the "The Gilt-Edged" road because of the fabulous amounts of coffee which are transported over it to Santos, the coffee port of the world. At Santos' fascinating harbor one sees ragged Brazilians loading bag after bag of coffee on the steamers of every nation which carry it to all parts of the world, but coupled with this old method is the most modern machinery which runs the bags aboard on long belts. The odor of coffee drenches the harbor; its aroma fills the streets and office buildings; the exquisite villas along the beach are perfumed by it, for ninety-seven per cent of the exports of this thriving town is coffee. In the streets oxcarts and modern trucks dodge one another with remarkable efficiency, and above all the turmoil and beauty, the picturesque women and sweating men, stands the Fortress Barre Grande to protect Brazil's fortune.

A TALE OF TWO CITIES

Bahia, another famous port of Brazil, is two cities really, for it is built on two distinct levels. Beneath, nestling close about the harbor, is the old commercial section with its narrow, crowded streets and its markets full of strange fruits—sweet ripe oranges, green in color, mangoes, and papayas. Above this level is the luxurious residential section, which, though less colorful, is cooler, has wider streets and more pretentious buildings. Here are the impressive government buildings and the homes of the wealthy. Bahia was the first important city in Brazil and until 1763 the capital. About her lingers the tradition, the romance of age. Her cathedral is the oldest church building in the nation; she has two ancient forts, and two old convents which are relics of the old Dutch and Portuguese traders. Though no longer the most important city of the state, Bahia is still prosperous and fascinating.

Homer Smith photo, Chicago

BRAZILIAN CACAO TREE

"WHERE THE NUTS COME FROM"

Everyone has heard of and eaten Brazil nuts, which are an important item in Brazilian forest industry and exportation. Another forest product is rubber, which is falling in importance because of the new value of plantation-grown rubber in the Orient. Palm fiber, Paraguayan tea, and vegetable wax are the other industries of the wooded sections aside from actual timber. Because of the difficulty and expense of transporting lumber to the coastal cities where it may be exported, there is surprisingly little lumbering done. When one considers that Brazil is blessed with what are probably the greatest timber resources in the entire world, such a fact is startling. But the industry, which is still young, has been growing in recent years, and it is quite possible that in time lumber will become one of Brazil's most important exports.

AGRICULTURE

The most valuable agricultural products of the country—which has not as yet nearly developed its potentialities to their fullest—are coffee, cotton, corn, sugar, rice, tobacco, beans, and cacao. Most of the tillable land is in the more habitable portion of the Amazon valley, or at least, most of the land that is actually under cultivation, for there is a very small proportion that is worked. And with agriculture one might include the important cattle-raising and meat-packing industries which represent a large proportion of Brazil's exports and wealth. These industries have been growing significantly in recent years, and not only are there large areas devoted to the raising of cattle and other livestock, but the most modern methods of breeding as well as slaughtering and meat packing are in use. In contrast, Brazil does not take advantage of her fisheries, and continues to import large quantities of fish each year.

The value of her gold mines has fallen off greatly since the eighteenth century when gold was so important to European and especially Portuguese trade. Nor are the diamond fields of as great significance as they once were. On the other hand, fabulously rich deposits of iron have been discovered, which constitute the most important ore resource of the country.

MELTING POT

Perhaps the most remarkable thing about the republic of Brazil is its solution of the racial problem. Or can one call it a solution? Probably not, for in reality hardly any problem exists at all. At first glance it would seem that, subject as she is to immigration from many nations, with a large Indian population and many Negroes, she would find the situation acute and the rather volatile

Homer Smith photo, Chicago

RECIFE, FORMERLY PERNAMBUCO, BRAZIL
Picture shows Commerce Square and part of down-town section of this city of 400,000.

South American temperament raising constant difficulties. But somehow all that is avoided. Race, color, and religion all fade into insignificance in a country where everyone is accepted.

In a town in the Plateau region a tall blond was asked if he were a German. He promptly denied that he was and claimed to be a Brazilian pure and simple, although upon questioning he admitted that his parents had come from Germany shortly before his birth. Perhaps the care which the government gives to the newly arrived immigrant is the clue to the situation, for immigration is encouraged by the state, and new arrivals are placed in colonies or on plantations where they are watched over until oriented and independent economically. After a lapse in immigration during and after the World War, it is again on the increase and will probably continue so for some years to come, because of the relatively small population of the nation and its need for more citizens.

As an advancing and prosperous nation Brazil has already achieved much. In the future she can hope for even more. With a sensitive population, one which is earnestly striving for improvement intellectually as well as commercially, she makes herself attractive to all—whether their purpose is merely a pleasant visit or a permanent home. The capital, Rio de Janeiro, can vie with any in the world in natural beauties, with its long avenues and canals bordered by towering palms. Brazil's natural resources are certainly sufficient to make her significant in world trade, even in their present undeveloped and unexploited state. She has not yet reached the stability of government which will be necessary for taking her rightful place among the nations of the world, but progress is being made toward that aim, and as the people become more literate there is reason to hope for greater achievements in the realm of politics. Brazil is certainly one of the most interesting of the new nations of the world, and one which should prove thoroughly delightful to the tourist regardless of his particular bent.

BOLIVIA: FROM PIZARRO TO THE CHACO

During the Incan days, Bolivia was an agricultural country; but when the Spaniards heard of its fabulous silver mines, they sent Gonzales Pizarro to look into the matter. Agriculture was forgotten, and the mining of silver became the country's chief occupation. Subsequently the silver mines of Potosí were discovered, two years after the arrival of the first Spanish viceroy in 1543. Pizarro rebelled against the homeland in 1546. The second substantial revolt against the Spanish rule came in 1780 with the Indian rebellion of Tupac-Amaru, a descendant of the last of the Incas, who was assassinated in 1571. The third revolt broke out in 1809. After a number of battles with the Spanish, Bolivia was proclaimed a republic in 1825. Then came a confederation with Peru and wars with Chile. Ever since the year of Bolivian independence the country has been bickering with Paraguay regarding the boundaries of the Chaco region, a sparsely-settled jungleland, for the most part. Open warfare was proclaimed by Paraguay in 1933. After a period of indecisive battles, the two countries agreed to a truce in June, 1935. Nothing, however, has been definitely settled.

A COUNTRY WITHOUT A SEAPORT

Although Bolivia is the third largest of the South American countries, it is the only one without an outlet to an ocean. Two chains of mountains, the Andes and the Cordilleras, flank its sides; and between these two chains is a plateau, which is Bolivia proper. The northern section of the country is fertile and contains most of the population; the southern part is an arid, uninhabited desert. Manufacturing is almost non-existent. Mining, agriculture, and frontier disputes seem to take up most of the Bolivians' time. The most important product is rubber; while second in rank is cocoa. The mining of copper, lead, and bismuth is conducted extensively.

Paul's Photos, Chicago

COTTON SPINNING IN BOLIVIA

A wire is the only implement used.

LA PAZ—CANYON CITY

The capital city, La Paz, is situated in a deep canyon of which the walls are surprisingly colored. A glimpse of the city from the heights reveals a panorama of red-tiled roofs, surrounded by imposing, high-flung walls of sheer, solid rock. Because the population is composed largely of Aymara and Quichua Indians, the native public market is a unique attraction. Indian women and children in their native costumes occupy the stalls, selling handwoven woolen goods, blankets, *ponchos,* and shawls, all executed in vivid colors. There are many fur shops in which are sold the rugs made of vicuña and alpaca skins. Facing the Plaza Murillo are the government palace, the congressional building, and a cathedral which has required 200 years to build. The University of San Andres is another interesting institution. A number of delightful, enflowered promenades beautify the city.

LLAMAS AND AIRPLANES

Other important cities are Cochabamba, Guaqui, Bolivia's port on Lake Titicaca, Santa Cruz de la Sierra, and Uyuni. The native markets in the latter are interesting, as are the immense droves of llamas which the natives use, much as the Mexicans use the burro, for transportation. The use of airplanes is rapidly increasing in Bolivia.

CHILE: THE "SHOE-STRING" REPUBLIC

Although Chile is fully two thousand miles in length, its average width is scarcely one hundred miles, thus extending as a long narrow strip along the southwestern coast of the continent. The Andes Mountains form a backbone for the length of the country and in some places almost reach the waters of the Pacific. The northern part is mostly desert land, but rich in nitrates. The central portion contains some of the most fertile land in the world, and a majority of the population lives here. The southern section is heavily forested and is one of the wettest regions in the world. A number of active volcanoes have plagued Chileans with eruptions. Agriculture, lumbering, and fishing are important industries; but the mining of nitrates in the deserts of Tarapaca and Antofagasta is still the greatest source of Chile's mineral wealth.

FROM THE ARAUCANIANS TO TACNA-ARICA

The Spaniards found Chile considerably more difficult to conquer than other American regions. In fact, the Araucanian Indians, a fierce tribe more closely resembling the savage tribes of North America than the advanced Incas to the north, were not suppressed until late in the nineteenth century. Although Diego de Almagro was granted this land and explored it, it was Pedro de Valdivia who effectually began the Spanish conquest in 1536.

The next era began in 1810, when the Chileans revolted from Spain. Up to the year 1868, when independence was recognized, there continued some desultory warfare between the two countries. Chile battled with Peru and Bolivia ten years later in their "nitrate war," which began the famous Tacna-Arica imbroglio with Peru, a dispute which lasted until 1929, when a peaceful arrangement was finally concluded. Meanwhile relatively few internal disorders shook the nation, though revolutions occurred from time to time. Today, after a try at socialistic government in 1932, the country has reverted to a constitutional form of government.

Situated on the slopes of mountains whose snow-capped peaks soar skyward behind it, the city of Valparaiso presents a delightful picture to those entering its harbor. From the heights on an overhanging hill, Cerro de la Artilleria, the Naval Academy rears formidably. On Los Placeres, another hill, near Viña del Mar,

Homer Smith photo, Chicago

SANTIAGO, CAPITAL OF CHILE
Grandstand of the Hipico Club race track.

stands the imposing edifice of the University of Engineering. "The Port," as the remnants of the old town are known, centers around the ancient church of La Matriz. The Plaza Sotomayor, instead of having the Bolívar statue found in so many South American cities, has one of Arturo Prat, a Chilean sea hero in the war with Peru. The Avenida Pedro Montt, the "White Way" of the city, with its Italia Park, opens into the immense Plaza O'-Higgins, both named after early statesmen. Errazuriz and Brazil Avenidas are two beautiful boulevards, lined with trees and many monuments. The Paseo Veintiuno de Mayo gives a fine view of the city below it and the far-flung shores of the bay; it is reached by taking an elevator from the Aduana Plaza. A number of similar elevators operate from the business section, which is on flat, man-made land along the harbor, to the residential section high on the slopes. Viña del Mar, Recreo, and Miramar are popular nearby resorts.

SANTIAGO

Santiago is the capital city of Chile. The Andes mountain peaks, towering in splendor, serve as a charming background for the city. Rising 400 feet high, Santa Lucia hill is a splendid place

Ewing Galloway photo, N. Y

FAMOUS "CHRIST OF THE ANDES"
Heroic bronze statue on boundary line between Argentina and Chile, symbolic of enduring peace between these two countries

from which to view Santiago and look down on the channel through which the Mapocho River flows, the five bridges spanning the river, the Alameda de las Delicias, a two-mile-long avenue which cuts through the entire city, Parque Cousino, Bruna Palace, Casa de la Moneda, and the many other beautiful buildings of the city. At the top of this hill is an enormous statue of the Virgin Mary. High up in the Andes, on the border separating Chile from Argentina, is an immense bronze statue of Christ. It was erected to commemorate the settling of the boundary dispute between the two countries.

Antofagasta, Talca, and Arica are cities in Chile, each with unique characteristics. The Chilean Lakes Region contains volcanoes, deep canyons, strange trees and flowers, forests, waterfalls, swift streams, and dozens of lakes. And over the entire area rise the volcanic peaks of Osorno and Calbuco, which still rumble and smoke threateningly.

PARAGUAY: INDEPENDENCE AND WAR

Having been one of the districts in the original Buenos Aires viceroyalty, Paraguay in its history parallels that of the other countries which comprised it. One thing, however, stands out, and that is the humane treatment accorded the native Indians by the governors, chiefly because of Jesuit intervention. As in no other Spanish territory, the Indians were treated as human beings, and the direct result was the long continuance of friendly relations between them and the Spanish without the warfare that accompanied all the other Spanish acquisitions. Paraguay declared its independence from Spain in 1811. Wars with Argentina, Brazil, and Uruguay followed, and the long dispute with Bolivia regarding the Chaco developed into actual warfare.

YERBA MATÉ

Since there are very few roads in Paraguay, the navigable rivers have been the main means of transportation. The airplane of late has supplemented some water travel. The forests are rich in *yerba maté*, a small tree from the leaves of which a favorite South American beverage is made. Sugar, tobacco, cotton, castor oil, and rice are important products. Cattle raising and stock breeding are also carried on extensively. Nandutí lace, made in Itaguá, is an exquisite product which the traveler will want to buy.

ASUNCIÓN

The only city of importance in Paraguay is Asunción, the capital. A broad curtain of hills rises behind the city, making a very picturesque background for the red tiles of the two-storied buildings which house most of the city's population of 95,000.

Homer Smith photo, Chicago

SKY LINE AND HARBOR OF ASUNCIÓN, PARAGUAY

The city boasts a number of beautiful plazas, particularly Plaza Uruguaya, and also quite a few well-kept parks, including the botanical gardens, a storehouse of rare and exotic flowers. Buildings of note are the government palace, the national library, the cathedral, and Encarnacion church. The Guaranís can be glimpsed at the central market, where they sell the usual collection of handiwork and agricultural products.

IGUASSU FALLS

Although Iguassu Falls are not in Paraguay, a visit to them can be made from Asunción. In the middle of a forest that is primeval, Iguassu Falls roar as the waters fall 210 feet, higher than Niagara Falls, over seventy different cataracts. Viewing from San Martín's Leap this majestic titan of nature's masterpieces, the surrounding trees filled with multi-colored, chirping and shrieking birds, the countryside a dense jungle of tropical growth, gorgeous flowers and hundreds of varieties of orchids, the sight-seer who is fortunate enough to be there takes away a memory of grandeur that can never be forgotten.

Posadas (from which the traveler to Iguassu Falls embarks), San Bernardino, and Concepción are additional cities of varied importance.

URUGUAY: MONTEVIDEO

The country of Uruguay for the first century of its history was the center of a bitterly fought rivalry between Portugal and Spain, because the portions of the New World assigned to them by the pope were separated by La Plata River, which each nation coveted. Then, in 1828, under the leader Artigas, Uruguay won its independence from Spain and was recognized by Argentina and Brazil.

The most important city is Montevideo. Its musical name comes from the tradition that one of Magellan's sailors exclaimed, "*montem video,*" upon sighting the round little *cerro* on the peninsula. The streets of Montevideo are broad and the houses are set back from the street, giving an impression of easy, carefree life. The most important of these streets is the Avenida de 18 de Julio, which extends through the city for two and a half miles. Its magnificent homes and smart shops make it one of the finest of South American thoroughfares.

PLAZA INDEPENDENCE AND 18TH OF JULY AVENUE, MONTEVIDEO, URUGUAY

Paul's Photos, Chicago

The pride not only of the Montevideans but of all Uruguayans is what is jestingly called "The Bulging Tower of Pisa," the tallest building in South America. It was started by an eccentric millionaire of Montevideo, who wanted to give his city the distinction of possessing the highest skyscraper on the continent; but, when the building was half finished, rumor reached Montevideo that some other wealthy man in a rival nation was planning a building which was to surpass the "Bulging Tower" by several stories. A series of frantic conferences between architect, builder, and owner resulted in a most amazing spectacle: several of the stories were made wider than others, probably to outwit the would-be rivals.

The citizens of Montevideo are great lovers of music. In their beautiful Solis theater, which can vie with any music hall in Europe, they enthusiastically receive the great artists of the world. So sure is their knowledge and appreciation of music that they dared hiss a world-renowned tenor who sang off-key in a performance of *Otello*.

A few mementoes of the past remain in Montevideo today. An old granite fortress still guards the harbor, as it did in the days when Spain ruled the world. An ancient cathedral vies with the modern "Bulging Tower" on the Plaza de Independencia, where it raises twin towers in an effort to reach the one misshapen tower of the skyscraper. The difference between the two ages represented in Montevideo is best seen from the top of the Cerro—the hill which called forth the Latin exclamation that gave the city her name. The new city is straight, clean, and modern, with broad streets; the old city has tortuous, narrow streets lined with flat-roofed houses, each with a roof garden of brilliant flowers. Which Montevideo is the more entrancing is impossible to decide.

The economic history of Uruguay began with the export of hides and salt beef, but modern science and American farm machinery have made Uruguay one of the world's centers for the manufacture and export of canned and frozen meats. The American manufacturers of farm implements easily hold the field in South America because of their willingness to teach the purchaser the use of what he buys. Such assistance has been invaluable to the republic, for the pampas are a splendid grazing area. The Uruguayans needed only the means of preserving their produce for export, to become one of the wealthiest agricultural nations of the world.

Uruguay may well be proud of herself, for, not only does the country have one of the most interesting of the many fascinating South American capitals, the most progressive schools, and the best financial record on the continent; but she is also more advanced politically and economically, as well as socially, than any other republic in South America.

ARGENTINA: THE COUNTRY OF SILVER

In 1515 Juan Díaz de Solís, one of the adventurous army of Spanish *conquistadores,* discovered the Rio de la Plata in his search for gold, silver, and precious stones. Ten years later Sebastian Cabot, then under the flag of Spain, following a voyage of Magellan, entered and explored that river while looking for a westward passage. Neither discovered what he was looking for, but found instead, a country that was to become one of the greatest sup-

Homer Smith photo, Chicago

HOTEL PUENTE DEL INCA, ARGENTINA
This point, near the Argentina-Chile borderline, is 8,975 feet above sea level, and is on the only railroad that crosses the Andes between the two countries.

pliers of hogs, sheep, cattle, corn, wheat, and wool for the world's markets. In the twentieth century Argentina exports no gold; instead, she receives it in payment for her agricultural produce which the rest of the world consumes.

Argentina owes its name to the search for silver (the Latin name for silver is *argentum*) in that country and to its Indian inhabitants' custom of wearing silver ornaments in the sixteenth century. Even the great estuary which leads to its capital city, Buenos Aires, is called Rio de la Plata (River of Silver). Argentina's northern frontier touches Paraguay and Brazil, its eastern boundary runs along little Uruguay and the Atlantic ocean, while along its whole western side it is bounded by Chile.

In the four centuries since Solís discovered the Plata, the Argentinians have driven off British and Portuguese invasions, taken territory from the country which is now Chile, and, inspired to an extent by the heroic revolution in the United States of America, have driven out the Spaniards in a desperate struggle for their independence. That was in 1812; five years later, in a daring military move of great brilliance, San Martín, the national hero, second only to the great Bolívar in the hearts of South Americans, split his small army into two parts and led them hundreds of miles over the high passes of the Andes to defeat the Spanish rulers for a final victory that was to insure the independence of the South American nations until this day.

Again, like her great northern sister, the United States, she spent the next sixty years in subduing the fierce Indian tribes of the Pampa and Patagonia. Like the other Latin-American nations, she has undergone several revolutions and dictatorships. In spite of these difficulties, Argentina has risen to the intellectual and political leadership of the A B C nations (Argentina, Brazil, and Chile)—the most powerful and advanced countries on the southern continent.

FROM TORRID TO FRIGID

Geographically the Argentine Republic is the most favorably endowed of all the South American republics, because so much of it lies in the temperate zone and so little of it is mountainous. It has several distinct and natural regions: the Andes, the eastern slope of the Cordillera to the Chilean border, the pre-Cordillera, and the Puma, or high plateau of the northwest. The Chaco is the forested northern plains, with a subtropical climate. The Entre Rios region lies between the Uruguay and Parana rivers. The Pampa is the economic and agricultural center of the nation, spreading fanwise three to four hundred miles from Buenos Aires and devoted to grazing and the raising of corn, wheat, and oats. Patagonia, or the southern plateau, is dry, sparsely populated, and largely given over to the pasturing of sheep. The few native Indians who still remain live here and go about practically undressed despite the severe cold of the winter climate. The island of Tierra del Fuego (the Land of Fire, so called because Magellan saw lights there) forms the toe of the continent. This island Argentine shares with Chile. This region has only 2,400 inhabitants, mostly aborigines, and is economically and agriculturally insignificant. Thus, in extending from twenty-two degrees to fifty-five degrees south latitude, Argentina experiences many types of climate from semitropical to sub-polar. In the north, palm trees and *yerba maté,* the South American tea, grow in profusion, while toward the south, where the climate is cold and dry, only scrub oak and pine are found. Also from east to west similar differences appear. At the base of the Andes there is a desert; while less than a thousand miles to the east one comes upon the rain-drenched Pampas, one of the granaries of the world.

In comparison with the United States, Argentina is about one third as large, but it has no transverse lengths of mountains like the Rockies. It is the world's greatest exporter of corn, producing some two hundred million bushels and exporting eighty per cent of it. In wheat it ranks sixth in the producing nations of the world, growing about a hundred million bushels per year. The country raises vast quantities of flax, practically supplying the world with linseed. Ranking very high among the sheep-producing nations of the world, it runs second to Australia. Argentina is fourth in the number of cattle and has more horses in proportion to its area than any other land upon the earth. The horses raised on the wide plains are among the fastest and the finest known, as witnessed by their winning the world's polo championship year after year.

THE CORN BELT

Advancing northward, the scenery undergoes a great change. There are larger cornfields, sugar cane begins to appear, and the region becomes warmer. In the province of Tucumán, the soil is so rich that it is able to produce more than one hundred bushels of corn per acre; while the climate is suitable to the production of enough sugar cane to satisfy the needs of the people of their whole country, with some left over to export. Farther north is the Chaco, a tropical country which produces quebracho wood, from which tannin is taken, and *yerba maté*, which is making its presence known in this country as a new drink. This is the tropical region of Argentina, much of it an impassable jungle, making it as yet difficult to explore or develop.

Several hundred miles south of the Pampas and Buenos Aires is Patagonia, a country not unlike the northern section of Nebraska, in that it is high, level, and dry. Because it is arid, crops cannot be grown; but sheep-raising is carried on.

CITY OF "GOOD AIRS"

Buenos Aires, the capital, is the first city, not only of the country, but of the whole continent. Buenos Aires is not alone the political capital of Argentina, but also the social, intellectual, economic, financial, commercial, and industrial center as well. Buenos Aires makes the laws, the manufactured products, the customs, the styles, and the news for the country as a whole. There is a saying in Argentina to the effect that, when Buenos Aires takes snuff, all Argentina sneezes.

The city is one of the most rapidly expanding, both in population and in area, in the world. In 1898 it scarcely exceeded 800,000; thirty years later the population exceeded 2,000,000; and it is growing at the rate of 100,000 a year. It now exceeds Philadelphia and is surpassed in the Western Hemisphere only by New York and Chicago.

KEEP TO THE LEFT

Buenos Aires is twenty-five miles in length and fifteen miles wide. It is much like any large, progressive city: its street-car service is fast and frequent; its taxis are numerous; subways are as good as New York's; the streets are as wide and straight as those of Chicago; in architectural grandeur, the public buildings equal those of Washington.

On the other hand, it is quite unlike any of the cities in the northern continent. There are no skyscrapers, because the law declares that buildings may be no higher than the width of the street upon which they stand. This gives a very pleasing effect of symmetry. Along these streets, usually in the late afternoon and early evening, pass great throngs of merry promenaders. On La Florida, the street which is the center of the capital's amusement, the crowd is so thick that automobiles are prohibited from using it. Here the young men go to see beautiful *señoritas* (usually carefully chaperoned), and here the *señoritas* go to be seen.

GRAIN AND CATTLE

Another notable feature of Buenos Aires is its harbor, which handles thousands of boats a year. The facilities of the port are excellent and impressive in size. Grain elevators are seen which hold a million bushels, granaries with a capacity of twice that much, a flour mill which cost three and a half million dollars to construct, and gigantic meat-packing plants, where daily many thousands of hogs, sheep, and cattle are slaughtered, frozen, and shipped to the markets of the outside world.

Buenos Aires is one of the largest Catholic cities in the world. It is therefore fitting that it should have an enormous cathedral

DURHAM CATTLE ON AN ARGENTINE RANCH

Homer Smith photo, Chicago

which covers more than an acre of ground and seats nine thousand people at one time. Right in the center of the city lies another city—this one being occupied solely by the dead—the Recoleta Cemetery. It has its own plazas and streets, its own houses and apartments. The houses are the private dwellings of the rich, while the poor are buried in the apartments, really enormous chapels, which are sometimes larger than churches and hold as many as fifteen hundred bodies.

ROSARIO—CITY OF ARGENTINA

Although Buenos Aires seems to lead everything in Argentina (it does have twenty per cent of the population and ninety-five per cent of the industry of the country), there are other beautiful and interesting cities and places elsewhere in the republic. Rosario, with a population of more than five hundred thousand, is the second largest city of the country. Its fame and importance come from the fact that, although it is five hundred miles by water from the Atlantic, it is one of the great wheat-shipping ports of the world. Boats, seeking wheat, sail 200 miles up the Plata and another 300 up the Paraná river to the steep bluffs upon which the city is built. There, along the river banks, stretch for two miles the wharves, warehouses, silos, and elevators.

Paul's Photos, Chicago

NATIONAL CONGRESS BUILDING IN BUENOS AIRES, ARGENTINA

THE OXFORD OF ARGENTINA

Two hundred and fifty miles north and west of Rosario lies Córdoba, the third city of the republic, with a population of 263,000. The city is justly famous for the beauty of its old buildings, for in point of age Córdoba is second only to Lima, Peru, the first city established by the Spaniards in South America. Its university, the oldest in the country, was founded six years before the Pilgrim fathers set foot on the shores of New England. There are many fine old residences of the colonial period. High houses of carved stone and grilled iron are built flush to the street; however, on the inside is the ever-present patio with its trees, bushes, birds, flowers, and all manner of green, growing things. Not only is the town charming in itself; but it is close to a region of beautiful mountains, lakes, and waterfalls, which make this area one of the sight-seeing centers of the whole country.

Other important cities are Santa Fé, Bahía Blanca, and La Plata; which are all cities of more than 100,000 and are river ports. The last named is interesting because it is considered the model city of the Argentine Republic. As it was founded as late as 1882, it contains wide, straight streets and modern new buildings.

MENDOZA, AN OASIS

In the far western part of the country, lying in the foothills of the mighty Andes and in the midst of a desert, is the very attractive town of Mendoza, founded in 1561, although it has a very new and fresh appearance. This is partly due to the fact that it was rebuilt in 1861 after a disastrous earthquake had killed more than half of the population. It is also partly due to the Mendoza River which runs through the town. This river resembles the Nile, because, with its irrigating waters, the people of Mendoza have been able to create a thriving, green oasis of vineyards in what was once a barren, sandy waste. So successful have they been that one can see nothing for miles and miles but grapes —grapes as delicious as any to be found in the world.

The neighboring province of San Juan also produces grapes, and so famous are these two regions that one of the popular sayings describes a drunken person as "*entre San Juan y Mendoza*" (between San Juan and Mendoza).

Mendoza is the first important town on the Argentine side of the railroad that slowly climbs its tortuous path over the Andes, one of the greatest mountain barriers of the world. The crossing is made at Uspallata pass at an altitude of 12,605 feet, higher than Fujiyama in Japan. And that is not the top, because the railroad tunnels some miles through the mountain. Two miles above it, on the roof of South America, stands the Christ of the Andes, a noble monument made of Argentine cannons and erected on the Chilean border to represent eternal peace and friendship between those countries.

In the distance can be seen one of the most magnificent sights in the New World, the peak of Mt. Aconcagua, standing in its majesty 23,000 feet above the level of the sea, the highest peak in the Western Hemisphere. Its symmetrical summit, a combination of jagged black rock and immense fields of white snow, makes a picture that will long be remembered by all fortunate to see it.

Such is Argentina, the land of thriving New World cities and farms, and yet full of Old World curiosities; the land of the highest mountains in the New World and, at the same time, of broad stretches of plains; a land of dry, sandy deserts, hot, rainy tropics, and cold, barren, rocky islands.

Black Star photo. By Pierre Verger.

AT A COCKFIGHT IN MARTINIQUE

In the foreground an injured bird is being given first aid, and in the background, center, a dark-hued enthusiast is placing a bet on his favorite.

BAHAMA ISLANDS

BEGINNING near the coast of Florida and extending for more than seven hundred miles southeast is a group of more than seven hundred islands, islets, and reefs belonging to Great Britain. Columbus discovered them in 1492, but they were first settled by the English in the seventeenth century. For a hundred years both the French and the Spanish fought with the English for the possession of these islands. Even the United States held Nassau, the capital, for a short while during the American Revolution. After the Revolution many American families who preferred to remain British subjects left America for the Bahamas. During the Civil War in the United States these islands were used by blockade runners aiding the southern states.

Twenty-five of the islands are inhabited; the most important being New Providence, Grand Bahama, Abaco, Andros, and Eleuthera. The city of Nassau or New Providence Island, lush with an abundance of tropical plants and trees, is typical of most of the cities. Fort Fincastle, situated on an elevation behind the city, is imposing. The government house on Mount Fitzwilliam affords another splendid view. Glass-bottomed boats offer the visitor an opportunity to glimpse the amazing undersea growths and fish life in the crystal-clear waters of the innumerable lagoons. The Bimini Islands, vividly set in coral reefs and resplendent with amazing bursts of tropical vegetation, are supposed to be the site of the legendary Fountain of Youth which Ponce de Leon so avidly sought.

CUBA

Columbus discovered Cuba on his first voyage in 1492. At that time it was known as Cubanascan by the natives, but Columbus called it Juana. It was not until 1511 that Diego de Velásquez settled a Spanish colony at Baracoa. It was from the Spanish settlements in Cuba that Cortés and De Soto sailed for Mexico and Florida. Negro slaves were introduced about 1523, and from that time on the native population decreased until now the whites form sixty-two per cent of the entire population, with the Negroes and those of mixed blood in second place with twenty-eight per cent.

Although Spain prohibited foreign commerce, illicit trade was carried on with the English, Dutch, French, and Portuguese. In 1762, the capital city of Havana was captured by the English under Admiral Pocock and Lord Albemarle. But, in the treaty of Paris the next year, the territory was returned to Spain. Cuba was one of the few Spanish possessions that did not take advantage of Napoleon's conquest of Spain to declare itself independent.

PIRATES!

Trade restrictions were eased during the Napoleonic wars; but later they were again severely enforced, and smuggling increased. The sixteenth and seventeenth centuries found French and English pirates using Cuba as a base for their operations. From the time that Cuban ports were opened to foreign commerce, in 1818, Cuban nationalists began to assert their demands for independence from Spain. Crushing taxation, unequal representation, rapacious cruelty such as the very early Spanish conquerors were capable of, all combined to create in the hearts of the Cubans a savage resentment against Spanish misrule. Finally, led by the agitation of Martí, the Cubans began a ten-year war, lasting from 1868 to 1878, in an effort to free themselves. Nothing came of this until 1898, when the United States warship, *Maine*, was blown up in the Havana harbor, and the United States declared war against Spain, winning independence for the Cubans.

"CUBA LIBRE!"

From then on, the Cubans were given the power to rule their own country, the United States under the Platt Amendment reserving only the right to intervene when necessary, and to lease land for naval stations at Guantánamo and Bahía Hondo. The Cubans, under further provisions of this agreement, were forced to keep governmental expenditures within the limit of their revenues and to continue the policy of sanitation begun by the American military authorities. Relations between the two countries, however, grew steadily worse. Revolution followed revolution, culminating in the deposing of the dictatorial Gerardo Machado in 1933, and the abrogating of the Platt Amendment the next year. Unfortunately, even these changes did not bring about political stability or a complete return of friendly relations with the United States.

The island of Cuba is divided into five provinces. The province of Havana, in which the capital city, Havana, is located, is thickly populated and is rich in sugar plantations.

Pinar del Rio raises the finest Cuban tobacco and has vast mineral resources. Santa Clara province has immense sugar and tobacco plantations and includes the city of Cienfuegos, one of Cuba's main ports. Camaguey, overspread with grazing land and forests, also has an important fruit industry. Oriente, on the east as the name implies, is quite mountainous and contains many natural wonders, including a number of limestone caverns which underlie a great deal of the island. Its fertile portions offer a fine soil for the growing of sugar cane and tropical fruit.

HAVANA

The old city of Havana, dating back to the Spanish conquerors, contains beautiful examples of colonial churches, fortresses, palaces, plazas, monasteries, and parks. The Prado is a parkway connecting the park system with some of the finest drives, the Paseos la Reina, Tacon, and Carlos III. In the magnificent harbor can be seen the grim outlines of Morro Castle, which was built in 1589 to repulse the attacks of French, Dutch, and English pirates. A marvelous view of Havana spreads out panoramically from the hill, outside the city, on which Príncipe Castle is built. A trip on the Malecon highway, which also acts as a seawall, will not only present a grand view of

HAVANA, CUBA
The capitol is at the left, in the center is a statue of José Martin, and at right is the National Theater.

Ewing Galloway photo, N. Y.

BUYING LOTTERY TICKETS IN CUBA
Lotteries are under government supervision.

Ewing Galloway photo, N. Y.

the ocean, but will lead to Vedado where an old cathedral and convent can be seen. The Town Hall and La Fuerza, another old fort, are to be found in the Plaza de Armas. The caves of Bellamar, near the Yumuri Valley, can be reached from Havana by railroad. Although the climate in this section is hot, Havana has become a favorite vacation spot.

HISTORIC CITIES

Formerly the capital of Cuba, Santiago de Cuba is now the capital of Oriente province. In the old days it was the center of the smuggling trade of the West Indies and was also the object of attack by pirates. It, too, has a Morro Castle, crowning a cliff that guards the landlocked harbor of Santiago de Cuba. Immediately across from it is La Sacopa. The largest church in Cuba, Santiago Cathedral, is pinnacled with two towers and a dome in true Spanish style. The harbor can be seen from the head of Marina Street. A drive along the Alameda takes the sight-seer into the lower part of the city and along the edge of the bay and affords him a splendid view of it.

Matanzas, too, was used by the early pirates as a haven from enemy ships. Now it is a thriving seaport that exports sugar in great quantities. Well-kept boulevards lead into the many plazas that dot the city. Close by, on a plateau, are the famed Bellamar caves, with overhanging formations. One of its chambers, 250 feet long, is so decorated by nature as to give it the appearance of a Gothic cathedral, which, by the wav. is the name the Cubans have given it. Matanzas is visited frequently by those who have heard of the splendid view that can be obtained of the entire Yumuri Valley from the top of a nearby hill.

Most of Cuba's seaports are protected by fortresses erected by the Spaniards to protect the harbors from pirate attacks. The Castillo de Jagua is one that was built to defend Cienfuegos in the province of Santa Clara. Rising to a height of 3,000 feet, the Trinidad Mountains can be seen from the harbor, and they present a majestic sight. A visit to the Arnold Arboretum, the field laboratory for Harvard students studying tropical vegetation, will be educational as well as entertaining.

Located on a cliff that overlooks Port Nipe, the city of Antilla, in Oriente province, affords the tourist a lovely view of the bay beneath. Guantánamo houses a naval training station of the United States and is a strategical position of defense. A few miles from Pinar del Río is Vinales, from which can be seen the scenery of the Vinales Valley. San Diego de los Baños, in keeping with its name, which means San Diego of the Baths, is a Cuban vacation spot because of its famed sulphur springs. Trinidad, founded in 1514 by Diego de Velásquez, still retains some of the antiquities of its past.

All in all, Cuba promises the traveler an exciting adventure without the attendant hardships of travel encountered in most tropical countries. In Havana, where the most modern conveniences are available, one can live comfortably, surrounded by the remains of a past that has known the blood-curdling cries of pirates, the swagger of Caribbean buccaneers, and the courtly grace of Spanish grandees.

HAITI

Haiti and the Dominican Republic share the same island. Two thirds of it belong to the former, the remaining third to the latter. Both are independent republics.

Here again Columbus discovered the land for the whites, who exploited the natives so outrageously that in a short while they disappeared completely, their places being taken by Negro slaves. French, English, and Dutch colonists came in; and in 1697 the Spaniards recognized a third of the island as being French. Continued cruelty to Negro slaves brought many insurrections, the climax of which was the one in 1795, led by the Negro, Toussaint L'Ouverture, who established Haiti as an independent republic.

LA CITADEL, HAITI

Courtesy Illinois Central System

Warfare with the French and English resulted in victories for the Negroes; and in 1804 they won their complete independence. Revolution followed revolution, and the country fell into a deplorable state until, in 1915, the United States stepped in, landing its marines to settle the financial and political difficulties. Since then matters have improved. The United States has withdrawn its forces, but some internal confusion prevails.

Port au Prince is the capital and main port of the republic. It has a population of about 120,000. The city has changed considerably since the American intervention, much work having been done in the paving of roads, the betterment of sanitation, and the erection of modern buildings. Earthquakes and fires, together with internal warfare, have taken their toll in the city. Cap Haitien, Aux Cayes, and Facmel are additional ports of importance.

DOMINICAN REPUBLIC

The history of Santo Domingo, as the Dominican Republic is known, is essentially the same as that of Haiti up to the time the Spanish gave up the western third of the island to France. In 1586, Sir Francis Drake looted Santo Domingo. During the French revolutionary wars, Spain was forced to relinquish its two thirds to France. But, in Toussaint L'Ouverture's rebellion, France, too, was dispossessed, and the entire island became an independent republic. Revolutions and internal warfare caused various separations and reunions until finally, in 1844, the Dominican

Republic was established. Like its sister republic, matters went badly in Santo Domingo; and in time the United States was forced to intervene as it did in Haiti.

Santo Domingo, now called Ciudad Trujillo, is the republic's capital and chief port. Founded in 1496 by Columbus, it is the oldest European settlement in the entire New World and still contains many relics of the ancient days. Even Columbus' body is said to be entombed in the cathedral, an ornate edifice. The ruins of Diego Columbus' house, the San Nicolas Hospital, and the Torre de Homenaje are sights to be viewed by the traveler. One of the first universities in the New World was established in Santo Domingo. The drive along the Malecon and the Plaza de la Independencia should be included in every visitor's program. Other important cities are Santiago de los Caballeros and Puerto Plata.

PUERTO RICO

Before Columbus discovered Puerto Rico in 1493 the island was known as Boriquén to its inhabitants, the Arawakan tribe. Here, as in the other West Indian Islands, the cruelty of the Spaniards killed off the natives, and today the population is mostly

Courtesy Pan-American Airways

SAN JUAN, LARGEST CITY AND SEAPORT OF PUERTO RICO
(Air view of business section)

mixed Spanish and Negro. In a like way, the Negroes were subjected to Spanish cruelty and inhumane treatment which, after a number of uprisings, resulted in a great Negro insurrection in 1816. The American fleet, under Admiral Sampson, attacked and took over Puerto Rico in the Spanish-American War. The country is still an American dependency, but the customary political dissension and demand for self-government continue among certain island groups.

Prominent in the mountainous country is El Yunque, which rises to a height of 3,700 feet. The climate, considering the tropical location of the island, is pleasingly temperate, especially in the winter months.

Puerto Rican lacework and embroidery, done by hand, is famous over the entire world. Cigars, cigarettes, and the usual tropical sugar and fruits are the most important commercial exports.

San Juan, the capital, is situated on an island connected to the mainland by a series of bridges. It, too, has a Morro castle, perched in a strategic position to protect the port from sea raiders. San Cristobal Castle is another stronghold. From the two castles the early Spaniards successfully fought off Drake and Hawkins in 1595. The islands later fell to the British, the Dutch, and finally, to the Americans. The governor's palace, La Fortaleza, is a fine old building. Ponce de León, the searcher for the Fountain of Youth in Florida, lies buried in the cathedral. A relative of his built Casa Blanca in 1525. The island has well-paved roads, over which most of the larger cities can be reached.

JAMAICA

Jamaica was another of the West Indian Islands that Columbus discovered on his second voyage. The island belonged to Spain from 1509 to 1655. English buccaneers long attempted to wrest it from the Spaniards; but it did not fall to the British until 1655, when Cromwell's West Indies expedition captured the island. Long before that the Arawaks, the native Indians, had disappeared completely and their places had been taken by Negro slaves. Twice the Negroes revolted under the British regime, their last attempt being completely suppressed by the British. But in 1833 slavery was abolished, and the insurrections ceased.

The roads in Jamaica are well paved, and a trip through the miles of sugar-cane land and coconut groves is well worth while.

Courtesy Illinois Central System

A FISHING VILLAGE IN JAMAICA

The countryside is filled with waterfalls, turbulent streams, and luxuriant undergrowth.

Kingston, the capital city, is clean and well laid-out, with about 63,000 people, predominantly Negroes. In this British colonial city even the Negroes speak with a broad, English accent. The officials are British; and, although an air of old Spain still lingers, behind it all is the spirit of black Africa only glossed over with civilization. Port Royal, across the bay, was once the capital and the stronghold of Caribbean pirates. It was completely destroyed by fire in 1703.

Other cities of importance are Spanish Town, Port Antonio, Falmouth, Port Maria, and Montego Bay.

Three zones of vegetation exist in Jamaica. Banana trees and palms grow along the tropical coast; a wide variety of semitropical fruits and flowers grow inland; and on the mountain lands the vegetation is that of temperate countries.

GUADELOUPE

After Columbus discovered the island of Guadeloupe in 1493, it was exchanged among the English, the Swedish, and the French several times. However, the French secured it permanently in 1818.

Paul's Photos, Chicago

Courtesy American Museum of Natural History

Above: MONT PELÉE IN MARTINIQUE

Left: WOMEN COAL THE STEAMERS IN GUADELOUPE

With the exception of a few whites, the population of 270,000 is entirely Negro or mixed. The western half of the island is mountainous, containing Grande Soufrière, an active volcano which erupted in 1797 and again in 1843.

With a population of 30,000, Point-à-Pitre is the chief city and port, located at the mouth of the Salée River. Basse Terre is the capital of the island. Le Moule, another port, is also of importance.

MARTINIQUE

Discovered in 1502 by Columbus, Martinique was first settled by a private company of Frenchmen in 1635. Forty years later the French government purchased the island for the crown. The Carib natives soon disappeared, and imported Negro slaves took their place. In the colonial wars between the French and the British, the latter held the island a number of times, but the French eventually won out.

The island has a rugged terrain and numbers an active volcano among its mountains. Mount Pelée, which erupted in 1902, killed more than 30,000 people in St. Pierre, the island's chief city. High plateaus, plains, jungles, and gorges are found here. Sugar refining and rum distilling are the chief industries; the usual tropical agricultural products are grown.

Fort-de-France, with a population of about 45,000, is the largest city on the island. It has a sparkling bay, well sheltered by a mountainous peninsula. Ste Marie, Le François, Trinité, and Gros Morne are other cities.

BARBADOS

Barbados was visited by an English ship in 1605 and claimed for the English crown. It has remained an English colony to the present day. The two English settlements located at Hole's Town and Bridgetown engaged in rivalry, even breaking out into war, for a long time. Additional disturbances were caused by the freeing of slaves early in the nineteenth century.

The inhabitants claim that the climate here is the finest in the West Indies, and the island has become a favorite vacation place. Scenic spots include the many coral reefs and Mount Hillaby, a thousand feet in altitude. In the years 1812 and 1902 the country was endangered with volcanic disturbances, when a heavy fall of ash issued from the volcano La Soufriére on St. Vincent. For

Courtesy Furness Steamship Lines

GREAT PITCH LAKE

years this day of terror, with the sun blotted out, was remembered.

Bridgetown, the capital, with a population of 13,000, is at the southwest corner of the island on Carlisle Bay. A few miles north is Speights Town, of only fifteen hundred population.

TRINIDAD

Discovered by Columbus in 1498, the Island of Trinidad was a Spanish possession for three hundred years, until the English seized it during the Napoleonic wars. The population is mostly pure Negro as well as mixed with a large amount of native Indian blood.

With the exception of a range of hills in the north, the island is rather flat. In the La Brea region is one of the natural wonders of the world, Pitch Lake, an immense surface of asphalt. It is liquid in the center, but hardens as it approaches shore line.

Port of Spain, the capital, with a population of almost 72,000, is the largest city. The sheltered harbor is not deep enough to accommodate the average-sized ocean liners, and so passengers who visit the island must disembark on small boats. The Botanical Gardens afford a fine view of the harbor.

The island of Tobago, rising like a mountain peak out of the ocean, adjacent to Trinidad, is the larger island's ward. It is a beautiful bit of land and, according to some stories, was the inspiration for Defoe's Robinson Crusoe island. Highly-colored birds of paradise have found one of the small islands off Tobago a safe haven.

Paul's Photos, Chicago

WATERFRONT OF NASSAU, CAPITAL OF THE BAHAMA ISLANDS

UFA Photo

ON A JUNGLE RIVER IN AFRICA

THE DARK CONTINENT

TO THE SOUTH OF EUROPE and to the west of Asia there lies a continent, three times as large as the United States, full of adventure, romance, and unexplored areas. This is Africa, the dark continent of contradictions, where civilization first arose and where some of the most primitive people in the world still live; where some areas are so barren that nothing can exist, while other areas yield billions of dollars' worth of products. As long as the mighty Congo flows to the sea, as long as the endless sands of the Sahara continue to be, and as long as man seeks adventure, Africa, the unknown, will always supply it.

Some clever scientist has shown that the peoples of the world fall into three different classes of civilization. There are the people who wear their shirts inside their pants, the people who wear them outside their pants and the people who wear no shirts at all. Africa contains all three classes. In north Africa you can see the Semitic Moslems whose robes are always outside their pants; in central Africa are the Negroes who wear no shirts, while in south Africa is the very civilized Britisher.

Along the Mediterranean coast is heard the soft wailing of melancholy pipes; along the Congo the steady beat of the tom-tom; and along the boulevards of Cape Town the blare of the latest American "swing" or the fine strains of a symphony orchestra.

Although Africa is the second largest mass of land in the world, only three small parts of it can be called independent. Of its millions of square miles, only Liberia and Egypt occupy territories which are considered free. The Union of South Africa, which is a British dominion, is actually an independent nation.

WHITE MAGIC AND BLACK

In this vast continent of long rivers, great deserts, high mountains, and strange people varied forms of adventure await the traveler. So let us go in search of some of the black magic in which Africa abounds. At the same time we must not forget to take along plenty of white magic with which to protect ourselves. White magic embraces such things as quinine and mosquito nets, rifles and pistols, canned food and bottled water, and no end of other things which have helped the white man in his conquest of this continent. In the line of white magic, we must not forget baksheesh (money), to be used in North Africa to open doors that otherwise stay closed.

TRIPOLI, CALLED LIBYA

Let us begin our search for magic and adventure in Italian North Africa, or what was once known as Tripoli. After Tripoli, in its long history, had passed from the hands of the Phoenicians to those of the Greeks and thence in turn to the Romans, Byzantines, Arabs and Turks, it fell to Italy.

The best port of entry into the country is the city of Tripoli. Here under a burning sun the traveler views from the sea tall

Homer Smith photo, Chicago

A LIBYAN "APARTMENT HOUSE"
Showing a well and water bags in foreground.

minarets which are glittering streaks in the azure sky. These colorful spires rise above the city's many mosques and stretch high above the low, flat-topped houses of the native quarter of old Tripoli as well as the more modern European section.

The most interesting building in the entire city is an old castle, where in the past the lords of the land ruled with a bloody scimitar. The castle was partially ruined by shelling in the war with Italy but has been restored and now serves more as a relic than as a protective feature. Yet a guard is maintained, and every afternoon with pomp and ceremony, with blaring trumpets and rolling drums, a detachment of khaki-garbed soldiers comes to change the guard. With its red fezzes and multi-colored belts, the procession is indeed a colorful one.

Another important building in town is the governor's palace. It is not especially interesting for its architecture, its age, or its history; but for the man who lives in it now. The man is Governor Italo Balbo, who made the startling flight from Rome to Chi-

Black Star photo. By Baron.

A MODERNISTIC HOTEL ON THE OUTSKIRTS OF TRIPOLI

cago in 1933. Tripoli, the capital of Tripolitania, and Benghasi, the capital of Cyrenaica, are the two most interesting towns in Italian Libya.

Let us go immediately to the really fascinating part of the country, the oases.

SAND AND ROCK

This, of course, means going into the desert, because, with the exception of the green strip along the Mediterranean shore, the rest of the country is a rocky or sandy waste. We can travel for days and see nothing but hills and mountains of yellow sand, or brown and red rock. Then suddenly in the midst of all this desolation there appears a shimmering, sparkling jewel, a perfect emerald. For a while we pay no attention to it because mirages are so common in this country. But we are not mistaken this time; for it is the green, palm-studded oasis of Bu Ngem.

MARKET DAY

For six days out of the week, Bu Ngem does not differ from other small, sleepy oasis towns that appear widely scattered over the Libyan desert. But on the seventh day, market day, the whole town is transformed. The central square is overflowing, the narrow streets are jammed with humanity, the coffee shops and the outdoor eating places are doing business. Everyone is enlivened with a holiday spirit and wears his finest clothes, for market day is a combination of the Saturday and Sunday of the Western World.

To the merchants who buy and sell everything, from camels to coconuts, time is nothing and money is everything. When you realize that the merchants sometimes haggle for fifteen minutes over something that may be worth a penny, you can imagine how long it takes to buy a camel. In the market the food bazaar is especially interesting, for its wide range of goods and smells. Side by side you see a breakfast food from the United States and a dish of fried locusts, just picked from the nearby date palms. Farther down there are aromatic spices, fresh dates, stale meat, baked eggs, delicious tea and coffee, rancid butter, strong cheeses, and dried meat.

DESERT MAGIC

Elsewhere in the town there are various kinds of entertainment especially gathered here for market day. In one corner of the central square sit the snake charmers. They are all competitors, but perform one at a time by blowing weird tunes on their pipes so that the deadly, hooded cobras in front of them stand up and writhe to the exotic music. After the performance one of the charmers will show that he is the best by putting the head of a cobra in his mouth and going through the motion of swallowing it. Farther down the line, in front of the main mosque, are magicians who swallow swords, eat fire, and apparently inflict punishment on themselves in many other ways. Next to them is a large tent in which the desert dancers perform.

FRENCH NORTH AFRICA

Lying just to the west of Libya is French North Africa, consisting of the three countries of Tunisia, Algeria and Morocco.

Black Star photo. By Baron.

BERBER HORSEMEN, LIBYA

They are considerably quieter and more developed than Libya. All the capital cities of the French territories, Tunis, Algiers, and Fez, are strange combinations of Paris and the Orient, although Fez has been least affected by the invasion of the French.

TUNISIA

In Tunisia there are three places of especial interest to the tourist. These are the holy city of Kairuan, Tunis (the capital city), and the ruins of the once mighty city of Carthage.

As in all the North African countries, the population of Tunisia is concentrated along the northern coast, while the desert hinterland is almost uninhabited. It is therefore strange to find, some 125 miles south of Tunis, a thriving city of 25,000. This is Kairuan, the holy city, founded by the great Arabian conqueror, Sidi Okba, in 670 A.D., when he and his hordes of Arabs were carrying the crescent of Islam across Africa. The holiness of the city comes from the fact that the Great Mosque of Sidi Okba is located there. To this enormous building, containing a huge courtyard and thousands of pillars, devout Moslems come on pilgrimages from all over North Africa. Unfortunately, however, a pilgrimage to Kairuan is only one seventh as holy as one to Mecca.

The first thing that the traveler notices about Tunis is the style of architecture used in the construction of its many mosques. Instead of the once familiar domes and slender spires of the minarets, he finds the open courtyards and square minarets of the Moorish mosques, entirely different from those in the rest of the Moslem world, but certainly with a beauty all their own. Another unusual feature which immediately strikes the eye is the great number of Christian churches and cathedrals. In Egypt the English have been content to let Egypt remain Egyptian, but the French seem to be bent on changing North Africa into a southern extension of France. A first glance at the city of Tunis reminds one of the Rue de Rivoli in Paris. A look at the people on the streets gives the traveler no clue as to their nationality, for of Tunis' 200,000 inhabitants, 15,000 are French, 25,000 are Italians and Maltese, 55,000 are Jews while the remainder are Arabs, Negroes, and Moors. However, at the top of the hill on which the city is built is the native quarter. In it are all those interesting features that the travelers attribute to an Arabian country. With the exception of the many mosques, in which Christians are most unwelcome, the most important feature is the Bey's palace, called the Dar-el-Bey. Its exterior is a perfect example of the charming Saracenic mode of Arabian architecture, but the interior leaves much to be desired.

Tunis lies on the edge of a large, shallow, salt lake which is connected with the sea and the port of Goletta by a long canal, through which ocean-going ships easily pass. Goletta is interesting because it is constructed of material taken from the ruins of Carthage near at hand.

ALGERIA

Passing westward into Algeria one comes to the ruins of the ancient Roman city of Timgad. This desolation of carved and polished stone is one of the most interesting places in Algeria. Here is a well preserved cemetery of an ancient civilization. Tim-

Homer Smith photo, Chicago

HARBOR AND SKYLINE OF ALGIERS

gad is a forest of stone that stretches as far as the eye can reach, with columns, a theater, a stadium, triumphal arches, a forum, roads and houses. Its great size and remarkable preservation are amazing, but even more amazing is the death-like quiet of the desert that surrounds it. Nothing is to be heard but the eerie soughing of the wind as it passes through the arches and between the many columns. Timgad is, indeed, a city of the dead; so let us take our leave and look for life which is very abundant in the hustle and bustle of nearby Algiers.

ALGIERS, THE WHITE

The view of Algiers from the sea is a spectacle. This city of white, with its milky triangle of the Berber town, the two prominent white mosques, its wide belt of modern buildings and spacious docks, and the dark green velvet that mantles its heights, forms a dazzling riot of color against a background of light blue sky and a foreground of dark blue water. Yet despite the many colors it is always the whiteness, intensified by the brilliant sun, that stands out in the observer's memory.

At first glance the city appears to be as modern as Marseilles; but a ten-minute jaunt through the European section along the waterfront brings us to the upper town, where the middle and lower classes live huddled together, an incredible mixture of Turks and Moors, as well as Kuluglis, Arabs, and Negroes. Let us search for and climb that steep ladder of small paving stones called the Rue de la Casbah, which will lead us to the heart of the ancient Berber maze. Here is something unique in Africa, of about the same size and no less amazing than the thousand-year-old labyrinths of Fez and Cairo. Here are streets as narrow as corridors, bathed in shadow and coolness; houses whose tottering walls are supported by many round, wooden struts, which, worn out by time, bend together as if seeking mutual support and thus form picturesque arches. Here in walls painted with a lime wash of white, blue or pink, are worn and broken doorways through which one can catch a glimpse of the narrow patio with its line of columns. Alternating with the doors are the narrow, grated slits of windows, through which one can see out but none can see in.

To obtain real adventure in the upper town you must visit it alone, retracing your steps continuously, losing yourself in tortuous streets, being brought to a stop by blind alleys, winding your way through a composite crowd of Moors and Arabs, Mozabites and Senegalese, Provençaux, Italians, and Maltese. You will also pass slowly moving figures of women dressed and veiled in white, who appear to be enormous but are light-footed under their *haiks,* wearing balloon-like trousers; small girls with henna-reddened fingers and hair plaited in pigtails, jabbering and bawling in the street and then suddenly disappearing through half opened doors; and beggars in *burnuses* lying motionless in shady corners.

At the same time you will notice many peculiar sights: a little mosque with a cross on it, an old palace which now serves as a police station, streets named "Beautiful France," or a blond French family living in a hovel, with Arabs and Sudanese for neighbors.

By no means is all of the country as French as Algiers is. Our next place to visit is a small village which lies across the dry and barren Atlas Mountains and on the northern border of the Sahara

Desert. It is such a charming and delightful spot that the Arabs named it Bu Saada, "The Place of Happiness." With the exception of some motor busses in the square and a new hotel, it is very similar to what it was in the days when the Arabs first came from the east, conquering all before them. However, we may be thankful that there are such things as motor busses, otherwise we should have to ride on camels.

Gladly we take the bus, and as we roll over the last mountain range we immediately recognize the streak of green in front of us as what it is—an oasis. Behind a large bank of light-colored sand, which seems to retain all the light of the passing day, the huts of the small town stretch away like a streak of white paint, overhung from end to end by a long frieze of tall palm trees, the whole picture being bordered by the deep greens and purples of the sunset. Such is Bu Saada at twilight. The village is engaged in its early evening occupations. In its narrow alleyways the dried earth huts have dark and low passages, propped up like mine galleries with smoky beams and twisted trunks of juniper trees. From behind windowless walls comes the dull sound of hand mills grinding grain for the evening meal. In a few stalls, primitive workers are fanning their forges, a handful of charcoal on the ground, by blowing through a long bamboo stick; or they are making braid for *burnuses*, the long Arabian nightgown-like gar-

Photo L'Ofalac—Algiers

ALGERIAN NOMADS (WANDERING TRIBESMEN) IN THE DESERT

Homer Smith photo, Chicago

VIEW OF THE EL ZOKÁ OASIS IN THE SAHARA DESERT

ment, by holding a hank of silk in their toes and twisting it with their hands. Soon it will be time for the muezzin, the Moslem priest, to give the call to prayer; and the village will become quiet for the night.

THE WITCHING HOURS

Night is the time when Bu Saada is the most attractive. When the sun has set, you can hear the tom-toms begin to throb and the pipes begin to cry and wail. This is the hour, the witching hour, when the Ouled-Nails, the famous dancing girls, go into their act. This is the time when crowds gather from afar to watch them go through their graceful movements, which are so pleasing to the citizens of the desert. Ouled-Nails are famous for two reasons: their peculiar dress and their graceful dancing. Their dress is odd because they wear all of their wealth around their neck until they are married. With the money they earn they buy jewels and coins in the form of necklaces, and when they are wed they must give it all to their husbands as a dowry.

MOROCCO

Underwood & Underwood photo

ABD-EL-KRIM, Great Moorish Chief

Morocco, Algeria's neighbor to the west, is well known for its cities, such as Mogador, Marakesh, Fez, Casablanca and Meknes. It is also unusual in that here Moorish architecture is at its highest, and French influence is at its lowest. Such monuments as the Hassan tower (an old minaret) at Rabat, the Kutubia (or bookseller's mosque) in Marakesh, the gate of Mansur in Meknes, and the Medersa Bu Inania in Fez are considered artistically perfect and have been reproduced in pictures and photographs thousands of times. Because the French did not take Morocco until 1911, the freedom-loving Arabs are still unused to foreign domination and thus revolt quite frequently. Therefore it is in Morocco where France has her greatest concentration of the Foreign Legion.

In this country of interesting cities, two stand out as especially interesting—Meknes and Fez. The first was a city built in a fit of anger. A long time ago Mulay Ismail, the sultan, asked Louis XIV for the hand of his daughter. Louis refused, saying that his daughter was accustomed to the comforts and splendor of Versailles and could not live in a town in Morocco which could not offer the same things.

The infuriated Mulay started to build a city that would surpass Versailles in splendor. He gathered mud and stone from miles around and built walls thirty miles long. Inside he built palaces, mosques, granaries, towers, stables and gates. But Meknes was a city of mud, and no Christian princess came to grace Mulay's court.

STRONGHOLD OF ISLAM

Fez is the most Mohammedan, and therefore the least modern, city in Africa. Everything that is strange and exotic in Cairo,

Homer Smith photo, Chicago

A DESERT NOMAD AT PRAYER

Tunis, and Algiers, can also be found in Fez. Within its walls, which were built a thousand years ago, there is nothing new. The foreigners live in the modern city about a mile away, while Fez sleeps within its walls as it has slept for the past ten centuries. Furthermore, as soon as a foreigner steps inside the walls he immediately feels that he is not wanted. But even though hard eyes stare at him hostilely, it is very much worth while to brave the stares in order to see the beautiful art work. Although he cannot enter any of the mosques, he can admire the beautiful tiles which are the basis of Moorish art and with which they are decorated.

The tiles are of all colors, but mainly blue and white. Everything is decorated with them—mosques, minarets, city walls, gates, fountains—until the whole city gleams and flashes like something from fairyland. Another feature of the architecture which is so distinctive is the pointed Moorish arch. This is also seen everywhere, from the smallest mud hut to the great mosque of Karueein, largest and oldest in North Africa.

Besides the pointed arch and blue tiles, Morocco has given us such names as mogador, the silk used for men's neckties, named after the city of the same name; tariff, from the city of Tarifa, which comes from the days when Moorish pirates forced all Mediterranean shipping to pay taxes; fezzes from Fez; tangerines, from Tangiers; and mascara, from Maskara, a town in nearby Algeria.

ALONG THE WEST COAST

As we go southward along the west coast of Africa we notice fewer and fewer Arabs and more and more Negroes. Indeed, we are passing into a very different part of the continent. Along the Atlantic shore are the foreign colonies: Rio de Oro, belonging to Spain; French West Africa and Senegal; Gambia, belonging to Britain; Portuguese Guinea; French Guinea, and the British colony of Sierra Leone. With the exception of Rio de Oro and French West Africa, the colonies are generally known as tropical. The two exceptions are hot and dry.

South of Rio de Oro it remains just as hot and becomes increasingly wetter. And the wetter it becomes, the worse it is for the white man because of the many diseases such as yellow fever, sleeping sickness, black water fever and malaria, which are prevalent. These are spread by the numerous insects, more numerous than the sands in the Sahara, and which play havoc with man in many other ways. There are the mosquitoes, carriers of malaria, tsetse flies, spreaders of sleeping sickness, red ants, devourers of food, cockroaches, eaters of books, and termites, destroyers of houses. In addition to these destructive ones there are scorpions, driver ants, chiggers and guinea worms whose bites, if not fatal, are extremely uncomfortable.

The intense heat, too, makes it impossible for a white man to stay here more than eighteen months at a time. Therefore, the whites rule for a while and then take vacations while the poor Negroes carry on in the plantations and mines from day to day.

THE NEGRO REPUBLIC

On the lower northwest coast of Africa is a place where Negroes are their own bosses. This is, of course, the Negro republic of Liberia where everyone takes life easy.

The Republic of Liberia was established by American idealists as a haven for slaves from the United States. When the slaves made their constitution, they decreed that no white man could hold office or own property in the new republic. As a result, no foreign countries could invest in the country, and Liberia was continually bankrupt. However, an American rubber company has now gained entrance and is operating large rubber plantations. The most profitable enterprise in the republic is the sale of its postage stamps to collectors. Every time a tourist boat docks at Monrovia, the capital, two persons always visit the ship: the American consul, who comes out to buy provisions, and the postmaster general who comes to sell stamps to the tourists. Whenever Liberia needs funds, all it has to do is to issue a new series of stamps.

THE GOLD, IVORY, AND MOSQUITO COASTS

Going eastward from Liberia, along the Gulf of Guinea, we pass, in succession, the colonies of Ivory Coast, Gold Coast, Dahomey, and Nigeria, and then southwards, the Cameroons and Spanish Guinea. With the exception of the last named, these colonies are divided, one by one, in the order named above, between France and Great Britain. They are much like the lands which we just left, except that here it rains every day in the year while the temperature seldom falls below eighty degrees. The Gold and Ivory Coasts are so named because gold and ivory were once shipped from there in days gone by. They were also the spots from which Negroes were shipped in the days of the slave trade. Now that the traffic in gold, ivory, and black ivory (that is to say, slaves) has ceased these colonies are relatively unimportant. This is not true for Nigeria, however.

NIGERIA

"Any person who . . . eats or receives for the purpose of eating any part of a dead human body is guilty of a misdemeanor and is liable to imprisonment for two years." Such is the decree of the British Colony of Nigeria, passed as late as the year 1922. However, Nigeria is progressive, with large cities, good roads, rich mines, modern railroads, and a population of some twenty-three million that speak as many as seventy-five different languages. There are the fierce Ashantis, the Hausas, who are thought to be descendants of the Ancient Egyptians; the Yorubas, marked with scars and with two front teeth missing; and many others.

Between North Africa and the Union of South Africa most of the cities on the continent are nothing more than a small collection of grass or mud huts, with thatched or corrugated iron roofs. Nigeria, however, has three really large cities and many others of a goodly size. The largest are Lagos, Kano, and Ibadan, the last having an estimated population of 250,000 people. Lagos is the capital and is located on the Atlantic coast, while the other two are far inland, near the border of the Sahara. They are the starting points or *termini* for the great caravans which carry the desert trade across the wide wastes of French West Africa.

FRENCH WEST AFRICA

One of the largest and most interesting French colonies in all Africa is the enormous expanse of territory embracing most of the Sahara Desert, the Ivory Coast, Senegal, and Dahomey. The Sahara, partly included in Algeria, stretches from the Atlantic to the Sudan; and from the southern boundary of North Africa to the vicinity of Lake Chad and the Niger River on the south. Contrary to general opinion, the Sahara is not an unbroken area of shifting sand. Numerous oases dot its great expanse from one end to the other. However, some of these oases are days apart, and caravans of camels are provided with plentiful supplies of water before attempting a crossing.

SECRETS OF THE SAHARA

The Sahara, in spite of popular beliefs to the contrary, is not flat, but presents a relief which varies greatly in altitude and in some places, such as the Tibesti mountains, rises to a height of 10,000 feet. The landscape is just as variable as the terrain, some sections being formed of reddish-brown, quartz sand hills; while others are bare mountains of solid rock. The picturesque yellow sand dunes are rare.

Water may often be found below the surface of the valleys, though frequently it is many feet down. In some spots there are large lakes, like the one near Timbuktu; and in other places there are dry lakes and marshes in which there is a residue of extensive

Courtesy Methodist Book Concern

SOCIAL LIFE IN THE DESERT CENTERS AROUND THE OASES

salt deposits. The temperature may vary as much as seventy degrees in a day, dropping from 100 degrees at noon to below freezing at night. In this combination of furnace and icebox live a great assortment of peoples such as Arabs, Negroes, Moors, Jews, Tibbu, and Tuaregs. Surrounded by Moslems, the Tuaregs stand out as having an interesting custom; here the women go about with uncovered faces while the men wear dark blue veils. The Tuaregs are among the most highly civilized people in Africa. Much of their ancient culture remains.

SHIPS OF THE DESERT

Though the camel is the chief means of travel, being known as the "ship of the desert," horses and mules are also quite extensively used. When two Beduins meet in the desert, it is customary for the higher to greet the lower with the salutation, "*salam aalikum*," meaning, "peace be upon you." By higher and lower greeting is meant that a man on a camel should greet a man on a horse, a man on a horse should speak first to a pedestrian. If a stranger does not receive such a greeting, he should be on his guard for a possible hostile attack.

THE RITUAL OF TEA

Another interesting desert custom is the great ceremony attending the drinking of tea. The sheik who entertains makes tea in the ordinary manner, pours the cups full, then tastes his own for flavor. All cups are then emptied back into the pot, and other elements are added. The staple food article in the oases is the date. November and December are the best months in the year for the desert people; because it is then that the harvesting ceremonies begin, and the buyers come in from the outside world. Nomads come from far and near to buy dates, and the sands of the Sahara around the oases resound with their shouts, as they prepare to camp for the night. Fires spring up, dates are fried for the meal, and then all is quiet as the men, huddled together for protection from the night cold, sink into slumber. Simple as it is, that is the life on the Sahara, and the nomads thrive on it.

FROM THE NIGER TO THE CONGO

We are now back on the Atlantic looking at the unhealthful, wave-washed, rain-drenched coast of the "corner of Africa" containing the Cameroons and Spanish Guinea. These are unimportant lands commercially, and as a result of this fact as well as of the poor climatic conditions few white men live here.

BAGIELLIS, BABINGAS AND BOMASAS

The above names are all given to a tribe of pygmies that live in this region, but the tribe prefers to call itself Akkas. Very little is known about these pygmies because they fear white men so much that they prefer to remain in the deep jungle. However, scientists sometimes win their confidence and make studies of their life.

FRENCH EQUATORIAL AFRICA

This is a strange colony because it stretches all the way from Italian Libya on the north to the mouth of the Congo on the south.

As might be expected, the lives of the inhabitants differ greatly over such a vast expanse of country. In the north they are desert nomads, while in the south they are naked savages living in the jungles. The mining industry has been developed in some regions.

THE JUNGLES

If any single area of Africa can be said to be typically African, or what people think is African, it is the Belgian Congo. Located in the densest of jungles, it is, nevertheless, one of the richest regions on the continent. Through it flows the great Congo River; and it is in the basin of the Congo that most of the farming of the country is carried on. Rubber, ivory, nuts, palm oil, cacao, and cotton are among the leading products. It is also very rich in minerals. In the Katanga region is the largest copper mine in the world; and deposits of gold, tin, and even radium are found there. The Congo was largely the personal property of King Leopold of Belgium, but was turned over to the country of Belgium in 1908.

Contrary to what might be expected of such a land, the trans-

Homer Smith photo, Chicago

A STREET IN LEOPOLDVILLE, BELGIAN CONGO

portation facilities are good. There are 2500 miles of railroads, and the Congo River is navigable for 1000 miles. Leopoldville, a city of 15,000, is the capital of this colony which extends over 918,000 square miles and contains 9,000,000 inhabitants, of whom 26,000 are Europeans. Although the Congo was discovered in 1482 by Diogo Cam, it was never explored until the Englishman, Stanley, traveled up it in the last century. About 1000 miles up the river are Stanleyville and Stanley Falls, both named for this daring explorer.

In the dense parts of the jungle the traveler comes upon "life in the raw." For it is here that the various tribal villages are found. Here the native worshipers of horrible fetishes, created by their medicine men, live in huts of grass. These denizens of the jungle wear but little clothing, although in the higher regions the nights may be quite cool. On such nights the various members of a family pack their bare, brown bodies into a small hut and thus keep warm.

BARTERED BRIDES

Marriage customs in the Congo are quite unusual. The brown-skinned bride and groom generally have little or no choice. In-

Homer Smith photo, Chicago

A NATIVE DANCE ORCHESTRA IN THE BELGIAN CONGO

stead, their fathers go into conference and bargain for a dowry, which may consist of as much as two cows. Neither the bride nor the groom has any voice in the matter and neither may dispute the father. Although the wedding ceremonies are very simple, the frenzied feasting and dancing that follow reach orgiastic heights and usually last the whole night through.

ON SAFARI

Hunting in the Congo is a great risk, for the animals there, especially the elephants and apes, are the most savage kind of game. Occasionally whole tribes go on safari hunting for elephants, most of which are killed for their tusks and skins, although some of them are trained to be used in lumbering. Occasionally, natives will come upon an elephant cemetery where the great beasts have gone to die. To find one is a great stroke of luck, for all that there is to be done is to pick up the valuable ivory tusks.

ANGOLA

Even though the Portuguese were the first to discover, explore, and lay claim to most of Africa, all that remains of their once great empire are the colonies of Angola, or Portuguese West Africa, Mozambique, and a few tiny bits of land elsewhere. Although Angola is close to the equator, it is considerably cooler and dryer than the country which we just left. The jungles have disappeared, which means that the natives live more in the open. Nevertheless they are of the same great tribe, Bantu, and are just as interesting.

POLYGAMY IN AFRICA

Africa is considerably different from several other parts of the world in that girl babies are more prized than boys. This is due to the fact that when the girls reach the age of eleven or twelve, which is the age of marriage in the tropics, they can be sold to a bridegroom's father for a good price. Their value is due to the fact that these natives, like many others in Africa, are polygamous. In fact, a male is not considered to be much of a man unless he has at least ten wives. In view of the fact that it is the women who do all the work, the more wives that a man can have, the richer he becomes. The women plow the fields, take care of the live stock, and bear children. Thus, the more corn, cows, and children the man has, the more prosperous and respected he is. The man's job consists of smoking, drinking, discussing ju-ju (a kind of black magic), and planning raids or wars on neighboring tribes. It is not surprising to note that the reason for the raids is to capture women, so that the raiders may have more wives. The wars usually come when the tribe which has been raided decides to raid in retaliation. All of this involves the use of ju-ju. The medicine man who knows the secrets of ju-ju the best is consulted as to the proper time of attack. The medicine man then dons his most impressive clothes, which usually include a stove-pipe hat, burns some magical powders and makes a very heavy smoke, throws some sticks into the air, and announces that the gods have told him that the best time to attack is just before moonrise. When the sharpening of spears, the filing of teeth, and the painting of the bodies are completed, the chief gives the signal to the drummers, who then start their monotonous and ominous booming. The rhythm is picked up by some other drummer in the forest, and then another and another, until the whole valley is vibrating with the beating of the drums. These are the friends and allies of the attacking tribe wishing them luck. Then the attack starts, and with many whoops and hollows the black warriors swoop down to fight and plunder.

On one such raid the attackers captured twelve women, two young men to use in an excellent stew, several dozen elephant tusks, and by far the best of all, two umbrellas, the dried head of an unfortunate white man, a white man's hat, and a pair of opera glasses. These last named articles were divided between the chief and the medicine man; the women went to the men who captured them; and everyone in the village had a share of the stew. The chief and the medicine man chose what they did because such articles are especially helpful in conjuring and ju-ju.

Although such raiding parties are very infrequent now, the blacks participate in another game which is just as exciting and has a certain element of justice in it. These are attacks which are unaccompanied by any beating of tom-toms or other extensive preparations. In fact, the only noise is the crack of a rifle. The result is a dead Portuguese officer with a bullet hole in the back of his head. The natives of Angola have no especial grudge against the Portuguese as a people, but they do intensely hate the officers of the Portuguese army. It is the officers who force the blacks, with guns and whips, to work in the fields or dig in the mines.

BRITISH SOUTHWEST AFRICA

Passing southward out of Angola, we notice that we are entering an entirely different kind of country. First of all, it is mostly a desert; second, it is under British administration, and the British are thorough-going colonizers in comparison with the indifferent Portuguese; third it is a country of many Bushmen and Hottentots, who are distinctly different from the natives of the rest of Africa.

MOBS OF MIDGETS

The Bushmen are not Negroes, but pygmies with yellow skins. Occasionally a giant Bushman is born, who reaches the towering height of five feet, but most of them seldom exceed four feet in stature. They never cultivate the land but gain their food by shooting game with bows and arrows. Since the white men—British, Germans and Boers (Dutch)—have taken all of the best land, the desert has been generously left to these tiny fellows as their hunting grounds. As a result they live on roots and berries, which leave them so undernourished that the race is dying out very rapidly.

Another people of this country, who are very closely akin to the Bushmen, are the Hottentots, a mixture of Bushmen, Negro and North African blood. They are not much taller than their Bushman neighbors but are sturdier and more healthy. The language of these two peoples is interesting because it contains many clicks, made with the tongue and teeth, and grunts. These noises are supposed to resemble the sounds made by some animals.

The white element in the population, living mostly near the Atlantic coast and along the rivers, produce for export sheep,

Homer Smith photo, Chicago

NATIVES OF THE KALAHARI DESERT IN SOUTH AFRICA

cattle, horses, goats, copper, lead, tin and diamonds. Incidentally, this country was called German Southwest Africa before the war.

THE HOME OF "SCOTTY" SMITH

Like Southwest Africa to the west of it, Bechuanaland is also a part of the Kalahari desert. Therefore it is not important for much except cattle raising and a little mining. Nevertheless, it has had a very interesting history, for it has been the playground for all kinds of bandits and robbers. The most famous of these was "Scotty" Smith, the South African counterpart of Jesse James. He was once an English soldier who came to South Africa to establish his peculiar custom of robbing the rich, helping the poor, and never breaking his word. His favorite prey were the diamond and gold trains from the mines, which he would swoop down on and rob, then return to his retreat in the desert among the natives. Bechuanaland at the time was full of many other freebooters and bandits, but "Scotty" was the most colorful. Other inhabitants were the Boers who had established a republic there. In addition to this, the freebooters had set up two republics and there was a Negro kingdom. They all met their master when Cecil Rhodes visited the territory, bargained for a week, and then returned to Cape Town with Bechuanaland as a part of the British Empire. Bechuanaland, like Southwest Africa, is ruled from the Union of South Africa.

UNION OF SOUTH AFRICA

South and east of Southwest Africa and Bechuanaland is the Union of South Africa. The Union is comprised of such states and territories as Cape Colony, Natal, Swaziland, Orange Free State, Basutoland and others: some taken from the Portuguese, some captured from the Boers, and the rest taken from the natives. The British began by taking Cape Town and then continued until they had control of all the country. Although the country is a dominion of the British empire, the Boers now have their share in local affairs, and the Boer language is spoken as much as English is.

CAPE TOWN

Cape Town is the oldest city in the Union and acts as the legislative capital of the country. The executive capital is in Pretoria, a thousand miles away. The same situation would obtain in the United States if Congress were to continue to meet in Washington while the President moved the White House to Des Moines, Iowa. Resting on a shelf between high mountains and the sea, Cape Town presents a picture that is difficult for any other city to rival. On its main thoroughfare, Adderley Street, one may hear twenty dialects used by the brilliantly dressed natives who stand there all day selling their flowers to European passersby. The buildings along the streets show an influence of modern English and colonial Dutch.

THE STREETS OF DURBAN

Durban, on the east coast, is considerably more picturesque than Cape Town as far as its inhabitants are concerned, although it does not lie in such a site of natural beauty as the capital city does. Durban's importance lies in the fact that it is one of the

Courtesy South African Railways & Harbours

BUSINESS SECTION AND HARBOR OF CAPE TOWN

Courtesy Union of South Africa

THE BAY AT PICTURESQUE DURBAN, SOUTH AFRICA

principal ports of the Union, the third city in point of population, and the favorite resort for many of the dominion's up-country residents. Its charm lies in the color that is found in its streets. It is said of Durban that, size for size, one may encounter here as much diversity of speech, race, color and clothing as one does in London, Paris and New York combined. In West Street you may meet in successive moments a young Kaffir girl in her beads and blanket and a European lady dressed in the latest from Paris. Here is a Mohammedan in brilliant gown and turban; there a Parsee, from India, or an Arab; yonder a Zulu house-boy in the neat tunic and knickerbockers which are the recognized clothing of the native domestic servant. Here may be noticed an Indian woman, bare of feet and poorly clad, yet with a wealth of gold ornaments at her wrists, neck and—nose! Yonder, again in striking contrast, glides an eastern lady of rank, richly garbed in silk, features thickly veiled, and with a male escort in attendance. Along stalks a Kaffir chieftain on one of his infrequent visits to town. He may have a wife, perhaps several wives, walking dutifully behind him as is the Bantu fashion. All around them are Zulu rickshaw boys with gorgeous trappings and heads bedecked with horns and feathers like their very warlike fathers.

CITY OF GOLD

Far inland, atop the high plateau which covers most of South Africa, is found the largest and busiest city in the Union—Johannesburg. Johannesburg has been described as the miracle city of the empire, and it certainly may be considered one of the wonder cities of the world. The development of the gold industry and the remarkable climate of the high-veldt have combined to turn what less than fifty years ago was barren prairie into a city whose real estate alone is worth $310,000,000.

As a result of its youth Johannesburg is very modern in an architectural sense and is certainly not African. Along its broad streets such public buildings as the City Hall, Law Courts, Cathedral, University, Railway Station, Stock Exchange, and other fine buildings give mute testimony to the march of western progress in the metropolis of South Africa. Johannesburg is no longer a gold camp where men rush to make money and then depart; it has become a fine city where the cultured work and live.

Homer Smith photo, Chicago

JOHANNESBURG, MODERN CITY OF SOUTH AFRICA

And all of this is due to that yellow, shiny, soft metal—gold. In the past fifty years there has been $5,000,000,000 worth of this precious substance taken from the deep mines near this city.

A CITY OF DIAMONDS

Another modern bustling city based on the mining of an even more glittering mineral, diamonds, is Kimberley. The products of these two cities make South Africa the treasure trove of the world, but one cannot help wondering what will happen to them when the minerals are exhausted.

Homer Smith photo, Chicago

A DAY'S WASH FROM A KIMBERLEY DIAMOND MINE

Courtesy South African Railways & Harbours

ABAKWETA DANCERS AT AN INITIATION CEREMONY
NEAR TRANSKEI, CAPE PROVINCE

MOZAMBIQUE

Lying along the southeastern coast of Africa, north and east of the Union, is the Portuguese colony of Mozambique, a country much more African than the one we have just left. Like Angola, on the western shores of the continent, Mozambique is a penal colony for Portuguese criminals and a prison camp for the natives. It is not unusual to have your baggage carried by a gang of chained Negroes.

The city of Mozambique is of interest, not because of its size, but because of its penal settlement, from which escape is almost impossible. Here, besides the old fortress, one sees the fine government house, an old cathedral, an arsenal, and other old buildings dating from the early days of the Portuguese conquest. Beira, a larger town farther down the coast, is even more interesting. Here is still in use a miniature railroad, and the city is a maze of narrow-gauge tracks. When two cars, coming in opposite directions on the same track, meet, the native boys merely lift one car off the track, run it around the other, replace it and proceed. Switches are unheard of.

Like many other hot African towns, Beira is more interested in sports than industry. There are no factories here, but there is a large golf course. It is amusing to note that the players here use two caddies, one to carry the golf clubs and the other to watch the flight of the ball.

NYASALAND

An interesting little protectorate, of small commercial value, is the territory of Nyasaland, the strip of land lying on the western shores of Lake Nyasa. Its exports consist of small quantities of cotton, tobacco, rubber, coffee, and beeswax, most of which is gathered by native labor for the whites living in the cool highlands. The natives who inhabit the hot malarial lowlands do little more than support themselves from their poor farms. During the World War there was a famous naval "battle" on the waters of the lake, when a small British boat engaged a German craft of the same size. The German gunboat now lies rusting in the deep waters of the lake.

RHODESIA

VICTORIA FALLS

Just as one associates the Alps with Switzerland, so are the Victoria Falls always associated with Rhodesia. If there were nothing else in the country but the falls, Rhodesia would still be

VICTORIA FALLS, SOUTHERN RHODESIA

Highest and largest falls in the world—the water tumbles 420 feet to the bottom of the gorge.

Homer Smith photo, Chicago

worth a thousand-mile trip across the jungly coastal plain, up the steep sides of the plateau, and across the thorny forest to the spot where the lordly Zambesi River leaves its flat course to plunge downward for a sheer drop of four hundred feet.

The natives call the Falls, "Mosia Tunya," which means "the smoke that thunders," and they have described it perfectly. After the waters have fallen the four hundred feet, which dwarfs the mighty Niagara, they strike the Devil's Boiling Pot at the bottom of the gorge with a force that sends up a roar and a mist that is reminiscent of an erupting volcano. When the water emerges from the clouds of mist, which unfortunately obscure the lower half of the Falls, it boils and rushes through that magnificent, foliage-covered gash in the earth which is the canyon of the Zambesi.

MAN VS. NATURE

A man-made spectacle which is alleged to rival the Falls for grandeur is the really magnificent bridge built across the mighty chasm to carry the trains of the so-called "Cape to Cairo" railway. Elsewhere the bridge would be instantly recognized as a miracle of engineering skill and brilliance, but next to the Falls it fades into an undeserved insignificance.

If we were to follow the Zambesi seaward, we should see such sights as colorful, tropical birds in flight, huge frogs that resemble half-grown kangaroos, hippopotamus and crocodile tracks on the muddy banks which are overhung with a dense covering of luxuriant tropical vegetation, and even a native chieftain in his royal barge propelled by dusky warriors dressed in scarlet capes and brilliant plumes.

TANGANYIKA, KENYA AND UGANDA

Instead of following the river we must continue northward across Rhodesia to Tanganyika Territory, the former German colony. With the acquisition of this territory after the war, Britain finally had a wide strip of lands that stretched from the Cape of Good Hope to the Mediterranean. This is the supposed route of the "Cape to Cairo" railroad. But to travel from one end of the continent to the other along this route, one must do a lot of traveling on foot, and by camel, donkey, and boat.

UFA photo

A SUCCESSFUL HUNT IN THE AFRICAN JUNGLE

A BIG-GAME HUNTER'S HEAVEN

Contrary to the general opinion, big game does not live, for the most part, in the tropical forests or jungles, but in the prairie lands of the big grasses. Therefore such grasslands as Rhodesia and Tanganyika are where American and European adventurers spend millions of dollars for equipment and licenses in order to bag a few elephants or lions. Just as one pays for a license to shoot ducks on the northern lakes of the United States, so must one pay the British government to shoot big game. The difference lies in the fact that it costs about ninety dollars for a license to shoot an elephant, as compared to perhaps two dollars for a duck license. Gorillas also abound in this region, but most of the time it is unlawful to shoot them, for their numbers are rapidly diminishing and some day they may be as extinct as the dodo.

Gorillas are not usually as savage as they are often said to be. Rather than attack, they will flee from man; although in covering their family's retreat they will drop behind and stage a frightening bluff. Nevertheless, many a man who has defied one was crushed to death in an ape's powerful arms.

THE PEARL OF AFRICA

Farther north in the Kenya-Uganda part of the territory is a region of unsurpassed natural beauty. Here are the lofty peaks of Mounts Kenya and Kilimanjaro, the highest on the continent. Uganda is called the Pearl of Africa because of the beauty of her many tropical lakes. To sail over the surface of these splendid pools is to see a picture of heaven on earth, and also, perhaps, to start an early trip to heaven via the jaws of one of the many hippopotami or crocodiles, which infest the otherwise placid waters.

ERITREA, SOMALILAND, AND ETHIOPIA

Formerly maps of Africa showed but two colored coastal strips as belonging to Italy—Eritrea and Somaliland. But now these two, with Ethiopia, form the new colony of Italian East Africa. Eritrea and the Somaliland are nothing but low, hot, and unhealthful strips of land along the sea. They both show a queer mixture of Negro and Arab, both in their architecture and in the faces of their people, who have been subjected to foreign conquest for ages past. Ethiopia, in contrast, was a land in which independence had been maintained since Roman days. Here was a land in which a semi-civilized people, riding wild horses and

Homer Smith photo, Chicago

BUSINESS SECTION OF MOGADISCIO, ITALIAN SOMALILAND

Homer Smith photo, Chicago

AIR VIEW OF ADDIS ABABA, (ETHIOPIA) ITALIAN ORIENTAL AFRICA

dressed in lion skins and chain mail, preserved their ancient freedom and Christian religion from attacks on all sides. But in 1935, following through its plan of colonial expansion, Italy invaded and conquered Ethiopia. These lands, along with British and French Somaliland on the coast, are of little commercial value. The land that is not desert is mountainous, so that almost everything produced is consumed on the spot.

As compared to the lands above, this large region is one of great fertility. Although it lies just to the west of Ethiopia, its northern parts are watered by the Nile, and its south is drenched with tropical rains. Meat, skins, rubber, ivory, tropical woods, and cotton are exported from here in sizable quantities. Strangely enough, much of the cotton is sent to the United States, the world's greatest producer of cotton. The reason is that the Sudanese fiber is longer and stronger than that grown in the States and is in great demand by the automobile tire manufacturers.

The Sudan, from north to south, is a parade of contrasts. From the Egyptian border as far south as Wadi Halfa the country is another Egypt. Great temples of ancient Egypt line the banks of the Nile, while the Sudanese brothers of the Egyptian fellahin cultivate the fields along the banks of this mighty stream.

THE MAD MAHDI

Farther south are the very Arabian and Moslem cities of Khartum and Omdurman, lying across the river from each other. It was here that General "Chinese" Gordon and the British garrison made their famous and final stand against the Mad Mahdi and his fanatical followers. It was also here that the British met the "Fuzzy-Wuzzy," the black and fuzzy-haired natives whose determined and fearless fighting threw the white soldiers into retreat. But the British returned, as they always do, with more men and better guns to establish an Anglo-Egyptian Condominium.

To the south the country resembles central Africa in every respect. Along the shores of the rivers one can see, under the tropical vegetation, natives who appear to have skins whiter than any white man. They are actually as black as any of their African brothers, but they delight in rolling around in ashes until they resemble very pale ghosts. Farther on we can see a scene which is so typical of the tropics—a crocodile sound asleep with his mouth wide open, so that little birds can fly in his cavernous jaws and pick the remnants of his last meal from his teeth.

MADAGASCAR

This island, the sixth largest in the world, is located 360 miles east of Mozambique. It is mostly inhabited by Hovas, a race of people who are not Negroes, but East Indians. They came to Madagascar many centuries ago in open outrigger canoes, all the way across the wide Indian Ocean. They developed quite an advanced civilization and were good fighters, beating off both Arabs and Europeans for many centuries. But finally the French conquered them, and these people, like the rest of the Africans, obey a foreign master.

Black Star photo. By Dorien Leigh, Ltd.

STREET IN THE BAZAAR SECTION OF CAIRO, EGYPT

Homer Smith photo, Chicago

GREAT HALLWAY OF THE TEMPLE OF HATHOR. DENDERAH, EGYPT

THE MYSTERY OF EGYPT

THE MYSTERY OF EGYPT has for centuries enchanted the world. No one has ever solved it, and probably no one ever will. Still this mystery is something which exists everywhere in Egypt. It is found in the dry desert air, in the bright moonlight that makes the ancient temples look like palaces of silver, in the smooth blueness of the Nile, in the sunsets at Assuan, in the tawny furnace of the Valley of the Dead, in the smile of the Sphinx, in the slow movement of a string of camels, black against a glowing sky, as they pass across a sandy dune into the silence of the desert.

A person becomes strangely aware of the mystery the first night he reaches Cairo. Just as dusk falls a drum begins to throb in the Muski or native quarter. Its pulsing rhythm is so steady that his curiosity will be aroused, and he will go out into the moon-bathed night in search of the throbbing. The path will take him past the broad tree-lined boulevards and impressive buildings of the modern section of the city into a maze of smelly, winding white streets, which rise steeply on flights of uneven steps.

On his way strange, hooded figures will brush past him; brown female arms, bare and ringed with bangles, will reach out from cell-like windows; dirty fingers will try to seize his coat; and strange guttural sounds will come to him out of the dark corners of these dimly lighted streets. But the solution to the puzzle is not to be found in the native quarter. It is only deepened there.

Nor can the answer be found at the pyramids, even though the traveler trudges through dark, dusty lanes to the old native quarter on the western side of the city, crosses the Nile, and plods through the sands to the base of these huge and ancient monuments that were antiquities while Moses was still a young student at the temple of Heliopolis. The secret is here just as it is everywhere along the Nile from Alexandria up to Assiut, Edfu, Luxor, or Shelal. It comes in the early morning when the Nile is like a sheet of pale blue glass; at midday when there is no sound but the creaking of a water wheel or the lazy cries of boatmen; at night when the sun has set in golden glory and boats with large sails come silently down the Nile in the dusk. Then the moon rises and someone plays a sad air upon a little flute, which gives forth queer, twisted melodies. Only the unspeaking Sphinx seems to know the answer; and the answer is carved on the rugged, stone face, in a cold, remote smile. No one has interpreted the answer. The riddle of the Sphinx remains unsolved.

EGYPT IS THE NILE

When one thinks and talks of Egypt, one is thinking and talking of the Nile, because it is the most important single thing in the country. The Egyptians have a saying which is in effect that "The Nile is Egypt and Egypt is the Nile." It is the river that has made Egypt what it is today and what it was 7,000 years ago—a narrow strip of cultivated fields on either bank of a long river. A mile to the east or a mile to the west is the desert. It is so close that it can always be seen even from boats sailing on the Nile through rich, green fields. The change is so sudden that it is possible to stand with one foot in a fertile field of wheat while the other foot sinks into the amber sands.

The fact that Egypt became a prosperous, unified, and civilized nation while the nations of Europe were nothing more than howling tribes of naked savages is very much due to the influence of the Nile. Although Egypt is 700 miles in length, the ease of communication along the river binds the different parts of the country together under a central government. In it also lies the prosperity of the country. The fertility of Egyptian soil is not due to rain, for there is none, but to the rich soil and the irrigating waters furnished every year by the annual Nile flood. Following the heavy rains in the center of the continent and in the mountains of Ethiopia, the river rises each summer, overflows its banks, and fills a web of irrigation ditches which spread this life-blood over the fields. When the flood subsides, the rich black earth is left on the land, thereby renewing the fertility of the fields which make up the real Egypt—real, because 95 per cent of the population live in the long and narrow Nile valley, while the remaining 5 per cent are Beduins who roam from one oasis to another in the bordering desert.

The Beduins dress in fine flowing robes and dash from one oasis to another on their camels or fast Arabian horses. They are known as sheiks. The real Egyptians, however, are the farmers or, as they are called in Egypt, fellahin. The sheiks are proud and insolent men, and they despise the lowly fellahin who do nothing but work from dawn to dark, but it is the latter who are the backbone of Egypt.

SEEDS OF CIVILIZATION

It is to the fellahin, of early antiquity, that we owe the study of astronomy. The early farmers, trying to determine the time of the arrival of the Nile floods, noticed that they came at the same time that the brightest star, Sirius, appeared in the heavens. Their study of astronomy grew until in the year 4241 B. C., the earliest fixed date in history, they made a calendar based on the sun. While other nations made their calendars on the basis of a four-week month, based on the moon, the Egyptians devised a twelve-month year, each month of thirty days, plus five extra days at the end of the year. This is the calendar that Julius Caesar introduced into the Western world; and, with some moderations, it is the same one that we use today.

Engineering also had its early start in ancient Egypt. When the Nile waters subsided, the early fellahin had to devise some method to raise the water to the fields. They did; and these methods gave rise to other inventions. The only trouble is that the modern Egyptians are still using the same shaduf, a simple pump, and the same water wheel that were invented in the days of the Pharaohs. Most of the modern inventions in Egypt are introduced by foreigners, especially Englishmen.

The more inventions the ancient Egyptians made, the richer they grew. The richer they were, the more leisure they had; and with this leisure they made more contributions to the civilization under which we now live. These contributions were in the form of writing, art, laws, architecture, and religion. These made them the greatest nation in the ancient world. After a few centuries it began to decline and was soon conquered by foreign nations and for hundreds of years could not be considered an independent country. In fact, it was not until 1937 that Egypt gained what may be called real freedom from foreign rule.

Authentic Egyptian history begins about 3400 B. C., when the kingdoms of Upper Egypt and Lower Egypt were joined into one under the rule of King Menis, the first king of the first dynasty. (Historians have divided the history of ancient Egypt into thirty dynasties or ruling families.) The first capital was in the city of Thinis, located in the middle of the country, near Abydos, and for nearly four centuries the country developed under a strong and efficient central government. Then the pyramid builders, Zoser and Cheops, moved the capital farther down the river to Memphis.

FROM MOUNDS TO MOUNTAINS

Pyramids first started out as tiny piles of stones which were put on the graves to keep the wolves away from the dead bodies. Thieves, who wanted to rob the dead bodies, found the stone piles no trouble to remove; so each succeeding king built his pyramid higher and stronger until we come to the Great Pyramid, that huge pile of stone raised by Cheops.

Then Egypt fell into black days and it was not until the coming of the Twelfth Dynasty, 2000 to 1800 B.C., under the kings Amenemht and Sesostris, that literature, architecture, art, and the sciences flourished again. Then came the first invasion, when the country was overcome by the Hyksos or Shepherd kings. They ruled for two hundred years until the warriors from Upper Egypt came down the Nile and drove them from the country.

Homer Smith photo, Chicago

EGYPTIAN AIR-LINER FLYING OVER THE PYRAMIDS NEAR CAIRO

In doing so the Egyptians learned the art of war and entered their greatest period of development.

During the next two hundred years the great Eighteenth Dynasty kings, named Thothmes and Amenophis, conquered a great empire, which included Nubia to the south and Palestine and Syria to the north. This was a period of wealth and splendor, notably under Queen Hatasu; a period of foreign trade with other countries, so advantageous that Thebes, the capital, prospered and enriched herself in her contacts with all parts of the world. To this day, the great masses of rocks which form the temples, tombs, obelisks, and halls at Thebes are the greatest reminders of ancient Egypt.

Then began a period of decay. Seti I and Rameses II tried to stop it, and in doing so they covered the country, from the Mediterranean to Wadi Halfa, with accounts of their magnificent deeds, written in hieroglyphics, the ancient Egyptian alphabet, on the temple walls.

A WAVE OF CONQUESTS

But they were too late. After they had passed into the hands of Osiris, the god of the dead, the country fell into chaos. A Syrian first seized control of the land; and then came, in rapid succession, the Nubians, the Assyrians, the Persians under their great king, Cambyses, and finally, in 332 B. C., Alexander the Great who made it a part of his empire. His successors, the Ptolemies, ruled it for 300 years until, in the year 30 B.C., Egypt became a Roman province.

Even though some of the conquerors destroyed when they entered this land, most of them made the country even more interesting for the present-day traveler, by adding to the already great number of monuments in which Egypt abounds. Alexander the Great established the city of Alexandria and made it the most important spot in the ancient world a thousand years before Cairo was heard of. The Romans and their successors, the Byzantines, covered the valley of the Nile with temples and churches, so that as Egypt stands today she is the biggest archaeological museum in the world. Stretched along her length are ruins left by dozens of different nations and peoples of the ancient world. That is not all. We have seen much of the mystery and beauty of Egypt is due to the old temples and the charming Nile, but what about the glories of the Arabian art and architecture?

Egypt saw the last of her old conquerors in A. D. 640, when Amr and his men rode down from the Arabian desert on their prancing chargers to capture the country, establish his capital at Fostat (now Old Cairo), and found the Arabian dynasties. These handsome and swarthy men of the desert were bent on conquering the world for Allah, and so they gave the poor fellahin the choice of becoming Mohammedans or of being beheaded. Most of the Egyptians preferred to keep their heads.

Under these new conquerors Egypt prospered, Cairo became the capital, and the famous university and mosque, el Ashar, was founded. From them came the glorious school of Arabian art and architecture which greatly influenced the mosques and public buildings of Egypt, and also the architectural works in other Moslem, and even non-Moslem, countries. These were the adventurous times of the Arabian Nights, when princes walked through the streets disguised as beggars; when palaces were built of jewels and gold; when anything could happen in the streets of Cairo. Strangely enough, though thirteen centuries have passed, the

Homer Smith photo, Chicago

QUAINT NATIVE EGYPTIAN VILLAGE ON THE NILE

streets of Cairo are just as fascinating now as they were in the days of the caliphs of old. In 1517, Egypt was again conquered, this time by the fierce Turks, and 1789 saw a brief occupation by Napoleon.

THE RISE OF MODERN EGYPT

After the massacre of the Mamelukes, or Turkish governors, Mohammed Ali, an Albanian, gained control, and under him the country advanced to prosperity. Under his successor, Ismail, railroads were constructed, trade and agriculture encouraged, schools built, and the Suez Canal opened. But these improvements cost the country so much money that it was soon swamped with debts and the European powers had to step in to put the finances on a sounder basis. This led to rebellion by the Arabs, military measures, and British control. Once more the country went forward; the Assuan storage dam and other diversion dams across the Nile were built, and irrigation thus became permanent and prosperity

Black Star photo. By Anne Wassell

NATIVE SAILBOAT ON THE NILE

followed. Then in 1914 came the World War and a British protectorate was established, which in turn was abolished in 1922, when King Faud assumed the royal title. And now, a far cry from the pyramid-building Pharaohs of the First Dynasty, the almost complete independence and future of his country lie in the hands of young King Faruk, who recently succeeded to the throne.

UP THE NILE

With this background in mind we can now start our journey up the Nile fully prepared for all kinds of conveyances. We shall start by rail, but may at any time shift to a steamboat or to a *gyassa* or a *felucca,* two kinds of sail boats that grace the Nile with their billowing sheets and jointed masts. Or we may take bicycles, camels, donkeys, and even ride on the broad, black back of some giant Nubian who carries his human cargo from boat to shore as easily as he would a basket of figs.

BAKSHEESH!

Before we start we must remember to be careful of one thing, and that is giving baksheesh. Baksheesh is money given as a tip, a present, or something extra after a purchase. It is the national word of Egypt. Naked babies, who are just learning to speak, young boys, village maidens, old men, and especially the guides and *dragomans* (porters), all storm the traveler for baksheesh. If you give it to a blind and crippled beggar, others just as blind and just as crippled will appear from nowhere to beg for themselves. If you happen to tip a boy for a small service, as surely as the sun sets in the desert behind the pyramids, twenty other boys will swarm around you, tugging at your clothes, flinging their dirty hands in your face, all crying in shrill voices, "Baksheesh, Mister, Baksheesh." There are supposed to be many curses which endanger the lives of the archaeologists and other scientists who open and explore the tombs of the ancient Pharaohs, but, to the traveler, there is no curse like baksheesh. If he gives it to an Egyptian, the Egyptian will want more and so will all his friends. If he gives no baksheesh, he will hear many guttural Arabic oaths and feel as if his head were going to be cut off. He is a clever man who gives just the right amount.

SLY MERCHANTS

The same is true when dealing with the street peddlers or the merchants in the bazaars. The former, sly fellows who walk the streets dressed in red tarbushes and colorful robes, are always on the lookout for the unwary tourist. They sight a tourist a block off and descend upon him in a mob to try to sell him their wares. They sell everything—postcards, scarabs, live parrots, mummified cats, maps, oranges, monkeys on a chain, mahogany tables made of stained pine, ancient bracelets made the night before, and authentic amulets from the tomb of some ancient king which they buy by the gross from some factory in Italy.

You cannot shake them off. They follow you for blocks. It

is useless to run into a shop for a while because they will be waiting for you when you come out. You might lose them for a little while, but they are sure to find you at your hotel that very same night. The only way to get rid of them is to buy something. Then the fun begins.

You may decide on a scarab, which is a stone in the form of a beetle, symbol of resurrection, used as an amulet. The peddler claims that the one he wants to sell you was stolen from the tomb of the great Pharaoh, Thothmes III, and that it should be in the National Museum because it is so valuable. He swears that it is absolutely genuine and that if he is lying he hopes that Allah will strike him blind, and his father and grandfather also. All the time he knows that the scarab was carved by his brother Ali, who sells relics to tourists visiting the pyramids.

Because the scarab is very old and also because business is so poor, he is willing to let you have it for only ten dollars, which is "very cheap, Mister, very cheap." The inexperienced tourist may pay this price; that is what makes tourists so popular with these rascals. On the other hand, the experienced traveler will look indignant or disgusted, or even laugh out loud at such a price. If he does, then the price starts to fall; and the more the prospective buyer shakes his head, the lower the price becomes. By this time a large crowd has gathered, for there is nothing an Egyptian loves better than watching an exciting sale. When the price has fallen to fifty cents, the peddler will call upon the crowd to tell the buyer that this is the greatest bargain in the whole land of Egypt. Then, when the price comes down to twenty-five cents, the sly rogue says that he hopes that Allah will make his right arm wither if he isn't losing money on the deal. Then, after the buyer offers a nickel for the wonderful scarab, the bargaining reaches a feverish height and ends with the peddler's swearing that he is ruined, but he sells it for a dime just the same. Then they part smiling, the traveler with a scarab which he doesn't want, but well satisfied with his bargain, and the peddler with a 200 per cent profit in his pocket and probably with some respect for the foreign effendi who made him drop so low in his price.

ALEXANDRIA HO!

With this advice on baksheesh and bargaining in mind, the traveler should be ready to step off his boat at Alexandria. But

Homer Smith photo, Chicago

MOHAMED ALI SQUARE IN ALEXANDRIA

what panic and pandemonium confront him as he disembarks at Egypt's leading port! At the gangplank is a milling mass of shouting and gesticulating dragomans and guides. They are dressed in red tarbushes or white turbans, and loose white robes or baggy brown trousers, wearing red sandals with up-curved toes, or barefooted. In one respect they are all alike: they are shouting, mostly in English, offering to be of some service to the traveler, and at the same time cursing each other in Arabic.

Woe be to the traveler when he marches down the gangplank to step among them! They grab him; they seize his suitcases and spirit them off to the customs house.

When you reach the customs house, you feel thankful that, at last, you have lost those terrible pests, the porters; but you have only stepped from the frying pan into the fire. The inspection of the Royal Egyptian government at the customs is an ordeal in itself. In your own country you may be a respected citizen, an honorable judge, a famous banker, or an earnest clergyman; but to the Egyptian officials you are a suspected criminal. You must open all your baggage in order that they may determine whether you are trying to smuggle opium, firearms, matches, cigarettes, playing cards, or such dangerous things as candy and popcorn into the country! After your underwear or your sweetheart's photograph has been pulled from the bottom of your suitcase, you are free to pack it again and then start to see Egypt.

ALEXANDRIA IS NOT EGYPT

Alexandria is the world. Here live great numbers of Greeks (descendants of Alexander and his followers), Italians, French, Germans, Swiss, and Levantines who belong to no country; Armenians with their language as queer as Arabic; Jews with derbies, and black curls hanging down their cheeks; Syrians; English, who are everywhere in the country, and a few Egyptians. If one were to walk down the street in Alexandria with his eyes closed, he could no more tell in which country he was than a blind and deaf man could. All languages are spoken here. Merchants have been known who would not go into business in this city because they knew only four foreign tongues!

In the city the tourist finds little that recalls the days of Greek rule when Alexandria was the first city in the world, and few things that recall the fallen glory of the Pharaohs. Instead, he finds an international quarter that might be a part of Paris, Berlin, or even foggy London. True, there is a native quarter, but the Egyptians who live in it feel that they are foreigners living in a strange land. In fact, this is the only city in Egypt in which it is possble to see more men on the streets in European dress than in the native Egyptian costume.

Although Alexandria has a charm and an atmosphere because it is such a mixture of West and East, it has only two really remarkable sights. The first is Pompey's Pillar, which is the only reminder of the architectural splendor of the city that formerly contained the famous museum, the great library that housed 700,000 manuscripts (burned in bonfires that lasted six weeks when the Arabs conquered the city), and the Pharos, a lighthouse which was one of the Seven Wonders of the World. The second sight is a bronze statue of Mohammed Ali dressed in a splendid Turkish costume and astride a horse of gigantic proportions. These sights are remarkable because the column is not

Pompey's, but one erected to a much less important dignitary, and the statue is a deliberate violation of Mohammedan law, which says that it is sinful to create any likeness of the human form. It caused quite a stir of protest among the Alexandrians when it was erected, and even now there are many who would tear it down even though Mohammed Ali was their greatest hero.

It was he who made Alexandria what it is today, and it was also he who made Egypt what it is today. As a clever Albanian soldier of the Sultan of Turkey, he came from the north to overthrow the sultan's viceroys and set himself up in their place. His sheer genius welded the fellah with the shiek, and the Arab with the original inhabitant of the Nile Valley, into something which approaches a nationality. His master mind recognized the need of a seaport, roads, canals, factories, public buildings, and a commercial crop, cotton. He gave Egypt these things and changed Alexandria from a city of 5,000 to one a hundred times as large. He was certainly the father of his country and a good step-father of *Iskanderieh,* which is the Arabian name for Alexandria.

FELLAHIN

So much for the city where Archimedes wrought inventions, where Euclid studied, where Cleopatra fascinated the world with her charms, and where St. Mark preached the gospel. Let us leave it for Cairo, in search of something purely Egyptian. On our way to the capital city let us go by canal in order to stop for a while at one of the small villages and see how the Fellahin live.

A MAGIC SONG

After gently drifting between fields of sugar cane and cotton for a few hours, our canal boat with its graceful, bellying sails comes to a stop at the creaking dock of the tiny village of Ityai el Barud. The sun is setting behind a row of palm trees on the other side of the collection of mud huts. Everyone is bustling with the activity of the early evening. Oxcarts are creaking; water is being drawn from wells; fires are being built, and the smoke of them is already covering the town with its bluish haze; our boatmen are cursing each other while they are busy tying up the boat, when suddenly—complete silence reigns. A magic spell has fallen over the town. Everyone is enchanted. Nothing is heard but the sound of a weird, wavering, song which floats over the housetops. The people around us must certainly be enchanted; for the woman who was drawing water is lying flat on her face, the driver of the oxcart is on his knees, and the boatmen are facing the east with their arms raised to the heavens.

Slowly the song becomes more insistent and more weird, until you feel cold shivers running up and down your back. Your stomach feels hollow, your hair stands on end, and finally you, too, want to face the east, fall to the ground, and pray to Allah; for what you hear is the call to prayer.

"ALLAHU AKBAR—ALLAHU AKBAR!"

The song you hear is that of the muezzin, the Mohammedan priest, who has climbed to the top of the minaret to call all the faithful to pray to Allah. He announces that Allah is the true God and Mohammed his prophet. At this time there are thousands of muezzins all over the Mohammedan world repeating the same words. In response, millions of Moslems, depending on where they live, are all turning to the east, west, south, or north, in order that they may face toward Mecca, the holy city of Islam.

The call to prayer is given five times between sunrise and sunset, but it is most effective when the sun goes down. When the stranger hears it at that time, he is charmed by its beauty and weirdness and must feel that, although these people are "heathens" and far different from him in every way, they have an extremely powerful religion.

When the last notes of the song have faded into the vast distances of the desert, the villagers pick up their tools and start to work again. Here comes a string of camels, their backs laden with goods from the next town, or perhaps they have just come from a nearby oasis in the desert and are carrying a load of figs and dates for the market of a nearby city. They are ugly, mangy brutes, with their hair falling off in big patches; they will tear the clothes off anyone who may be so unfortunate as to come within reach of their stained and yellow teeth. In Cairo, foreign women are in especial danger because the camels seem to have developed a great fondness for Paris hats.

ON TO CAIRO

A glance into one of the little huts, made of sun-dried brick, will show the poor Fellahin family squatting on the floor, eating their rice or beans and, if they are fortunate, a piece of lamb. If they see you, they will invite you to share their simple meal because, in such villages as Ityai el Barud where there are no tourists, the peasants are very hospitable. Charity is one of the fundamentals of their religion. It is the same everywhere along the Nile, except in the large cities where the beggars constantly shout "baksheesh" in your ears. But we can stay no longer with the people of Ityai el Barud unless we want to sleep in one of the native huts. Of course we should be most welcome, but we should also have to sleep on a dirt floor and be devoured by mosquitoes,

Black Star photo. By Fritz Henle

A SECTION OF CAIRO, SHOWING SOME OF THE CITY'S GRACEFUL MINARETS bed bugs, lice, and fleas. No, thanks; we'll take the night train to Cairo, which is only an hour away.

If the traveler happens to buy a third-class ticket, he has a further adventure in store for him. As the train stops, he is swept from his feet and borne along by a swarm of natives, all of whom are looking for a seat next to the window; for nothing delights the childish native more than to watch the scenery rush past his window. The traveler, after having been pushed up the stairs and hurried into the car, finds that all the seats seem to be taken. However, by deftly moving a crate of tomatoes from the wooden bench, pushing some chickens under the seat, and shoving a goat out into the aisle, he can easily clear a seat for himself. Undoubtedly the desert giant, next to whom he must sit, will reek of garlic and dirt and will grumble at him gutturally for moving his possessions; but that is to be expected, for this is Egypt, and more than likely, if the big fellow knows any English, he will engage the traveler in conversation and they will soon be fast friends. After a short ride the traveler can gaze out of the window into the desert moonlight and see the magic city of the East—Cairo.

MOONLIGHT MADNESS

Surely what he sees can't be true. It is nothing but a mirage, or a picture from one of the pages of the Arabian Nights. First is seen the Nile, silvery now, a thousand feet wide and dotted with the sails of numerous small craft. Beyond, white buildings and flat roofs extend, with here and there a group of green palms higher than the rest. Everywhere are white domes with slender spires standing next to them, punctuating the landscape like so many exclamation points. These are the hundreds of Cairo's mosques and minarets. Farther in the distance the ground rises; on an eminence is seen the Citadel, and from within its walls, the magnificent inverted bowl and slender minarets of the great Mosque of Mohammed Ali. Behind, lofty yellow cliffs—the Mokattam hills—glisten in the light of the moon.

As the traveler feasts his eyes, the train slips into the sordid outskirts of Cairo and the fantastic sight disappears. He shakes his head. He must have been dreaming, or perhaps the cigarette which his Arabian traveling companion gave him was loaded with hashish, the narcotic which is so much used in Egypt. But no, there it is again. It may be magical, but it is not a dream. Then the train screeches to a halt in the station, and the spell is broken for a time. Once more there are the clamoring shouts of the guides, dragomans, and hotel porters who are willing to take a person and his money to any part of the city.

After the usual arguments, bickerings, and distribution of baksheesh, you climb into a horse-drawn cab and find yourself in the streets of fairyland once again. Although on your way to the hotel you don't approach the really mysterious native quarter, modern Cairo is fascinating enough by itself for the first night. Along streets lined with towering palm trees, past brightly lighted saloons and dance halls, through crowds of excited people, mostly foreigners it seems, your cab makes its way until it draws up before a hotel.

After showing your passport, signing several papers, and feeding many hungry hands with piasters, you are finally left alone to enjoy your first night's sleep in this magic land. Your dreams—and you will certainly have them—will be crowded with strange sights; you may be chased down dark alleys by Arabs with long mustaches or charmed by Egyptian dancing girls; you will hear strange sounds like the call to prayer or growling curses; and then you will hear, "*Neharak-said!*" The dream is over because the room is being flooded with brilliant sunshine, and near the head of the bed stands a giant black servant clad in a red fez and flowing robes. It was he who said, "*Neharak-said!*" which is the Arabian equivalent of "Good Morning!"

A CITY OF CONTRASTS

After a breakfast which is an exact duplication of the kind that is served in London, you are ready to see the meeting place of the East and the West. Cairo is a wonderful mixture of occidental and oriental culture and people. Beside the modern streetcars, automobiles, and taxis are seen camels, donkeys, and oxcarts. Porters, carrying heavy loads on their backs, are passed by up-to-date motor trucks. Men dressed according to the latest Fifth Avenue fashions brush shoulders with natives in dirty white robes.

Probably the greatest contrast is between the foreign women who copy the latest thing out of Paris and their dark-eyed Moslem sisters who wear the same costume as was worn in biblical times. This consists of a voluminous black robe and a veil which hangs, from just below the nose, all the way to the feet. It is attached to the head by strips of tape and a small piece of ornamented wood that lies lengthwise over the nose. All that remains to be seen are the hands, feet, and eyes. The hands and feet are usually dyed a sickly reddish-yellow, but in the deep, liquid, exotic, brown eyes lie all the mysteries of the Orient.

Cairo! What wonderful visions are conjured up by the mere mention of the name, and what colors are brought to mind by only thinking of the streets! Cairo is a city of color, deep-blue skies and white, billowy clouds that are found only in desert countries; brilliant yellow sunshine followed by floods of white moonlight; a clear atmosphere in which it is possible to see for miles, and then brown sandstorms as thick as pea soup. Along the streets there are beautiful palms and brightly colored houses, while the sidewalks are crowded with Nubian Negroes, yellowish Coptic Christians, dark-skinned Arabs, Sudanese, Armenians, Syrians, Greeks, and others from almost every race, nationality, and religion imaginable.

IMPORTANT AT LAST

Let us take a walk through the streets and see how these interesting people spend their time, remembering, however, to ignore the many guides, salesmen, donkey-boys, and beggars who consider us as being sent by Allah to be their legitimate prey. Ahead of us such a crowd has gathered that it seems that there is an accident, a bargain, a fight, or perhaps the king is going to his mosque. No, it is only a funeral. In the elaborate coffin may be the body of some poor beggar who was pushed around the streets every day of his life, but now that he is dead it appears that half of the city is mourning him.

At the head of the procession comes a crowd of poorly dressed men and women who are moaning, screeching, and crying as if the deceased had been their lifelong friend. On the contrary, they have been hired for the occasion and are out to earn a few coppers by wailing until they can no longer speak. Behind them comes a far more respectable-looking crowd. These are wearing their holiday finest, some in rich robes, others in black frock coats with embroidered jackets, and all in red tarbushes, or fezzes, which look like inverted, red flower pots with a black tassel hanging down the side. The coffin, the object of all the commotion, is draped with a gaily colored cloth and is carried on the shoulders of four or six men.

While the procession passes by, the hawkers and refreshment sellers are making a great profit out of the interested throng. Some of them carry little tables of sweets and candy, which are usually covered with flies. Others have goatskins on their backs, or on the backs of their donkeys, from which they sell lemonade or water to the thirsty. All of them constantly cry, "*Ya au wud Allah!*" meaning, "Oh, may Allah reward me!" However, if we are thirsty, it is best that we visit the nearby coffeehouse.

TRIC-TRAC, TOBACCO, AND TALK

The coffeehouse, or café, is the common club throughout the Near East, and Egypt is no exception. Here men come to smoke, talk, drink coffee, sip brandy, play games, and read the daily newspapers. In one corner two dignified Arabs are playing *tric-trac* (backgammon). They are very quiet, making only a clicking noise with the pieces, but next to them are four of their companions who are wildly excited about some game of cards. They slam the cards on the table with much gusto and laugh loudly when one makes a good point. Nearby, an interested spectator watches them and smokes one of the queer contraptions so typical of the Near East.

An Egyptian does not carry a pipe, although he usually has a package of his favorite tobacco somewhere in his pockets. When he wants to smoke, he merely goes into a coffeehouse and rents a "hubble-bubble," or waterpipe, for a few cents. He gives his tobacco to the waiter, who stuffs it into the bowl, drops a hot coal on it, and presto! a pleasant half-hour's smoke is ready. The pipe resembles a huge hair-tonic bottle; it stands on the floor and has a long hose which reaches the smoker's mouth. When it is puffed, the smoke passes through the water in the bottle and reaches the mouth in a cooled and sweetened form. While he smokes, he may order *baklava* or *kadaif*, which are eastern pastries, the sweetest things imaginable. They are so sweet that many are served with butter and hard sauce to make them slip down the throat without sticking.

NO HARPS OR HALOS

Incidentally, when a Mohammedan dies, he expects to go to heaven as a matter of course, but not to wear a halo, play a harp, or fly with wings. Instead, he has been taught that heaven is the place where one wears fine silk robes, sits on soft cushions, watches pretty dancing girls, smokes a hubble-bubble, and eats *kadaif* and *baklava* all day long. He much prefers such pleasures to harp playing or flying. In the olden days the best way to reach heaven was to be killed in battle while fighting for Allah. Now that most of the Moslems have ceased to be such warlike people, the next best way to attain this end is to build a mosque. All that the poor man can do is to pray five times a day and to hope for the best. Then, too, all good Moslems must make at least one pilgrimage to Mecca before they die. They dress in *ihrams,* which are two white cotton cloths, one worn over the back and left shoulder and the other wrapped around the waist and upper legs. These cloths must contain no hems or seams, because, as most tailors are Christians, the *ihrams* would be soiled by their touch. Thus attired, they go off for their long journey in the desert to the holy city, where they pray in the great mosque, kiss the Kaaba, the huge black rock which is supposed to have fallen from heaven, visit the sacred tomb of Mohammed, and then they may feel reasonably sure of seeing the dancing girls when they die. Anyone who has made a pilgrimage to Mecca is called a Haji, and he adds this prefix to his name. Thus, a man by the name of Baqir becomes Hajibaqir and is respected by his friends and neighbors forever after.

TURKISH COFFEE

But it's a long way to Mecca from where we are sitting in the café. Coffee, like the hubble-bubble, is very popular in Egypt and other sections of the Near East. So much so, that there are said to be over fifteen hundred coffeehouses in Cairo alone. The drink, which is known as Turkish coffee in the Western world, is a constant delight to Egyptians. Many foreigners, on the other hand, compare it to sweet mud, while others go as far as to say that the dregs could be used for paving streets or for caulking canal boats. As a matter of fact, it is a very delicious drink, being made of equal parts of coffee and sugar, which are boiled and then served in a cup that holds about four thimblefuls.

Because it is against Moslem law to drink any alcoholic beverages, coffee is a very good substitute. Its counterpart in America would be a glass of beer over which good-fellowship reigned. The Arabs drink it while entertaining their friends, beating their business associates in a close bargain, or arguing politics. A cup of coffee is an absolute necessity to a business deal that is going to take more than three minutes to negotiate. Before anything is discussed, the coffee must be brought in and the time of day must be passed. Thus everyone is put into a good humor. In politics the effects are not so fortunate. All Egyptians are politicians, and when two of them meet over a cup of coffee, the argument that follows is tremendous. It may end up by one of them throwing his cup at the other's head, but happily the cups are small, and the Egyptian's aim is notably poor; so one is seldom hurt. Strangely enough, the two may be found the next day sitting at the same table in the same café, drinking together as if nothing at all had happened.

THE CITADEL

Although the Egyptians are a fascinating people, we must leave them and their café to see some of the sights in their interesting city. The first to be visited is the Citadel, which, built on a small hill, towers above Cairo as if it were a watchdog guarding the city at its feet. That is exactly the reason that it was started by Saladin in the year 1176 with stones taken from the pyramids across the Nile. Before it was finished this great Arab was called to Palestine to ravage the Christian crusaders and finally drive them from the Holy Land. He did so by capturing Jerusalem, but died before he could return to Cairo, the city he loved.

SANTA SOPHIA

In the far western corner of the Citadel stands that famous edifice erected to Allah, the Mosque of Mohammed Ali. This superb structure, without a doubt, takes its place beside those

MOSQUE ON THE CITADEL, CAIRO

Black Star photo
By Fritz Henle

other gems of Moslem religious art—Santa Sophia and the Blue Mosque in Constantinople. To approach this mosque in the early morning when it is partially veiled in the mists that arise from the desert, to see the many domes which form its roof rising one above the other like so many bubbles, and to see its tall, slender minarets stretching to the heavens until their tops are lost in the grayish fog, is to realize that here is one of the most awe-inspiring creations in the whole world.

A SUN BATH

In a little while the sun rises from behind the Mokattam hills and dissolves the early morning mists which have made Mohammed Ali's mosque a fairy palace. In its place there now seems to be a palace made of pure gold. The golden rays of the sun shining on the yellow alabaster, of which the mosque is constructed, produce this splendid effect.

The sun also throws the awakening city of Cairo into a contrasting picture of light and shadow. There lies at our feet the largest Mohammedan city in the world, the largest city on the continent of Africa and the largest city in the Near and Middle East between Naples and Bombay. Immediately below us are the tombs of the Caliphs and, in another direction, those of the Mamelukes, all elaborate tombs, of which little appears to be known. They are badly disintegrated but enough is left standing to give one an idea of how impressive they must have been in the past, when they were kept in repair by sheiks and attendants who lived in them.

THE END OF THE MAMELUKES

As a matter of fact, very few of the bodies of the Caliphs, who were the rulers in the days of Arab supremacy, are to be found in these tombs. Most of them were buried in mosques in different parts of the city. The bodies of the Mamelukes, with the exception of a few hundred of the last ones, are actually buried in their tombs. These Mamelukes were Turkish slaves introduced at the time of the Turkish conquest. They soon became powerful and, in the absence of anyone more potent, they elected sultans from their own number. Thus, they ruled Egypt for six centuries until Mohammed Ali appointed himself sultan. They were still a thorn in his side; so he invited some four hundred to dinner one night, and just as they were entering his palace on the Citadel his soldiers mowed them down with rifles and cannon. Thereafter Mohammed Ali was all-powerful. These unfortunate Mamelukes are the ones whose tombs we do not see, for they are buried—no one knows where.

MOSQUES

This should not trouble the traveler too much as there are thousands of tombs in Cairo. Every mosque is a tomb of some-one, and the city has more mosques than Pittsburgh has smoke-stacks. As we gaze at the city below us, we see another mosque and its companion minarets at every glance. Some are huge hollow squares, built in the fashion of the great mosque at Mecca; some are of the Turkish type with their bubble-domes and, as a contrast, sharp thin minarets that look like well-sharpened pencils; some are massive squares that resemble the Taj Mahal in India; and the rest, by far the most numerous, are the true Egyptian mosques built after the style of architecture developed in the days when the Arabs were the most civilized people on the earth.

MOSQUE EL-AZHAR

Mosques of this last type are really the most beautiful but, because there are so many of them, they receive but little attention. Their minarets are the graceful, scalloped ones with much ornamentation. Their walls are full of elaborately carved niches and slender windows showing the pointed Arab arch. Their doorways, bedecked with gold figures and verses from the holy writings of the Koran, the Moslem Bible, are entrances to some mystic cave. Inside, the walls are covered with the same fantastic ornaments, while the floors are an expanse of deep and soft oriental rugs of rare beauty. No matter where the mosque lies or in which direction it faces, the rugs in all mosques are laid in the same direction—toward Mecca.

Perhaps the most famous mosque in Cairo, and certainly the most important to Moslems the world over, is the mosque of el-Azhar. It is on the large open square that lies to our right. Now that the desert sun is rather high, the open spaces of the Citadel are growing very warm; so let us go to the cooler sanctuaries of el-Azhar.

The reason for el-Azhar's greatness is that it is the most important educational institution in the Moslem world. It is the foremost university for Mohammedan students. To enter this great center of learning (and the same is true of all other mosques) we may leave our hats on, but must take off our shoes, for such is the custom of Islam. After shuffling about for a few minutes in our stocking feet and hearing our guide translate some of the lectures, we begin to realize that this is not a university in the Western sense but rather a sanatorium in which the half-dead arts and sciences of the Middle Ages are kept alive. Everyone agrees that the Arabs of the seventh and eighth centuries were far advanced culturally and that it was from them knowledge came to illuminate the Dark Ages of Western Europe. But they are still teaching the principles of the seventh century, while the rest of the civilized world has progressed to the twentieth century.

STILL THE DARK AGES

Moslem professors are not allowed to teach anything that does not come from the Koran. Barefooted Moslem students from all over the world squat around their teacher and learn to recite the Koran by heart. When the many thousand students gather together to chant their verses in unison, the sound is like the roar of the sea. They chant much about not eating pork, but nothing about brushing their teeth. They know everything about the happy life after death, but nothing of the life which they live. To attend el-Azhar is to commit intellectual suicide. Fortunately, there are now in Egypt many American, English, and other foreign schools and colleges where a modern education may be had. Also, Egyptian public schools have improved so that it is possible for a lad of thirteen years, who has gone through grammar school, to know more about the world than a professor in the famous university of el-Azhar.

In contrast to the noisy voices of el-Azhar, the other mosques are very quiet. Here the faithful come to pray, bend, lie on the floor, and kiss holy stones. In one mosque there is an especially holy stone which, if the sufferer licks it enough, will cure his indigestion. Another mosque has marble pillars in it which are set very close together. If a man cannot walk between them, he is too fat to pass the gates of Heaven. Therefore, he must exercise; and the best way to exercise is to pray, because praying consists of standing, kneeling, crouching, and falling to the ground. It is a good exercise and holy.

DERVISHES

Another exercise which is also holy is that done by the dervishes. There are two kinds of dervishes, the howling variety and the whirling variety. They are to be seen in the mosques, but only on Friday because that day is the Moslem equivalent of the Christian Sunday. It was on a Friday that Adam, one of the six great Mohammedan prophets, first saw the light of day; it was on a Friday, too, that he died. It is interesting to note that in towns like Alexandria, where there are a great many different sects, many stores are open only from Monday to Thursday, be-

Homer Smith photo, Chicago

NATIVE MERCHANT IN ASSUAN, EGYPT

cause Friday is the Moslem holy day, Saturday is the Jewish Sabbath, and Sunday is, of course, the day of worship for the Christians.

So the dervishes gather on Friday to pay homage to Allah. A few are so religious that they honor their God by thrusting nails in their eyes and arms, putting weights, large enough to kill an ordinary man, on their chests as they lie on the floor, and eating burning charcoal or ground glass. A more common sort are those who sit on their haunches, rock back and forth, and howl prayers. They do this until they work themselves into a frenzy, foam at the mouth, and faint. But no one takes any notice of them; so they are left on the floor until they recover their senses. These are the howling dervishes, so called from the way they howl their prayers. The most interesting kind are the whirling dervishes.

They perform in a circle, a few yards in diameter, marked on the floor of the mosque. The whirlers enter the circle dressed in very full, white dresses and wear white, conical hats, like a dunce's cap. In the center of the circle sits their sheik or leader, and after a few prayers from him an ear-splitting din commences. That is the music. The musicians seem to use only two kinds of instruments; one which is shaped like a Hallowe'en horn, and sounds like one; and the other, which is very much like a tom-tom.

Most Egyptian music is beautiful in a weird and exotic way, but this racket sounds like a combination of New Year's Eve and an Apache war dance.

Nevertheless, it has a beautiful sound for the dervishes who start their whirling with the first note. Around and around they go, slowly at first but gradually increasing their speed until they are doing fifty to sixty revolutions a minute. They do it by standing on one foot and pushing themselves around with the other. Not only do they revolve, but they also rotate. What a fantastic sight they are! Their wide skirts slowly spread out until they stand out straight from their bodies. At the same time, the conical hats on their heads are also making circles, so it is almost impossible to watch them without becoming dizzy oneself. Why they don't fall over from dizziness is hard to understand because they do it continuously for as long as twenty minutes. Furthermore, even though there be as many as six or seven dancers in the small circle, they never collide with one another.

THE SUPERB MOSQUE

Before we finish our visit to the mosques of Cairo, there is another that we surely must see. The Egyptians call it the "Superb Mosque," while it is known to the tourist as the Mosque of Sultan Hassan. Although it is over six centuries old, the passing years have added to and not detracted from its beauty. On the outside, its immense sheer walls stretch upwards for a distance of four stories, and the tall windows and door are only a little less than that. Just to see it, you think, "Here is one of the most impressive scenes in Cairo." But on the inside your thoughts fail you. You can only feel. Surely Allah must be watching you from some high corner of this beautiful and enormous room. Legend has it that Hassan, who was a very cruel man, cut off the arms and put out the eyes of the architect who designed the mosque so that the architect would never again be able to create such a wonderful structure.

THE CENTER OF MYSTERIOUS CAIRO

After seeing the great examples of Arabic architecture we must now turn our attention to the way that most Egyptians live. To find this out we must visit the Muski or native quarter. We leave our hotel in the late afternoon, cross the Sharia Ibrahim

Pasha, the main street, pass, on our right, the grand opera house, which looks like the important civic building in any town in America, continue another block past the Gardens of Ezbekiyeh, the famous park and zoo, and lo and behold! we have come to a different city. Surely this can't be Cairo. But it is Cairo and, what is more, the real Cairo. This is the Cairo of the Egyptians and Arabians; the Cairo of the strange sights, sounds, and smells; the city as Mohammed, Harun-al-Rashid of the Arabian Nights, or any of the sultans of Turkey would have known it. Here are the narrow streets, the winding alleyways full of reeking humanity, the low, two-storied houses made of mud bricks, and the old stone arches and covered bazaars of the ancient city.

As we make our way through the crowded lanes, hawkers cry to us to buy their excellent wares, children follow us demanding baksheesh, dusky figures in windows beckon to us, while camel drivers shriek, "For the love of Allah, clear the road!" We pass all sorts of tiny shops displaying their wares in the open air. There are spices from the Far East, silk from Japan, woolens from England, olives from Greece, coffee from Brazil, and a familiar brand of sewing machine from America. Imagine the different smells all mixed together. Some are pungent, some are sweet, and some are of the kind that makes the stranger sick to his stomach. The food and goods are all uncovered, despite the fact that there are clouds of dust always arising from the unpaved road. Flies and bugs are everywhere. A native woman, in a dress that has not been cleaned for a year, sits in the gutter and picks lice from her child's head. A little farther down, a leper with his nose gone drinks out of a common drinking cup. Woe be to the traveler who wears a white suit in the native quarter! He will be covered with fleas before he has taken ten steps.

PANDEMONIUM

In addition to the strange sights and smells there are noises of every description, and the whole clamor is beyond description. The street is, of course, narrow, and resounding from the walls of the surrounding stores and houses come the sounds of a donkey being whipped and urged to a greater speed, camels being guided and heartily cursed, money changers jingling their coins, storekeepers shouting the excellence of their goods, and even the singsong chant of a teacher instructing his students on the sidewalk.

When we go farther down the road, new noises come to our ears. There is a clanging of metal on metal in the Suk en-Nahhassin, the bazaar of the coppersmiths, or the clack-clack of the looms in the rug bazaar.

If you should close your eyes and listen, you would believe yourself to be in a madhouse on fire. Yet with your eyes open for thirty minutes (time enough to become somewhat accustomed to the dirt and smells) you begin to realize that you are a witness to a scene that is certainly worth coming thousands of miles to see.

But the scene is not like a picture because it is constantly changing. Now that it has grown darker and the sun has set, we hurry to the nearest mosque in order to hear the muezzin give the last call to prayer, which occurs about an hour after sundown. Here is the Red Mosque, one of the most beautiful in Cairo. We can hardly see the priest on the tiny balcony near the top of the minaret, but we can certainly hear him; for suddenly ring out those magic words, "Allahu akbar!" (Allah is greatest), and around us the noise of the city ceases as all start to pray.

But this time the flickering lights of the gas street lamps have been turned up so that the prayers in their movements cast long, black shadows on the walls, which make the street seem very ominous. In fact, it *is* ominous; for over there are two black-bearded Arabs, with daggers in their belts, scowling at us and wondering what Christian dogs are doing at Moslem prayers.

A NATIVE MEAL

Before they have time to scowl again, we suddenly remember that we have an appointment to meet our guide, who is going to take us to a native restaurant for a real Egyptian meal. We arrive at the appointed spot, take one look at the eating place and almost lose our appetites. Before us is an open store full of tables, flies, natives, and unsavory odors. But all of Egypt cannot be seen from the street; so we bravely march in over the dirt floor, to a table which has been reserved and, upon which a clean table cloth has been placed in our honor.

As this is a low-priced restaurant, the meal that is served is an oily and highly seasoned one, consisting of lentils, stuffed cucumbers, goat's milk cheese, bread made of corn, eggs, and rice. It is not really a bad meal but merely cooked in a manner that foreign taste finds strange. After the dishes have been cleared away, a small glass of colorless liquid is placed on the table. One sip of this dissolves the oil that clings to our mouths, the second makes us forget the sting of the many spices we have eaten, and the last actually makes the room in which we are sitting seem like a first-class restaurant in Paris. We refuse a second glass of the stuff (it is called *arak*) for fear that, on drinking it, we might imagine ourselves to be in some sultan's palace in the time of the Arabian Nights.

Thus refreshed, we return to the street to find that again the scene has changed. A bright moon is flooding the almost deserted alleyways with a light that hides the dirt and grime. The noises have disappeared, but in their place is a plaintive wailing of pipes and the muffled beating of a drum, both very strange sounds but far more pleasing than the music which we heard played for the dervishes. This odd, oriental tune appears to be coming from a dimly lighted hole in the wall at the end of the street—a native cabaret. A glance inside shows a shadowy cavern lighted by an occasional candle, the faltering light of which weakly falls over the tables and chairs, a group of musicians huddled in one corner, the audience and a sinewy figure gracefully moving in front of it.

LITTLE EGYPT

The figure is that of an Egyptian dancing girl, whose bodily movements seem to have entranced her watchers. Her arms are slithering snakes transmitting their wavering motion to her quivering shoulders. The motion flows down her body in increasing rhythmic undulations to die out at her feet, which remain rooted to the dirt floor. As the pipes become shriller and more piercing and the drums more booming and insistent, her body responds with greater intensity. Then her lips open and from them comes a ghostly wail which rises and falls with a measured rhythm. She is telling a story of the olden days when heroic Arabs mounted their white steeds and set off into the desert, bent on conquering the world. To relate their successful deeds her voice is low and electric; when in turn, their failures and deaths, her song slowly mounts to a dreadful climax of wails.

The effect of such singing and dancing upon her audience is remarkable. They squirm in their chairs, follow the rhythm with their arms, sink to the floor in ecstasy, and finally as the entertainer is writhing and shrieking the climax, they writhe, shriek, bellow, or moan in unison with her. Such is their way of showing appreciation.

Leaving the Egyptians in their trance, we return to the street flooded with moonlight and, noting its brightness, realize that this is the proper time to see those ageless monuments, the pyramids. So we turn to the west and head for the European quarter, but just before we reach the section of bright lights and broad streets, strange music again comes to us. It is as weird as anything that we have heard before but much more barbaric, much more African. This is undoubtedly a Nubian or a Sudanese orchestra, something from the lands that lie far to the south. But no, for as we come closer we hear clarinets and cornets, and the jungle music turns out to be an old friend, "St. Louis Blues." It comes from a dance hall nearby, where natives and foreigners dance with each other. It is especially patronized by American tourists who are not interested in native music but want to dance to tunes from their homeland.

DESERT SANDS

We board a streetcar, cross into modern Cairo, which is a thousand years newer than the native quarter we have just left, ride for half an hour and finally come to the site of a civilization some four thousand years older than modern Cairo. Here we leave the Egypt of the present and the Egypt of the Arabs far behind us as we cross the desert sands to the burying place of the ancient Pharaohs. Of course, we are traveling in a modern trolley car, but we soon forget it when we see those gigantic mountains of stone, the pyramids, towering above us.

THE ANCIENT PYRAMIDS

In the moonlight they seem to be taller than any peak in the Rocky Mountains, and yet they were built by men as a final resting place for another mortal. Elsewhere in the world nothing as massive or as impressive as this is built even for the worship of gods. Close examination of the pyramids shows that they are not smooth-sided as they seem to be in pictures, but consist of hundreds of steps to the top. Each step is a solid piece of rock weigh-

"THERE IS NO GOD BUT ALLAH, AND MOHAMMED IS HIS PROPHET"

People of the desert offering a prayer.

Homer Smith photo, Chicago

ing over a ton, and the great pyramid of Cheops, is composed of over 2,300,000 of these pieces. The engineering knowledge of these ancient Egyptians is a marvel to our modern architects.

CHEOPS' RESTING PLACE

The entrance to the great pyramid is on the north side. With lighted candle the explorer enters the passage and walks, stumbles, and crawls for a thousand feet upward. Along the route there are passages which shoot off in all directions. Most of these are either air-shafts or false alleyways to throw thieves off the trail. Another passage goes down and down, seemingly into the bowels of the earth, to a secret, subterranean chamber. These passages are avoided by the explorer, who follows his tortuous path ever upward until he no longer feels the narrow walls next to him. His footsteps create loud echoes, which sound like noises from the land of the dead; so he knows that he is in the burial chamber. By holding the candles high above his head he can see, in the middle of this enormous room, an empty sarcophagus, once the resting place of Cheops. But Cheops has been gone for thousands of years, having been removed by grave-robbers when Egypt was still a young country; so the explorer thinks that it is time for him to go too, for he has never been in such a spooky place.

HEAD OF A MAN—BODY OF A LION

In the moon-cast shadow of the pyramids there is another figure which was considered by the ancients, along with the pyramids, one of the Seven Wonders of the World. This is the Sphinx, with its head of a man and its body of a lion, which has crouched on the desert sands countless thousands of years. He was old when the pyramids were built and two thousand years older than that when the ancient Greeks were founding the basis of the civilization which we now enjoy. As the moonlight illuminates his face, his famous smile of sad wisdom can be seen. Who would not smile like that and be wise after so many years?

DESERT GOLF

After a last look at these wonders we make our way back to the streetcar. On our climb down from the small plateau on which these monuments stand we suddenly realize why night time is the best time for visiting them, for there at our feet lies a product of the nineteenth century—a golf course. Imagine visiting the oldest graveyard in the world, seeing the most impressive sights, and losing oneself in the mists of history only to see a golf course!

MUMMIES AND SARCOPHAGI

The final object of interest in Cairo is also connected with ancient Egypt. This is the National Museum. Here the Egyptian government has preserved the splendors of the ancient land. In it are perfectly preserved statues of wood, stone, and metal, mummies, sarcophagi, models of tombs, ornaments of alabaster, gold, and silver, and other objects whose value is computed in millions of dollars and whose historical value can never be measured.

Probably two exhibits stand as the most interesting. The first is the complete furnishings taken from the tomb of Tutankhamen and placed in the museum as they were found in his tomb. This is unusual because most of the tombs of the Pharaohs have been disturbed or robbed at one time or another. The second exhibit of interest is the one containing the unwrapped mummies of Seti I and Rameses II. Seti, the father, raised Egypt to one of the highest levels ever attained by that country, while Rameses, the son, ruled it for three score years when it was at the height of its glory. The art of mummifying was at its zenith in their time, and so their bodies are almost perfectly preserved. The unusual thing about the two mummies is that Seti's body seems strong and straight and there is a look of youth on his face while Rameses' mummy is that of a wrinkled old man, weak and feeble. This is explained by the fact that the father died when he was very young while the son lived to be over ninety.

TO THE PHARAOHS

With this introduction to ancient Egypt we must now visit the places where the ancient Pharaohs lived and ruled. This means going into a new land as different from Cairo as modern Cairo is different from its native quarter. There are those who say that Cairo is not Egypt but merely the gateway to Egypt. If this be so, then let us board a Nile steamer and see the real Egypt now that we have passed through the gate.

Our first stop is a little way south of Cairo at Sakkara, the village which has given its name to one of the most famous pyramids—the step pyramid of Sakkara. This was part of the cemetery of the famous city of Memphis, the ruins of which lie between Sakkara and the western bank of the Nile at Bedrashen.

It is difficult to realize that the fields around Sakkara through which we are passing were formerly occupied by one of the most important cities in the ancient world. Memphis was the second capital of Egypt in order of time, and reigned supreme from the time of King Zoser, 2900 B.C., until Thebes conquered it 700 years later. Even then it was a town of importance, surviving the Ethiopian, Assyrian, and Persian conquests, until the Arabian conquerors finally transferred the capital to nearby Cairo. Of all its greatness there now remain two gigantic statues of Rameses II, one broken, the other intact but lying on its back, and an alabaster sphinx standing in a pool amid a grove of palm trees.

To many it comes as a surprise that the great pyramids near Cairo are not the oldest monuments in Egypt, although such is their reputation the world over. The step pyramid at Sakkara, built by King Zoser as his tomb, is a hundred years older than the great monument erected by Cheops. Zoser had as his assistant a remarkable man by the name of Imhotep. This man was so famous for his knowledge of medicine, architecture, and proverbs that, twenty-five hundred years after his death, he was made the god of medicine. A set of surgical instruments, carved on the side of the temple at Kommbo, belonged to him.

The religious thought of Memphis centered around the god Ptah, the god of architects and master-workers. Later, the sacred bull was worshiped as Ptah incarnate, and in the cave at Sakkara the bulls were buried. This subterranean cavern, hewn out of solid rock, dates from the days of Rameses II.

There are also two very early tombs which were dug in 2700 B.C. They are especially interesting because they contain wall-paintings (the best examples of ancient Egyptian art yet found) which show such activities of those long-dead people as boat-building, sailing on the Nile, plowing, reaping, and sowing.

Homer Smith photo, Chicago

PORT SAID, EGYPT, GREAT PORT OF THE SUEZ CANAL

CAVES OF SPEOS ARTEMEDOS

Our next stop is Beni Hassan. This is the landing stage for our visit to two points of interest. We mount the long-suffering donkeys that are awaiting us, and are carried first through green fields and then along the edge of the desert. Our first objective is the cavern of Speos Artemedos, which contains inscriptions from the time of Queen Hatasu. From here we continue to a hillside where, cut out of the rock of the towering cliffs, are a number of tombs belonging to noblemen of the dynasty of 2000 B.C. These tombs have wall-paintings depicting the manufacturing, commercial, agricultural, fishing, and hunting activities of Ancient Egypt. In one cave there is a picture of a caravan from the eastern countries which has come to Egypt to sell its goods.

AMENOPHIS' GOD

Tel-el-Amarna, some two hundred miles south of Cairo, is not especially famous for any ruins to be found there. It is true that there are some notable rock tombs, but its importance lies in the fact that it was the capital of one of the most unusual rulers that Egypt ever had. This was Amenophis IV, who, in 1375 B.C., conceived the idea of a single god. He therefore overthrew the many gods of his fathers and substituted in their places a single deity, the sun. This was a new and revolutionary idea, and like so many new ideas the great mass of the people refused to accept it. They preferred their old gods of life, death, wisdom, luck, and the Nile. So they revolted, overthrew Amenophis IV, and Egypt had to wait until the days of Christ before they accepted the idea of a single God. The city of Akhenaton, which was established by Amenophis as the capital of his new religion, was attacked by "time" and the priests from Thebes until it was destroyed. All that remains is a pile of dirt on which is built the village of Tel-el-Amarna. *Sic transit gloria mundi*—so passes the glory of the world.

CEMETERY CITY

The next city up the river is Asyut, where a great diversion dam stretches across the Nile. At this point the cliffs that line the Nile valley come very close to the river and so are very easy of access. They are interesting not only for the rock tombs, dating from the Eighth Dynasty (2450 B.C.), but also for the excellent view of the Nile valley which they afford. At the very base of the cliffs there is a Moslem cemetery which looks like a small city in itself, because each grave has a small tomb over it. From a distance the tombs all look like houses. At some distance across the Nile there is a small village of mud houses where, a little more than a hundred years ago a company of Napoleon's soldiers was deserted by him on his flight from Egypt.

Asyut is the most important educational and commercial center in Egypt south of Cairo. It contains a large American mission college where many Egyptian children are taught to speak English. After learning it, the children proceed to make life miserable for the tourist by their incessant requests to enter into conversation in the language which they have learned.

BEAUTIFUL ABYDOS

Nearly a hundred miles south of Asyut lies the ancient town of Abydos, site of some of the most beautiful ruins in the Nile Valley. Abydos lies about thirty miles from the Nile on the spot where the desert touches the flood plain of that river. Here is the temple of Seti I, the loveliest and holiest shrine of Ancient Egypt. It was erected in 1300 B.C., during the period when, under Seti, art in Egypt reached the highest point in its climb to perfection. Seti's early death prevented his completing it, and so the work fell to his son, Rameses II. Most temples have but one sanctuary; but this has seven, six of which are dedicated to gods and the seventh to Seti himself as a god.

The original pylon (entrance gate) of the temple disappeared centuries ago. Behind the site of the original pylon there are two open courts whose sheer walls are covered with engravings. In back of these are two hypostyle (pillared) halls whose beautiful columns reach skyward to support a roof which has long since fallen in. The first, which was built by Rameses, is nothing exceptional; but the second, the work of Seti, is what makes the libations before the two gods, Horus and Osiris, and his offering of a tiny kneeling figure, the goddess Maat (goddess of truth), to temple famous. On its walls are bas-reliefs showing Seti pouring Osiris.

CORRIDOR OF KINGS

Still farther back are the seven sanctuaries and the long corridor of the kings. In the hall of the sanctuaries the art work shows the different ceremonies proper to each god. This is done in the graceful style characteristic of Seti. The long corridor of kings is also very beautiful, but its especial value is for the archaeologist rather than the artist. In it Seti attempted to pay proper respect to his ancestors, and in so doing he listed the seventy-six kings of Egypt who preceded him in the order in which they reigned. Thus, he has given to history a chronology which is the framework upon which the whole story of Egypt is built. Close by the temple is a monument to Seti which has all the appearances of a tomb. It is remarkable for its walls which are covered with inscriptions from the Book of the Dead, the ancient Egyptian Bible, and for its ceiling which has sculptures showing the sky-goddess Nut, with her lovely form and outstretched arms, being supported by Shu, the god of the air. Although this temple at Abydos is not so well preserved as the one at Dendera, which we shall soon see, or as impressive in size as the ruins at Karnak, it still ranks first as the temple containing some of the finest art ever achieved by the Egyptians.

TWO THOUSAND YEARS NEW

The great temple at Dendera is unique for several reasons: It is very new, according to Egyptian standards; it is perfectly preserved; it contains sculptures of Cleopatra and her son, and its walls are covered with drawings of objects of astronomical interest. It is considered new because it was built as late as the first century B.C., only two thousand years ago. The gigantic portraits of Cleopatra and Caesarion, her son, on the outer walls of the temple are among the few of this famous queen that have come down to us. Because the temple was dedicated to the goddess Hathor, it is of great interest to astronomers. This is due to the fact that the festival of the goddess came at the same time as the Egyptian New Year, which was in turn connected with the first appearance of the star Sirius, which heralded the coming of the flood of the Nile. Because of all this, the ancient artists covered the walls of the temple with numbers relating to astronomy, and also the famous signs of the zodiac. Thus, the Ancient Egyptians have given us the basis of both the pure science of astronomy and the so-called science of astrology.

Homer Smith photo, Chicago

RUINS OF THE TEMPLE OF AMMON, LUXOR, EGYPT
On its walls are remains of scenes depicting events of early Egyptian history.

The perfect preservation of the temple is probably its greatest attraction; for it is so intact that it is possible to follow in the steps of one of the old ceremonies in which the goddess Hathor was joined to the sun god Ra. This can be done by climbing the ramps from the pitch-black darkness of the temple rooms below to the sun-flooded roof above. It was along these same steps that the ancient priests imagined that they carried the goddess from the darkness below to the golden light above.

LUXOR THE MAGNIFICENT

We, as travelers, have realized by this time that there have been three phases to the history of Egypt. The first that we saw was the modern, as represented by Alexandria and European Cairo; the second phase is that of medieval, or Arabian, Egypt which we saw in the native quarter in Cairo and in the villages of the north. Although the third or ancient phase is scattered all along the Nile valley, its center is located in the area around Luxor, which is our next stop. Here is the great concentration of the magnificence and glories of the ancient empire—the land which was the first civilized area on this earth.

There is as much to see in the ancient capital of Egypt, Thebes (more commonly known as Luxor, the name of the modern town on the site), as there is in the modern capital, Cairo. What was once included in Thebes is now broken into distinct units called Luxor, Karnak, the Colossi of Memnon, the Valley of the Kings, the Valley of the Queens and the necropolis of Thebes itself. In the village of Luxor there is a temple by the same name. It was built by Amenophis III (Eighteenth Dynasty), at the time when Thebes was becoming the greatest city in Egypt. If it were located anywhere else in the country, it would be considered a great temple (it is 625 feet long and 180 feet wide), but being so close to the magnificent piles of rock at Karnak, it is dwarfed into insignificance.

Karnak must not be thought of as one temple. Instead, it is a great collection of temples erected by the different Pharaohs in honor of many gods and goddesses. The approach to it is a road from Luxor lined on each side by rows of small sphinxes. This leads through a gigantic portal which towers into the air several hundred feet. Behind the portal is the first massive pylon, which acts as the outside wall for the main part of the temple area. Throughout the temple there are ten other gigantic pyons which separate the adjoining courts and sanctuaries.

Homer Smith photo, Chicago

STATUE OF RAMESES II
LUXOR, EGYPT

THE GREAT HYPOSTYLE HALL

The second court is the most famous throughout the world, for this is the Great Hypostyle, or columned hall. When the ancient Greek explorers first saw it, they immediately agreed that it was one of the Seven Wonders of the World. All travelers who followed them have thought the same. One hundred and thirty-four pillars, each seventy feet high and twelve feet thick, stretch up like enormous trees to spread their beautiful capitals against the sky. Here is something as impressive as the pyramids, but even more bewildering. There are several theories as to how the pyramids were constructed; but no one, as yet, has explained how the ancients, without the aid of modern machinery, constructed such a massive, and yet beautiful, forest of columns.

Over the rest of the temple area there are scattered several smaller temples and huge piles of rocks, representing great buildings which have fallen before the attacks of time, fire, or earthquakes. A very interesting object in this area is the obelisk whose needle-like form stretches above everything else around it. It is one of the few obelisks left in the land. Most of its sister pieces have been carried away to such distant places as London, Paris, Rome, and New York.

THE COLOSSI OF MEMNON

At the time of its greatest power, Thebes covered wide areas on both sides of the river. If we cross the Nile now, to its western side, perhaps we can determine what those two huge statues are. By tramping through some poor fellah's cornfield, we see in front of us two mammoth seated figures. They are massive piles of rock delicately sculptured to represent Amenophis III, but are known to the world today as the Colossi of Memnon. Although these twelve-hundred-ton statues were once within the city of Thebes they now stand quite by themselves, surrounded on every side by cornfields.

Homer Smith photo, Chicago

THE COLOSSI OF MEMNON, THEBES, EGYPT

VALLEYS OF KINGS AND QUEENS

A donkey ride to the west over the range of hills, or mountains, as they are called in Egypt, brings us to the famed Valley of the Kings; and a half mile farther on is the Valley of the Queens. In this region are many ancient tombs of kings and queens. The great valleys themselves are hot, dry scars in the earth, and no one would ever think of them as graveyards. That is the exact reason why the Theban Pharaohs used them for such. They knew that the great pyramids built in the north had not protected their ancestors' mummies, so they decided to have tombs which were invisible. They commanded their architects to burrow rather than build; and they cut long tunnels sometimes five hundred feet in, and the same distance down, for the beautifully decorated tombs. The tombs and the tunnels were then decorated with important scenes from the lives of the kings, filled with their treasures, stocked with small statues of themselves and their servants (who were to take care of them in the next world) and finally sealed after the dead kings' bodies had been properly placed inside. The entrances were then covered with great piles of loose stone and gravel, and this system foiled all attempts at robbery for many centuries, although the modern archaeologists solved the secret.

The remaining wonders of Thebes are all close to the Nile and consist of a great number of temples, some erected to the various gods, and some built to honor the kings who reigned at the time. As we leave Thebes for a refreshing ride up the Nile, we leave with very definite impressions in our minds—great heat, great expanses of sand, and great heaps of temples.

ELEPHANTINE ISLANDS

This part of the Nile voyage is especially delightful because of the number of small islands which dot the river. Each of them is a lovely jewel, with its bright, green palm trees. On the banks we pass the great temples of Edfu and Kom Ombo—the first dedicated to Horus, the falcon-headed god and the second to Imhotep, the god of medicine. Finally we see Elephantine Island in the distance, and on its shore the Nilometer where the rise and fall of the Nile have been measured since the days of the Romans. Across the river is the village of Assuan, which has given its name to one of the most famous dams in the world.

Paul's Photos, Chicago

ASSUAN ON THE NILE, NEAR THE GREAT ASSUAN DAM

ASSUAN DAM

The dam is one of the great monuments to the engineering skill of the modern world. It makes the land south of it a vast reservoir, some two hundred miles in length, just to serve the needs of the Egyptian farmers. It is here that the irrigation waters are stored during the rainy season of the lands to the far south. Then, when the Nile is running dry, they are released so that the fellahin may have water for their lands the year 'round. The sight of the dam and that from the dam alone make the trip up the river worth while.

A walk across this solid wall of rock, stretching a mile and a half from shore to shore, affords a picture of great contrast. To the south there lies a solid sheet of water broken only by the lovely temple of Philae which is flooded most of the year. Nothing else can be seen but water reaching from desert cliffs to desert cliffs. From here there may be found many places of great loveliness. Here are numerous isles, some tree-covered, some rocky, separated from each other by the rushing torrents of the cataracts. On the shores of each side are rich green fields which finally blend into dunes of golden sands. It is around Assuan where the desert of the story books exists. Here are the high mounds of colorful, shifting sands, while elsewhere in Egypt the desert is nothing but a rocky waste.

A small side-trip into this wonderful desert takes us to a small quarry in which still lies an old obelisk. Some ancient king ordered it for one of his monuments, and so it was quarried and cut; but for some reason it was never taken from the quarry. There it lies as a sad reminder of the unhappy fate of Ancient Egypt.

"WHOSOEVER DRINKETH OF NILE WATER . . . ."

We, too, are sad and unhappy, for we know that our most delightful trip has come to an end. In a few weeks we shall be hearing church bells rather than the magic call to prayer. Where in our country can we find a river like the palm-lined Nile? We return to Assuan deep in melancholy, for it is from here that we shall take the boat down the river again, and that means leaving this mysterious land.

". . . MUST RETURN"

But, just as we are ready to depart, something happens which makes us very happy. An Egyptian friend rushes up with a tray of glasses and a bottle. The latter contains Nile water. He fills the glasses, and we drink a toast by quoting the old Egyptian proverb, "*Lishrub moyet en Nil awadeh.*" Now we can smile and be content with our lot, because the old proverb means in English, "Whosoever drinketh of Nile water must return."

Courtesy Matson Navigation Company, Chicago

THE RUGGED SCENERY OF BUCKLAND VALLEY, FROM MT. BUFFALO NATIONAL PARK, AUSTRALIA

ISLAND CONTINENT OF THE SOUTH SEAS

ALL OF US have felt the strange fascination of far-off lands. At one time or another we all dream of journeys to remote lands, which by their very remoteness suggest romance and adventure and awaken in us dream pictures and wanderlust. Such a land is Australia, the island continent which, with little Tasmania to the southeast, lies completely within the Southern Hemisphere. This continent, the last to be discovered and opened to civilization, is geologically the oldest in the world. Most of it was dry land when great parts of Europe and Asia were still under water. Here are produced unique trees, flowers, plants, and animals, which long ago vanished from other parts of the world. Here, too, are found aborigines who still live in the manner of people of the Stone Age. Vast tracts of sparsely populated country and solitary expanses challenge our imagination. Australia's history abounds in exciting stories of heroic exploration, of tragic settlements by deported British criminals, of the feverish rush for gold, of brave, enterprising, and persevering pioneers, who, in less than one hundred and fifty years, have built a modern and progressive country from a wilderness land.

THE LONELY CONTINENT

At once the largest island and the smallest continent in the world, Australia lies remote from all other lands. Even New Zealand, which we regard as its neighbor, is over a thousand miles away. Lying between the Indian and the Pacific Oceans, Australia is some three thousand miles from Japan and twenty-five hundred miles from India. Ships leaving London for Australia via the Suez Canal must traverse eleven thousand miles, and the traveler going from Californian ports to Australia via Samoa, Fiji, or Tahiti covers a quarter of the circumference of the earth.

AUSTRALIA'S CONTOURS

The shape of Australia has been likened to that of the boomerang, the unique and efficient weapon invented by the aborigines of that continent. Although Australia is bounded on all sides by water, it has very few indentations, and its miles of coast are singularly limited in port facilities. Nevertheless it has several spacious harbors.

A vast country, its topography is unusually regular. The continent is for the most part an immense plateau, high in the east, becoming increasingly lower toward the center and the west. A succession of mountain chains parallels the full length of the eastern coast and part of the southeastern coast as a result of the continual elevation of these marginal portions of the continent. Vast basalt "floods" covered the features of these mountain ranges, filled in the valleys, and the ranges were leveled into a plateau. The whole of this mountain system is named the Great Dividing Range and is also known as the Eastern Highlands and the Southeastern Highlands. In the southeastern section is the highest summit of Australia: the granite-capped Mount Kosciusco, over seven thousand feet high. The mountains of the southeast rise bleak and solitary, lonely and denuded. In contrast are the mountainous sections of the northeast, blanketed with tropical vegetation. There a few naked crags seem to lift themselves from a sea of lush greenness. Extending twelve hundred miles along the northeast coast is the Great Barrier Reef, greatest of all coral reefs, separated from the coast by a channel over sixty miles wide.

The eastern and southeastern coast, where the greater portion of Australia's population lives is well-watered. Australia's area is large enough to experience a great differentiation in climate within its various regions. The interior is generally hot and arid; the tropical portion is drenched with monsoon rains during the summer and parched by drought in the winter. The high and rocky coast of the Great Australian Bight in the South is dry and devoid of streams.

Australia's seasons are the reverse of those in countries of the Northern Hemisphere; the summer months are December, January, and February, and the winter months, June, July, and August. Along the eastern and southeastern coast, the warmth of summer is tempered by sea breezes, while the nights are almost invariably cool. The extreme north is tropical, and some parts of the interior are too hot to be favorable to white inhabitants. Generally, however, the climate resembles that of California, Southern France, and Italy. In the mountainous and temperate sections, snowstorms are common in winter. Approximately thirty-eight per cent of this continent is situated in the tropics. The northern third of this region has mean temperatures in the summer months of 80 to 85 degrees Fahrenheit, in the winter months of 55 to 75 degrees Fahrenheit; and in the southern third 80 degrees to 65 degrees and 55 to 50 degrees in the same months respectively. The southeastern parts, including Tasmania, are the coolest. This is because of the presence of highlands. These highlands in southeastern Australia and Tasmania are the only parts where snow falls, and there it lies for months. The northeast Queensland coast has the heaviest rainfall and the region about Lake Eyre has the least. Tasmania has a climate like England's; it is moist and mild, unreliable, expanding and shrinking according to the amount of rainfall. In the interior are found a number of salt lakes, many of which disappear in times of drought. Fortunately there are great artesian basins underlying nearly one-third of the surface of Australia, and many wells have been opened throughout the country, reclaiming vast sections.

LAND OF LIVING FOSSILS

Curious and interesting forms of plant and animal life are found in Australia. Cut off from other lands millions of years ago, Australia has preserved living specimens of animal and vegetable life which disappeared from the remainder of the earth untold ages ago. Isolated, Australia not only retained its own strange primitive natural life, but it also kept from its shores the more advanced forms of life which gradually began to inhabit other lands. Here are no native pigs, elephants, bears, or monkeys, nor any of the higher mammals to be found elsewhere. So unique is Australia's animal kingdom that scientists sometimes divide the animals of the world into two classes: Australian and non-Australian. The ants and termites are destructive pests, and the rabbit, fox, sparrow, and starling have been added to the list of pests.

Typical of Australia is its national animal, the kangaroo, "the animal that jumps when it runs, and stands up when it sits down." The kangaroo is one of the "marsupials," a peculiar primitive type of mammal. All marsupial mothers have a pouch or fold of skin upon their abdomens in which they carry and nurse their young. Except for the opposums of America, which are marsupial, there is no other living marsupial known outside Australia. The kangaroo has over a hundred relatives, varied in size and habits. Among them are the rock wallaby or wallaroo, the tree kangaroo, and the rat kangaroo. Some of the marsupials burrow in the ground, some roam the woods or barren lands, and some live in trees. One group lives on grasses, other groups eat insects, flesh, roots, or fruits. Of all the marsupials the most lovable is the koala, known as Australia's bear. Looking every bit like a toy Teddy bear, the koala, a soft, fluffy, gray-colored creature, whimpers or cries like a baby, when molested. To wipe away his tears he rubs his little black beady eyes and rubbery-looking black nose with his paws, like a tired, peevish youngster. Lazy in habits, the young either ride in their mother's pouch or climb upon her back, to be carried up a lofty eucalyptus tree for food or rest.

THE PATCHWORK ANIMAL AND HIS BROTHER

Two queer primitive mammals found only here are the platypus, or duckbill, and the spiny anteater, or echidna. Both lay eggs but suckle their young. The platypus is the odd patchwork creature which has baffled scientists. It has webbed feet, the tail of the beaver, a bill like a duck's, soft fur like a seal's, and poison spurs, and is perfectly at home on land or in water.

The echidna possesses a long sticky tongue, with which to catch ants. Of all the animals introduced into Australia, the rabbits

FEEDING MRS. KANGAROO AND "JOEY"

(Baby kangaroos are called "Joeys" in Australia.)

LIVING "TEDDY BEARS"

The Koalas, like the kangaroos, carry their young in pouches.

THE LYRE BIRD

Mimic of the Australian forests.

Pictures on this page courtesy Australian National Travel Association. Los Angeles

have had the most notorious history. Multiplying at an appalling rate, they overran the country. To combat the rabbit pest, Australia has built miles and miles of fencing; one fence, alone, in Western Australia is eleven hundred miles long.

THE BIRD WORLD

Australia is filled with brilliantly colored birds with sweet voices and strange habits. The emu, called the "Australian ostrich," is the national bird. Its likeness, along with that of the kangaroo, appears on the common-wealth coat-of-arms. On the vast plain of the interior the traveler can see the emu, which does not fly because its wings have degenerated, scuttle along the ground at a fast pace, unconcerned by a drove of kangaroos leaping by at a distance. Along the east coast we find the bower bird, which builds a playhouse, or garden. To this playhouse it brings all sorts of bright objects, shells, seeds, and flowers, which it arranges artistically and with great care. Inside this bowered retreat, the male birds bow and dance and court their mates with great ceremony. Truly exotic is the lyre bird which spreads its tail into the form of a perfect lyre. A skilled mimic, it can imitate the songs of other birds, the sound of the axe, the barking of dogs, and even the blare of a horn. A bird well-remembered by any traveler is the kookaburra, known as "the laughing jackass." Not a bit bashful, it will come from "the bush" into the city's boundaries and startle the peacefulness with boisterous, mocking laughter. Cockatoos are as familiar in Australia as crows are in the middle west of North America. Brilliant hues are not confined to the birds. There are many kinds of highly colored reptiles in the country, and fishermen find gorgeously colored fish. The leathery turtle has been found in some of the coastal seas.

LAND OF PRIMEVAL FORESTS

To see the wonderful woods of Australia is to understand why Australians love their trees. There are many growths of bygone ages which have no counterpart anywhere else in the world. Entering the forests, we lose all consciousness of the present and feel ourselves in a landscape of the shadowy past. It is as if we moved through the idealized pictures of prehistoric forests. The woods of Australia are not damp and shaded, nor monotonously regular. Here, rather, we see forests within forests—groves of straight

TOWERING EUCALYPTUS OR GUM TREES IN THE CUMBERLAND FOREST, MARYSVILLE, VICTORIA

Courtesy Australian National Travel Association, Los Angeles

soaring eucalyptus trees of many and varied species, surrounded by other forests of shorter trees, tall grasses, and towering ferns. These forests are strangely well lighted; the leaves of the eucalyptus grow somewhat vertically, so that light and warmth can trickle through and nourish the other, smaller growths. The eucalyptus or gum tree is an evergreen which sheds its bark but not its leaves. The many species of gum trees include some of the tallest trees in the world. The towering karri pines dominate in many of the forests. Throughout are seen great tree ferns, which exist elsewhere only in fossil form, and grass trees, peculiarly Australian in aspect, with stems, hardly thicker than a walking stick, surrounded by clumps of wirelike leaves. These rise to a height of ten or twelve feet and have a long spike at the top, studded with white blossoms. Then there are the gouty trees, with trunks of pyramidical shape, rising sometimes twenty feet and topped with straggling branches which bear a scanty crop of leaves and star-shaped sweet-smelling blossoms. The bottle tree is distinctive; its trunk looks something like a graceful vase or bottle with a plant stuck in its neck. Here, too, we see many forms recognized as tulip, lily, honeysuckle. But these are not trees as we know them, rather are they huge, impressive, bewildering giants.

"A JOY FOREVER"

Throughout Australia grows a species of acacia known as "wattle," sweet-smelling and colorful, covering valleys and gullies with golden brilliance. Brightening many a landscape are the romantically named flame trees, with their crimson-red flowerings. All through the "bush," or country, we find blankets of brilliant blooms—lavishly tinted orchids, splashing red banksia, pitcher plants, kangaroo's foot, boronia—a vast array, their beauty a delight to the eyes and their names a joy to the imagination.

THE ORIGINAL AUSTRALIANS

Remnants also of bygone ages are the Australian aborigines, called "blackfellows." Like the continent's flora and fauna, they too are unique. Deep copper or chocolate-colored, they have black or dark auburn hair, wavy but not woolly. Their range of height is similar to that of Europeans. While some individuals are sturdily built, in general only the upper part of the body is well developed. The muscular development of the rest of the body is poor. The legs especially are long and thin, the calves slight and inconspicuous. The aborigines have broad flat nostrils, thick lips, and large, black, deep-sunken eyes. When Australia was discovered, they were living in almost prehistoric savagery. Their numbers have greatly dwindled since their contact with the whites, and now only about sixty thousand of them remain. Of this number a few thousand are employed by the white population to perform various light tasks. They are, for the most part, however, disinclined toward steady work, and great numbers of them still live in the remote regions of the interior, following their strange primitive mode of life. Marriage is permitted between persons of the same tribe who stand in a certain blood relationship. Usually the old men have the highest authority because of their greater magical powers. There are many tribal rites. There are initiation rites for both men and women; there are rites which are performed for the totem animal or plant.

These blackfellows wear no clothing in summer; in winter they usually put on the skins of animals. They wear no elaborate head ornaments. Sometimes they wear in their hair a bunch of feathers or the tail of some small animal. For beauty purposes, they make many gashes on their breasts or backs, rub these incisions with dirt to induce infection, and finally are happy when their bodies are covered with varied patterns of raised scars. Sometimes they anoint themselves with ill-smelling fish oils.

These tribes have no fixed settlements and no agricultural life. With their crude weapons—war clubs, spears, shields, wooden axes—and their effective invention, the boomerang, they roam through the country in search of food and sustenance. They make no pottery. In bad weather they build rude tem-

Courtesy Australian National Travel Association, Los Angeles

ABORIGINES OF CENTRAL AUSTRALIA, CARRYING THEIR PECULIAR WEAPON, THE BOOMERANG

porary shelters of bark or logs. For transportation across streams they construct rude canoes. They have no extensive possessions, and in their nomadic wanderings, they carry on their person all they own. Yet they are the most capable of hunters, amazingly skillful in tracking down animals.

We would not heartily approve of their tastes in food. They eat anything from kangaroo meat to lizards, caterpillars, and beetles, cooked or raw, and plants and roots of all kinds. Cannibalism is not regularly practiced, but, when food becomes scarce, the blackfellows will eat enemies who are killed or persons who have died of disease. Sometimes parents to forestall starvation will kill their infants for food. These aborigines prefer the flesh of the vegetable-eating native, the Chinese, or the Malay to that of Europeans, which is tougher and more salty. These native peoples of Australia are dangerous to strangers, not because they are "degraded savages" and of evil intent, but chiefly because they are ignorant, suspicious, and perilously dependent on the unreliable bounty of nature.

BEGINNINGS OF RECORDED HISTORY

The first discoverers of Australia are not recorded in the pages of history. We do know, however, that the continent was sighted by a Portuguese, Manoel Godinho de Eredia, and by a Spaniard at the very beginning of the seventeenth century. Repeated visits were made by the Dutch during the following hundred years, and by 1665 the land was named New Holland. Tasmania, the island which geographically belongs to Australia, was discovered in 1642 by the man whose name it now bears, Abel Janszoon Tasman, and who first named it Van Diemen's Land. In 1688 the first Englishman to stand on Australian soil was William Dampier, who reported that it was a country "sandy and waterless," with stunted trees, and inhabited by the "miserablest people in the world."

The name most closely associated with Australia, however, is that of Captain James Cook. In his craft, the *Endeavour,* he sighted the eastern coast; cruising northward he finally dropped anchor on April 28, 1778, in Botany Bay, so named by him because of the surrounding strange vegetation. Cooking over an open fire nearby were natives, now known as the Australian "blackfellows," who strangely paid no attention to the anchorage. Just as Cook gave orders to land, two natives suddenly appeared on a projecting rock, each armed with a bundle of sticks to use as weapons. Here, too, was first seen the boomerang, the curved "throw-stick" weapon peculiar to the Australian aborigines. When the natives made threatening signs, a musket was discharged; but they remained unconcerned. Finally one of the blackfellows threw a stone toward the boat. The British fired a shot, hitting him in the leg. Both natives quickly disappeared, only to reappear shortly, equipped with shields made of bark to protect themselves. Thus ended the first encounter of Cook and the blackfellows.

Although Cook landed a number of times, he was unable to establish friendly relations with the natives. Finally, he hoisted the British flag on Cape York, and Great Britain took possession of the land.

THE THREEFOLD STORY OF AUSTRALIA

The saga of Australia is woven around convicts, sheep, and gold. Curiously enough the history of the United States determined the future of Australia. After the American Revolution, the English could no longer send to this country the undesirable and criminal population they wished to deport. Australia offered a solution, and in 1788 ten hundred and thirty-five convicts under military escort landed at Sydney Cove. The first colony of New South Wales was established, and Australian history began. Then began a series of explorations into the interior, and in the wake of heroic expeditions, suffering, and death. New lands were opened. Convict laborers built roads, bridges, and routes into the heart of the continent. Hardy pioneers discovered rivers and great salt lakes far inland. Interwoven with these discoveries are tales of courage, of lonely treks into inhospitable hinterland where roamed thousands of primitive natives. Part of the colorful history of Australia is told in the exciting story of the mutiny of the *Bounty*. Admiral William Bligh, set adrift in 1789, finally returned to England. In 1805-1808 he was made governor of New South Wales. There his soldiers mutinied and kept him as a prisoner until 1810. On Pitcairn Island still lives a group of descendants of Tahitian women and British sailors who were mutineers of the famous ship *Bounty*.

The next most important step in the history of Australia was the introduction of sheep raising in 1803 by one Captain John

McArthur. With the discovery that the climate was admirably suited for the growing of the finest grades of merino wool, new and enterprising settlers entered Australia. Now the sheep of Australia yield more than one-fourth of the world's wool, including more than one-half of the world's finest quality merino wool. The most important product in the agriculture industry is sheep.

The peacefulness of Australia was startled by the discovery of gold in 1851. The country teemed with feverish activity. Immigrants of all races and from all parts of the globe poured into Australia; each week saw the arrival of about two thousand persons. Shops, pastures, ships, were all deserted; everybody was searching for gold. Even government officers and policemen forsook their regular duties, and soldiers were brought from Tasmania and England to keep order.

The findings justified the frenzy. One gold nugget was found at Ballarat in 1858 which weighed 2,159 ounces and was sold for $50,000. Echoes of the fabulous yields of the mines of Victoria, Queensland, and West Australia were heard all over the world, and Australian agricultural and industrial life, born now and richly nourished, began a steady growth. With the removal in 1870 of British troops whose chief concern had been the criminal population of Australia, the way was opened for the country's steady, progressive development.

The Commonwealth of Australia was proclaimed by the British parliament on January 1, 1901. It is comprised of the five continental states of Victoria, New South Wales, Queensland, South Australia, Western Australia, and the island of Tasmania. Up to 1927 Melbourne was the temporary seat of the federal government. Since then Canberra has become the capital.

UNDER THE SOUTHERN CROSS

Three-fourths the size of all Europe, Australia has a population smaller than that of Holland. The continent has nearly seventeen times as many sheep and twice as many cattle as people. Beside its harbors and coastal rivers have grown thriving modern cities, but a major portion of the continent is uninhabited. Australia is the most sparsely populated continent with 2.23 people per square mile. However, the population is increasing due to "natural" increase and immigration. It is the policy of the governments in Australia to encourage closer settlement on the land. A settler receives many concessions in paying for his land, implements, seed, and in credit, because he is regarded as an asset.

Its ideal being "a white Australia," strict laws exclude the entrance of colored peoples, and 98 per cent of its total population is of British stock; of these, 85 per cent are Australian born. Few are descendants of the convict settlers; they were an unproductive group. It is rather paradoxical that, although Australia's chief wealth lies in its agricultural, pastoral, and mineral districts, almost half of its entire population is concentrated in the six principal cities. Despite its small population, totaling slightly less than seven million, two of its cities, Sydney and Melbourne, each have more than a million inhabitants.

SYDNEY

Beginning our tour of the capital cities, we enter through the Heads, the glittering, cobalt-blue harbor of Sydney, the capital of New South Wales. Its shoreline is scalloped with picturesque bays and fingers of land upon which nestle houses with red-tiled roofs and lovely gardens extending to sandy beaches or rugged cliffs. Spanning the harbor is a magnificent arch-suspension-type bridge, the largest and widest ever built. Opened in 1932, it now accommodates a steady stream of motor, train, tram, and pedestrian traffic.

Sydney is a mixture of new-world modernity and florid Victorianism. Because it expanded without any definite plan, its streets are winding and irregular. Many of its old buildings are being torn down to make way for sleek new structures. Already possessing a number of modern edifices, it still retains the romantic picturesqueness of a Renaissance town hall, a Byzantine market, Gothic churches, and a government house that resembles a Tudor castle. A city with Parisian flair for gaiety, Sydney has neon-lighted nightclubs, theaters, motion-picture "palaces," and such American institutions as the soda fountain, fruit-juice stands, light-lunch counters. Yet there are no drug stores, but, instead, "chemist shops," which sell only drugs; cigarettes are purchased from tobacconists.

Sydney's populace, like that of all Australia, has found the happy medium between work and play. Businessmen take time out for morning and afternoon tea; yet work does not suffer.

Courtesy Australian National Travel Association, Los Angeles

PORT JACKSON, HARBOR OF SYDNEY, AUSTRALIA
One of the most beautiful seaports in the world.

All have learned the art of enjoying leisure, of basking on the shores of the sun-drenched Pacific, of surfing, boating, playing. Sydney and its vicinity offer to its sun-loving inhabitants a choice of no less than twenty beaches. Manly, a popular resort near Sydney, has a five-acre pool with a shark-proof net. So mild is the climate that many Australians swim throughout the year. About twenty per cent of the city's area is devoted to open-air spaces, used for recreational and educational purposes: municipal parks, cricket grounds, botanical gardens, and a zoölogical park. For week-ends, one can take delightful trips to many nearby points of interest and beauty; the most popular and stimulating are the fantastically beautiful Jenolan Caves and the scenic Blue Mountains.

GATEWAY TO THE TROPICS

From Sydney we can reach Brisbane, capital of Queensland, by boat, train, or airplane. In this city with its flavor of Hawaii or the West Indies we see graceful palms, gorgeous, flamboyant flowers, stalls piled with tropical fruits of all kinds; and, over all, the air is heavy with exotic fragrances. The mildness of the climate, too, has had a profound effect on the style of the houses; many of them are built on stilts to permit a free circulation of air, giving coolness in summer time and dryness during the season of heavy tropical rains.

The chief pride of Brisbane, a city of 300,000, is its city hall, which occupies more than two acres. Of Italian Renaissance style, it is built from Queensland granite and freestone. From its lofty tower one views a magnificent panorama of the city and its suburbs, built on many hills through which winds the Brisbane River. Below lies the main business street, Queen's Street, lined with the city's tallest and newest buildings. Along the waterfront are busy warehouses, from which is shipped much of the state's wool and sheepskin.

"MARVELOUS MELBOURNE"

Called by its proud citizens "marvelous Melbourne," this lovely city of beautiful boulevards and garden homes recently celebrated its hundredth birthday, with the Duke of Gloucester, from England, attending to represent the royal family. Unlike Sydney, Melbourne reflects the neat orderliness of long and careful city-

Courtesy Australian National Travel Association, Los Angeles

HENLEY DAY ON THE YARRA AT MELBOURNE

planning. Centered within a relatively small area, its business district is bounded by streets ninety-nine feet wide, leading into broad spacious parkways. The charm of its outlying parks and boulevards more than makes up for the monotony of its business district. Across the Yarra Yarra River stretches tree-lined St. Kilda, an avenue of rare beauty.

Once the center of the wild boom days in the gold rush, Melbourne has outgrown its youthful impetuosity and has become, in appearance and spirit, a city breathing English conservatism. Bourke Street, in Melbourne, is still the scene of old-fashioned cable trams; its streets are deserted on the Sabbath day; its populace observes a quiet, substantial life. Like all Australians, the citizens of Melbourne love sports; summer finds them playing cricket, golf, and tennis, or picnicking in the nearby Dandenong Mountains; winter finds them skiing at Mount Buffalo, only a few hours away.

Twice a year Melbourne awakes from its quiet life. Henley Day on the Yarra River in November is the scene of a colorful spring-time regatta. Gaily bedecked houseboats line the river-banks to watch the festivities; down the placid Yarra floats a continual stream of elaborately appointed canoes bearing stalwart young men and prettily dressed young women shaded by bright parasols. All Melbourne answers the call of this brilliant carnival-fashion show.

All roads lead to Melbourne during Cup Week. The Melbourne Cup is Australia's sporting classic, and the first Tuesday in November each year witnesses a huge crowd at Melbourne's Flemington racecourse. Great horse-lovers, Australians of every age, rich and poor, throng the tracks. Here, where a gently rising hill provides a natural amphitheater, as many as 120,000 people have gathered, all gay, enthusiastic, relishing the sport of a good race.

TASMANIA'S CAPITAL

Tasmania, Australia's island state, is separated from the southeastern tip of the continent by the two-hundred-mile-wide Bass Strait. Its capital, Hobart, reminds one strongly of southern England: stone houses, dotting its smiling hills and valleys; rivers, willow-bordered; and sweet-smelling hawthorn hedges. Yet its venerable eucalyptus and radiantly golden wattle preserve an unmistakable air of Australia. Because of its temperate climate, many Australians spend their summer vacations here. The city, on the shores of the River Derwent, rises slowly on low hills against the background of Mount Wellington, snow-capped several months of the year. On a hill overlooking the river stands the Government House in proud isolation amid extensive gardens. In this section are the zoölogical park and botanical gardens. Most of the public buildings are located near the wharves. The museum is of great interest to all who visit Hobart, for the remains of the last full-blooded aboriginal Tasmanian, who died in 1876, are here preserved. According to many scientists the Tasmanian aborigines were even more primitive than the aborigines of Australia's mainland. When Truganini died in May, 1876, her race became extinct. She was the heroine of many romances with white and black heroes.

THE GARDEN CITY AND PERTH

Adelaide, the capital of South Australia, can be reached overnight by train from Melbourne. In its setting of emerald parks it reflects the careful city-planning which has made of it a veritable garden spot. Its center is a square mile of business blocks, surrounded by a belt of park-land, two thousand acres in extent. Flanking this are twenty-one municipalities and residential districts. The Torrens River, artificially dammed to form a lovely slender lake, curves through the city, between the commercial district and the chief residential section, North Adelaide. Immaculate gardens pattern the banks of the river. On the North Terrace stand the stately parliament buildings, Government House, the library, the museum, Adelaide University, and the School of Mines. Many of the suburbs have in their very hearts vast blossom-laden squares, and one often sees stretches of green pastures where horses and cattle lazily graze. Because of its many schools and churches, Adelaide is often called the "Cultural City of Australia."

It is a three-day journey by train from Adelaide to Perth, the capital of Western Australia. Smaller than the other capitals, except Hobart, it has a population of 180,000. Changing from a village into a city since the gold findings of the nineties, Perth possesses few outmoded buildings in its business district. It is nestled on the sloping bank of the Swan River. In front of the city lies Perth Water, the lake fashioned by the widening river. Along the water's edge is an esplanade where thousands of young and old promenade. West of the city, along the river bank, is a thousand-acre reserve of native "bush," called King's Park. Here the amazing, beautiful wild flowers of Australia are preserved and protected.

INFANT CAPITAL OF THE COMMONWEALTH

The capital city of the Commonwealth is Canberra, like Washington, D.C., a made-to-order city. Its architect is a Chicagoan, Walter Burley Griffin, whose plans were selected from many in a world-wide competition. Opened in 1927 as the seat of the Commonwealth government and the home of the Governor-General, Canberra now has a population of nine thousand. Miles of broad thoroughfares, straight avenues, circles, and curving drives radiate out from Capitol Hill. No other city in the world has its vast expanse of park-lands. On the summit of a ridge overlooking the valley stands the Parliament House, a two-story structure, covering an area of four acres. Here have been planted

Courtesy Australian National Travel Association, Los Angeles

GARDENS AT PARLIAMENT HOUSE, CANBERRA, NEW CAPITAL OF THE AUSTRALIAN COMMONWEALTH

more than three million shrubs and trees of all species. Unforgettable are the sight and scent of Canberra's radiant springtime, a fragrant season full of the luscious blooms of golden wattle, cherry, peach, and almond. A city of low, scattered buildings, of winding streets and flowering trees, Canberra, the beautiful infant capital, challenges the future.

THE GREAT "CUTBACK"

Not to visit the great "cutback" or the "bush," popularly meaning the country sections, is to miss the real Australia. Inland from the mountains extend vast sheep and cattle ranches, known as "stations" or "runs." Many of these are complete communities in themselves. In a typical large station we find a graceful home surrounded by beautiful gardens, the Australian counterpart of an old English manor. Behind this are built full barracks and houses for the station hands and their families, stables, blacksmith and machine shops, a butchery, a laundry, and a bakery. Here, too, are post-office, telegraph station, and power plant.

Life in general is unhurried, but, when necessity demands, everyone is ready to work long and hard. In these interior parts there is time, too, for polo, tennis, golf, books, and music. Despite the immense number of sheep grazing on a great station, a person can travel long distances without seeing a single sheep.

Courtesy Australian National Travel Association, Los Angeles

ON A VAST SHEEP STATION IN NEW SOUTH WALES

In this vast region, known as "back of beyond," neighbors living a hundred miles apart converse with each other by hand-operated radios. Vast distances here are spanned by that remarkable, heroic organization, the Australian Aerial Medical Service. A sick person can, by radio, describe his symptoms to a doctor hundreds of miles away and receive in answer the needed medical advice. Here we see the modern miracle of "flying doctors," who daringly respond to urgent calls by climbing into their planes and speeding hundreds of miles to save lives and bring new lives into the world. "The Bush" is truly the scene of much of Australia's grandeur, romance, and drama.

With regret and wistfulness the tourist leaves Australia, newly discovered veteran of continents, land of golden beaches, modern cities, and sparsely peopled open plains, land of age-old vegetation and unique animals, land of endless contrasts.

NEW ZEALAND

Black Star photo By E. D. Hoppe

MT. EGMONT, NORTH ISLAND, NEW ZEALAND

A BRITISH DOMINION

New Zealand is one of the dominions of the British Empire and consists principally of two islands called, simply enough, the North Island and the South Island. These islands lie about twelve hundred miles to the southeast of Australia, and are bounded on the north, east, and south by the South Pacific Ocean, and on the west by the Tasman Sea. Their climate and position in the Southern Hemisphere correspond to Spain's and Portugal's in the Northern Hemisphere.

The history of New Zealand before the coming of the white settlers is lost in the mists of time. The first definite knowledge relates to the peopling of the islands by the Maori, who came in the fourteenth century in a great wave of migration, possibly from Tahiti in the Society group of islands. Overpopulation was probably the principal reason for the migration, and certainly warfare preceded it. The actual trip was undertaken in large canoes, which bore such poetical names as "Storm Cloud," "Face of God," and "Shade of the South." Tradition has it that the Maori used a chart that had been handed down from their ancestor, Kupe, who had visited the islands centuries earlier.

ADVENT OF THE MAORI

The Maori came to shore about 1350 A.D. on the east coast of North Island and soon spread throughout the land. The members of each tribe continued to associate their identity with the canoe to which they had entrusted their lives and most valuable property. For centuries these various tribes fought among themselves, mainly uninterrupted in their warfare. It was not until 1642 that the islands were seen by a white man, the adventurous Tasman; and it was as late as 1769 before Captain Cook began his exploration of New Zealand, astounding the natives, who little dreamed what changes his visit presaged.

The earliest white men to visit the islands, other than explorers, were enterprising sealers and whalers. They, in turn, were followed by traders and missionaries, and finally by settlers. The English were slow to lay claim to New Zealand. It was not until 1840 that settlers began to come in numbers and that the British Government was led to take possession of the islands through fear of French intentions. Twelve years later, in 1852, they were made a separate self-governing colony and in 1907 were officially designated as "The Dominion of New Zealand," thus taking rank with the dominions of Canada, Newfoundland, Australia, and South Africa.

BY LAND AND SEA

Both islands are generally mountainous, the mountains extending the entire length of each island. Numerous long spurs reach toward the sea, with the result that there are no broad coastal plains. North Island, however, has a long and narrow peninsula that is rather low and is indented by numerous bays. There are, indeed, a great many sheltered bays on all the coasts, and in the southeastern part of South Island there are many fiords of scenic grandeur. Both the islands have lakes of striking beauty and many fine rivers that course through verdant, well-watered valleys. North Island possesses a fascinating region of active volcanoes, hot springs and lakes, and spectacular geysers. In the mountainous southern portion of South Island there are many long, narrow, and winding lakes similar to the Finger Lakes of New York.

The present population of New Zealand is more than one and a half million people; of this number, the native Maori account for only about 82,000. The Maori are a branch of the Polynesian race, and are a people of great physical beauty. In their appearance and life they are much more like the people of the South Sea Islands than the natives of Australia. Their clothing is brightly colored and pleasing to the eye, and they have developed such arts as wood carving and painting to a high level. The Maori were originally divided into some twenty clans, similar to those of the Scottish Highlands. In respect to civilization they rank high among the colored peoples of the world. Many of them at the present time are distinguished not only in education and agriculture, but in government as well, and in this respect, they differ from the natives of Australia and Africa. Until 1871 a large proportion of the natives were in active opposition to British rule, but since they have bowed to the inevitable and have largely blended with the general population. Their tribal organization consequently has largely disappeared. Maori members are now elected to the house of representatives according to the proportion of Maori in the whole population.

By far the great majority of the white people of New Zealand are of British stock. Other nations are represented in limited numbers, however. From European countries have come Austrians, Germans, and Scandinavians; and from Asia have come Chinese, Hindus, Syrians, and half-castes. Although the first European settlements were made on North Island, the actual spread of colonization was much faster in the early period on South Island. Here was more rich and accessible land. The Maori were peaceful, and later the gold fields drew a horde of such rough and picturesque adventurers as invaded California in the days of '49. Near the end of the nineteenth century, however, there began a trend toward North Island, and at the present time this part of New Zealand has the greater population.

The cities of New Zealand are like those of Australia—new and bustling, yet retaining English characteristics in their street names, architecture, and inhabitants. The important center, Auckland, is a typical example. The first impressions are of tall buildings, modern tramways, and motor service. Auckland is famous for its splendid harbor, its many miles of sheltered waterways, its beautiful parks and gardens. Overlooking the city is Mount Eden, an extinct volcano. But within and around the city of Auckland there are still found reminders of New Zealand's short but exciting history. In the Bay of Islands, in the beautiful North Auckland country, can be seen on "Maiki" Hill the flagstaff around which the ferocious warriors of Heke swarmed when the embryo village was sacked by the Maori, and not far away is the old church at Russell, still showing the marks received in battles between the increasing white men and the brave but faltering natives.

BEAUTIFUL SPOTS

South of Auckland one can travel through many interesting resorts which attract people to New Zealand from all over the world—Rotorua, the great thermal center; Waitomo Caves; Taupo and Tongariro National Parks; Lake Waikaremoana; and the Wanganui River; and Mount Egmont. Of these, Rotorua is especially striking with its chain of beautiful lakes. Southward are the Wairakei Valley, with its volcanic activity, and Lake Taupo, the largest lake in New Zealand, covering an area of 238 square miles. Near the outlet to Lake Taupo are the imposing Huka Falls where the river plunges with a thunderous roar into a swirling pool. To the south of the lake is the Tongariro National Park, with its three volcanic peaks. Here is a region of snowfall and thermal eruptions, including the huge active cone of Ngauruhoe Volcano. To the west of Lake Taupo is another lake that rivals Taupo in its wild beauty, Lake Waikaremoana, the "Sea of Rippling Waters."

Not far from Lake Waikaremoana is the wild and rugged Urewera country, where the Maori people lived until they were driven out recently by the relentless encroachments of gaily dressed tourists and eager travelogue photographers. Mount Egmont, too, was a favorite resort of the New Zealand aborigines. This lonely peak rises from the midst of a magnificent forest reserve and is a favorite resort of visitors who throng the comfortable hotels that surround it.

Paul's Photos, Chicago

WELLINGTON, CAPITAL OF NEW ZEALAND

WELLINGTON

A tour of North Island normally comes to a close at the city of Wellington, the capital city of the dominion. Wellington is situated at a magnificent and bustling harbor and is surrounded by high ranges of impressive hills. It is nearly in the center of the country and is separated from South Island only by the narrow Cook Strait. Wellington, like Auckland, possesses a great many modern and beautiful hotels, office buildings, and theaters, not to mention its parliament buildings, the Town Hall, the Victoria University College, and the National Museum.

New Zealand is a country of startling contrasts, and this is never more evident than when one goes from North Island to South Island. The latter has for a great backbone the Southern Alps, which extend from one end of it to the other and form an impressive background to the wide-extending landscapes on the eastern side. On the west of the island, towering mountains crowd in upon the coast, their snowfields and dazzling white glaciers contrasting with the green of the surrounding forests and the deep blue of the sea.

ENGLAND TRANSPLANTEL

From Wellington the traveler usually takes one of the comfortable and fast express liners, which leave in the evening and reach Lyttelton, the port of Christchurch, early the following day. Here he transfers to an electric train for a short trip to the city. Christchurch is perhaps the most English city outside of England. Through it winds the beautiful River Avon, lined with willow and oak trees, and flanked by fine gardens, manor houses, and parks. The English atmosphere is further emphasized by the impressive cathedral on the busy square, and the Tudor-period buildings of Canterbury College. The population of Christchurch is already about 120,000 and promises to increase greatly in the future; in this it is less English than in other respects.

MORE CONTRASTS

Communication has been opened between Christchurch and the renowned West Coast glaciers. These are reached by a long tunnel under the Southern Alps, the longest tunnel in the British Empire. These West Coast glaciers descend to within a few hundred feet of sea-level, and their termini can be easily approached by the pathways that extend to them from the nearby hotels. There are two great glaciers here, the Fox and the Franz Josef, acknowledged by experienced travelers to be the most beautiful in the world.

From Christchurch one may go also to the orchard country of Marlborough in the northern half of South Island. In the midst of the orchard country is the residential and holiday city of Nelson.

South of Christchurch is the city of Timaru, near Mount Cook, New Zealand's highest alpine peak, reaching 12,349 feet into the heavens. From this great mountain the traveler normally goes to the port of Dunedin, a busy city of 85,000 people, situated at the head of Otago Harbor. From here one may travel to the Southern Lakes region, between deep water and jagged peaks.

NEW ZEALAND FIORDS

Along the shores of the southern West Coast are the famous fiords, similar to those of Norway but believed to be more beautiful by many who have seen both. These deep arms of the sea have been formed by ancient glacial action, and the bold patterns of land and sea seem to represent both the beauties and the powers of nature's forces. Milford Sound was reached for years only by the famous Milford Track, an excellent road that winds through high mountain ranges, over rushing torrents, and along the bottoms of picturesque valleys.

Black Star photo By Fritz Henle

THE BEAUTIFUL TAJ MAHAL, AGRA, INDIA

INDIA

Courtesy Methodist Book Concern

TEMPLE RUINS AT DAWARAHAT, INDIA

THE "Brightest Jewel in the British Crown," India is perhaps the most amazing country on the face of the earth. Separated from its neighbors by vast mountain ranges in the north, it juts southward from central Asia, forming a great triangular wedge between the Arabian Sea and the Bay of Bengal. Within its borders is to be found a truly old civilization, for the history of India can be traced back five thousand years. Here Eastern and Western culture meet, although they rarely mix; for the Hindu fakir who has lain for a score of years on his painful bed of spikes cannot be expected to be disturbed seriously by a passing automobile.

India is the land of contrasts. Portions of it offer the traveler some of the most magnificent scenery in the world. In other places the country presents a dreary and desolate picture. Indescribable dirt and squalor lie just outside the beautiful palaces and temples of polished marble. Contradictions and inconsistencies meet the visitor on every hand. But from the exotic brilliance and color of the tropics to the snow-clad splendor of the Himalayas, India draws the traveler with the irresistible lure of the mystic Orient.

A world within itself, India contains more than forty-five different races, speaking twelve distinct languages in two hundred dialects. It is only two-thirds the size of the United States, and yet it contains almost three times the number of people. Among these millions are more than two thousand separate castes and tribes, each adhering zealously to its own religious beliefs and social customs. It is not strange to find extremes of every kind occurring there.

In India, where a well-developed civilization flourished long before the time of Christ, only about one-tenth of the inhabitants know how to read and write their own language. Here also, where a few are rich beyond the dreams of Midas, many do not get enough to eat. Sacred cattle walk unharmed through streets where food is as scarce as money. Strange and incredible things take place in this land "East of Suez." Marriages are arranged by parents. Men torture their own bodies in a frenzy of religious fervor.

AN ANCIENT BATTLEFIELD

India has a fascinating mixture of many different civilizations and influences. It is an ancient battlefield whose history is represented by a long series of invasions. Who the first people were and where they came from, no one seems to know. India's remote past is lost in the dim ages of long ago.

Among the first inhabitants that we know very much about were the Aryan invaders who swept down from the north nearly twenty-four hundred years before the time of Christ. For nine centuries this Aryan movement continued. Religion takes a greater part in the social system of India than in European or American countries. The caste system, for instance, is vitally important to the Hindu. Brahmanism persisted as a religion even after the rise of Buddhism in the sixth century B.C. But Hinduism in turn became generally prevalent.

Alexander the Great invaded the country in 327 B.C., bringing with him much of Grecian culture. If the visitor to India is puzzled when he sees a typically Grecian face on some old Buddhist statue, he should remember that Alexander once ruled here. But his stay was brief, and when he withdrew into Persia, India became a prey to other conquerors. Dynasties were established only to disappear again into oblivion. In the fifth century A.D., art, music, science, and literature flourished in the "Golden Age of Hinduism." Then this enlightened civilization was swept away by five hundred years of conflict and strife.

In the eleventh century, less than one hundred years after the death of Mohammed, Arabs swarmed into the disorganized country, spreading Mohammedanism and Moslem culture. That they gained a substantial foothold during the following three hundred years, is amply proved by the fact that there are almost eighty million Mohammedans in India today.

In 1398, the fierce Mongol horsemen under the leadership of Tamerlane invaded the land. They were ruthless fighters, and their advance through the country was accompanied by great bloodshed and cruelty. After sacking Delhi, Tamerlane withdrew his forces, leaving a devastated land to the bickerings and quarrels of the local rulers. But a descendant of his entered India in 1525 and established the Mogul Empire, an empire which became, under Akbar the Great, one of the strongest in India's history. With the death of Akbar's grandson in 1707, however, the power of the Mongols rapidly diminished.

EUROPE TAKES A HAND

The voyage of the Portuguese explorer Vasco da Gama, in 1498, marked the beginning of modern European influence in India. Portugal for the next hundred years was almost exclusive in her enjoyment of the fruits of Da Gama's discovery. Then at the beginning of the seventeenth century came the British, the Dutch, and the French. The power of the Portuguese was waning and the British, who in an attempt to find a better route to Japan had almost stumbled upon India, set about the task of establishing themselves here. The Dutch, who became important rivals of the British during the next century, were finally forced to retire from the country after suffering a severe defeat at the hands of Robert Clive in 1758.

The occasional clashes between the French and the British became increasingly numerous during the eighteenth century and led at last to open conflict for supremacy. In 1751, Clive, who rose from service as a clerk for the East India Company to be champion of the British interests, established his fame by the capture of Arcot. But not until ten years later, when the French under Lally were decisively beaten by Colonel Coote, did British influence become wholly dominant.

THE BLACK HOLE OF CALCUTTA

Probably few incidents have captured the Western imagination like that which occurred at Calcutta in 1756. At this time the British were not only being threatened by their European rivals, but were being endangered by uprisings among the native rajahs. Suraj-ud-Dowlah attacked Calcutta in June, and the superiority of his forces made it necessary for the hundred and forty-six British survivors to surrender. Their ruthless captor forced the entire number into the "black hole," a practically airless cell in Fort William. The heat was terrific, and only twenty-three survived.

To avenge the horrible death of his countrymen, Clive organized his forces and attacked Calcutta. The young rajah retreated, and the city was taken without much resistance. Clive pursued his enemy, and a series of brilliant victories for the British was finally climaxed at the battle of Plassey in 1757. Clive, with a small force, defeated the numerically stronger troops of Suraj-ud-Dowlah and laid the foundation for the British Indian Empire.

Throughout the following century, the British East India Company, acting for the government, continued to further British interests in India. More territories were annexed and the semi-independent native states were brought more completely under British domination. Occasionally uprisings would occur, and the British government's forces would become involved. The Sepoy mutiny of 1857 marked a turning point in British policies. In the following year, by an act of Parliament, control of India was taken from the Company and vested in the London government.

THE SEPOY MUTINY

Because of the annexation of lands and the forced introduction of Western customs, many of the natives grew hostile to the British. Even the Sepoys, Indian soldiers under British command, joined in this rebellious sentiment, and many of them mutinied in May of 1857. Owing to the number of Sepoy regiments which had mutinied, the British forces were greatly reduced, and the rebellion was at first successful. Delhi, Lucknow, and Cawnpore were taken, the government treasuries were looted, and many isolated groups of Europeans were slain.

The task of regaining lost ground was a slow process, hampered by the small number of British troops available, by disease, and by the difficulties of transport. More troops had to be brought from England, South Africa, Singapore, and Burma. The railway system extended only 120 miles from Calcutta to Raniganj, and beyond that point men were obliged to march under the hot Indian sun. Munitions and food had to be conveyed by road for almost 800 miles to Delhi.

At Cawnpore, General Wheeler and his small force were captured and treacherously murdered; and the women and children, taken prisoners. General Havelock hurried from Delhi, hoping to save the defenseless survivors. After forced marches, he arrived within 22 miles of Cawnpore. When he learned that there was still a chance of rescuing the white prisoners, he made his men march another 14 miles that night. In the battle of the following day he defeated the mutinous Sepoys and took Cawnpore, only to find that the women and children already had been massacred.

Delhi was the first important stronghold to be regained by the British. The capture of Cawnpore came next and after an interval, the famous relief of Lucknow. Everywhere, the British forces were fighting against vast odds. The burning Indian heat and the ravages of fever and cholera made their task doubly difficult. The defense and final relief of Lucknow is an epic in military history. The thrilling events that occurred here can be realized only when the visitor beholds the well-preserved ruins of the Residency, where a handful of white soldiers and a few loyal Indians battled against overwhelming odds for 140 days.

INDIA THINKS FOR HERSELF

With the transfer of power in India from the East India Company to the British Crown, many changes gradually took place. Western influence became more pronounced. Trade with the outside world increased, missionaries entered the country, schools were opened, and new ideas were introduced. A spirit of self-sufficiency and nationalism grew and flourished. Religious leaders rose to speak for the abolition of the caste system and for the birth of a new and more democratic Hinduism. Enlightened natives wanted independence and control of their own affairs. In fact, so pronounced did this new spirit become, that, at the start of the World War, riots against the British were not infrequent.

During the World War, India rallied to the British cause and demonstrated her loyalty with money and troops. In England's time of need India was not found wanting, and it was not until 1919 that revolt against British domination again swept the country. Mahatma Gandhi at this time rose to lead the movement in his campaign of passive resistance. The response of the Indian people was great and immediate. Communication was obstructed. All the wheels of industry and government turned more slowly.

The British government, while taking steps to allow a greater freedom for the Indian people, realized the difficulties and problems which complete independence would present. India, as we have seen, is composed of a vast number of different peoples, very few of whom are educated. The caste system and major religious differences are stumbling-blocks in the way of unified progress. So, while granting some of the requests of the Nationalists, England still retains a considerable control in Indian affairs. The constitutional reform of 1935 was a step in the direction of Indian self-government. And a blow to the caste system was delivered when, in 1936, the Maharajah of Travancore decreed that any or all of his four million subjects, regardless of birth, caste, or community, might enter any of the state temples. India, however, is an old country and the problems which it faces are numerous.

INDIA HAS VARIETY

The country is divided geographically into three general divisions: the main peninsula in the south, where a tropical climate prevails throughout the year; the vast and fertile plains of the Indus and the sacred Ganges; and the elevated tracts of the Himalayas. The Himalayas stretch in a line of majestic, lofty peaks for over a thousand miles. Here is to be found Mt. Everest, the highest mountain in the world. All the rivers of northern India have their sources in these mountains and flow through the comparatively level plains in the most thickly populated section of the land. The southern portion of the peninsula has two mountain ranges—the Eastern and Western Ghats—running parallel to the eastern and western coasts. These mountains are only moderately

GERSAPPA FALLS, INDIA—830 FEET HIGH

Courtesy Methodist Book Concern

high, and the territory between them forms a hilly plateau. At the southeastern extremity of the peninsula and separated from it by about twenty-two miles of shallow water lies the beautiful island of Ceylon.

India's climate varies, from the tropical heat of Ceylon and the south to the temperate coolness of the hill country and the northern mountains. The varying seasons may be classified as either cool, dry, or rainy. Winds, called monsoons, ordinarily alternate in sweeping over the land in southwest and northeast directions; but the moisture-laden southwest monsoons sometimes fail to arrive, and the soil becomes parched and dusty. When this occurs, crops wither and agricultural India suffers a famine. In spite of the progress made by the British in building dams and irrigation canals, many districts are still in great need of water.

FARMING WITH A WOODEN PLOW

The great majority of Indians make their living from the soil. Wheat and rice are the main crops, although sugar cane, jute, tea, and cotton are also cultivated. The Indian peasant uses a primitive wooden plow that is effective only when the earth is softened by a heavy rain. He still makes his cattle tread the corn out of the ear and has it ground in a treadmill, as his ancestors did. Modern agricultural machinery is relatively rare except on government farms, and transport away from the railways and main roads is by slow and clumsy bullock carts.

SNAKE CHARMING

Much of India's backwardness may be charged to the caste system, which elevated the learned professions and debased the useful and necessary trades, such as laundering and tanning. The educated Hindu father would rather see his son a humble clerk than the head of a shoe factory or a sawmill. Hence, Indian recruits for many of the despised but essential occupations come from the lower and less intelligent castes. The art of making things by hand is passed down from generation to generation. Under the caste system, it is fairly easy to predict what the son will do if his father's occupation is known. Among craftsmen like goldsmiths, weavers, and embroiderers, the skill which this hereditary system develops is sometimes very great. In India even such occupations as juggling, hairdressing, and snake charming are hereditary.

BOMBAY IS THE GATEWAY TO WESTERN INDIA

More visitors arrive at Bombay, the second largest city in India, than at any other port in the country. It is the main gateway to India, and on its busy streets are to be found representatives of most of the races of the world. Bombay covers an island of almost twenty-two square miles, and it is hard to believe that this modern port with a population of over a million was once leased to the British East India Company for ten pounds a year.

Courtesy Methodist Book Concern

HINDU WITH CASTE MARKS ON FOREHEAD

Courtesy Methodist Book Concern

HINDU ASCETIC SITTING ON BED OF SPIKES

The visitor to Bombay will find few ancient temples or picturesque ruins; but its sheltered bays, wooded hills, magnificent public buildings, and interesting bazaars will well repay the time devoted to them. The native market offers all the sights and sounds of the Orient. It is the gathering place of merchants. Here one may see the pearl buyer from the Gulf, the wily Arab horse dealer, and the hardy Afghan who has transported his bales of rugs and embroidery through the bleak passes of the northwest by camel caravan. One sees displayed for sale here superbly designed carpets, exquisitely embroidered shawls, gold and silver ornaments of delicate workmanship, and jewels of unsurpassed beauty.

TOWERS OF SILENCE

Beyond Malabar Hill, where the visitor can get an excellent view of the city, are the Towers of Silence, resting-places of the Parsee dead. The Parsees are the present-day followers of Zoroaster, worshiper of the sun; and it is because of their reverence for the three major elements, earth, water, and fire, that the bodies of their dead are never buried. Corpses, which must pollute neither the ground by burial, water by commitment to the waves, nor fire by cremation, are placed on iron grills in these towers and left to be devoured by birds. The beautiful garden surrounding this curious place, from which may be obtained a wonderful view of sea and mountain, provides an ideal spot for the meditations of the relatives of the departed.

Six miles across the water from Bombay lies the island of Elephanta. In its caves the visitor will see many interesting carved statues of Siva, the Hindu god of destruction. These and other stone images of the ancient Hindu deities are products of the expert craftsmen who dwelt here as early as the eighth century.

BURNING GHATS

Before the visitor finally leaves Bombay for the Indian mainland, he should get his first view of the burning ghats of the Hindus. A ghat is a landing place along the water front and should not be confused with the coastal mountains of the same name. The burning ghats, of which there are many throughout India, are places of cremation for the Hindu dead. Unlike the Parsees, the Hindus burn the bodies of their deceased. The usual location for this ceremony is the water front. Broad flights of steps lead from the edge of the water to platforms, where the bodies are consumed by fire and reduced to ashes. These ashes are then cast upon the water, in accordance with Hindu ritual.

INDIA HAS ITS "FOUR HUNDRED"

Almost directly north of Bombay lies the picturesque city of Udaipur. Its ruler, the Maharana, is probably the foremost figure in India's aristocracy. Prominent Americans may trace their ancestry back to the landing of the Mayflower; but this prince of Udaipur is said to be a direct descendant of the Sun god!

Udaipur was founded in 1568, and legend tells us that Udai Singh, its founder, might have been murdered had it not been for the remarkable loyalty of a family servant. So great was the devotion of his nurse that she, upon hearing of the plot to murder the infant prince, substituted and sacrificed her own son in order that the royal child might survive.

The city is situated on the western shore of a beautiful blue lake. On a high bluff overlooking the lake is the royal palace, an imposing edifice of granite and marble. It overlooks several exquisite marble pavilions rising out of the clear waters like fairy palaces floating in a huge sapphire. One of these island palaces is said to have been erected by an ancient ruler of Udaipur for his homesick bride, a place where she might worship as she had done in the house of her father.

The Maharana's palace, with its rich apartments, its fine terraces, and its splendid view, well rewards the visitor to this interesting spot. In the court of this palace are to be found a number of arched gateways. Under these in days past the kings of Udaipur were accustomed to have themselves weighed, and the solid gold which these proud rulers used as a counterweight on the scales was afterward given away to the poor.

Among other places of interest is the Odi Khas, a large tower at the southern extremity of the lake. Here the visitor may observe the traditional evening feeding of the wild pigs. At this tower it has been a custom of long standing to distribute several bushels of corn each night to wild pigs, which come unbidden from their jungle retreats. The visitor should be sure to see the Jagganath temple and the Slave Girl's Garden, delightful havens on the lakeside.

Courtesy The Art Institute of Chicago

PARSEE TOWER OF SILENCE, BOMBAY
Vultures consume the flesh of the dead, placed on the walls of this tower.

JAIPUR

Between Udaipur and Delhi, the capital of India, lies the "pink city" of Jaipur. Luring the visitor with its pink-tinted streets and buildings, its magnificent palaces, its mixture of oriental splendor and poverty, and its rigid adherence to the caste system, it offers a typically Eastern atmosphere. Of comparatively recent origin, as Indian cities go, Jaipur was founded about two hundred years ago by a native ruler who devoted much of his spare time to the study of the stars. The division of the city into regular rectangular sections and the obvious planning of its broad, straight streets, indicates the founder's mathematical and astronomical turn of mind. Although astronomy and astrology have from early times been interesting subjects to the East Indian, and although many natives still turn to the stars for guidance in their daily problems, Jaipur is the only purely Indian town laid out in accordance with a preconceived plan.

From the pink and white washes which brighten Jaipur's buildings to the brilliant green, yellow, and red costumes of its inhabitants, the place is a riot of gay colors. The streets of the town, except during the extreme heat of noonday, provide an oriental setting for a veritable pageant of India. Goats, donkeys, bullocks, camels, and massive elephants, weave through crowds of men, women, and children. All castes and classes, from ragged, naked beggars to resplendent noblemen, dressed in golden cloth and glittering jewels, pass in review.

The town is noted for its jewelry, brassware, and carpets. The gold enamelwork done here is the best in India. Here, also, is produced much beautiful tied-and-dyed silk cloth. Jaipur is the center of a great number of thriving industries, and few visitors can refrain from buying something that is made here.

In the time of Queen Elizabeth this town and most of India were ruled by Akbar, the Mongol conqueror. Unlike his ancestors, Akbar was a constructive ruler, building many palaces, establishing schools, and preserving the peace. Near Jaipur may be found several intricately carved and highly decorated palaces dating from the sixteenth century.

The Maharaja's palace, built much later, still gives in its fortified wall and battlements, mute evidence of the turbulence of the times. Seven stories high and standing in the center of the town, it commands an excellent view in every direction. The Diwan-i-Khas, the beautiful audience hall of white marble, is especially fine.

Adjoining the palace is Jai Singh's observatory, in which may be found several of the Maharaja's original astronomical instruments. The royal stables are built in circular fashion around an inner courtyard. At one end stands a great platform from which the ancient rulers were wont to observe feats of horsemanship. The "hall of winds" is a queerly constructed palace, standing at the intersection of two main thoroughfares.

AMBER

From Jaipur to Amber is seven miles. There, if the visitor wants to see the greatest glory of this beautiful but deserted city, he usually gets on the back of an elephant and is taken up a steep and winding road to the palace. Beyond a massive, fortress-like wall is the palace, untenanted now, but at one time the thriving capital of Jai Singh. One sees here reminders of the faded but magnificent glory of India's past.

At a short distance from the main entrance stands a temple. Here each morning a goat is killed as a sacrificial offering to the goddess Kali, for this is one of the few places in Amber still occupied by men. To the visitor, the daily slaughter of a goat is a startling reminder of the ancient days when this same temple was the scene of human sacrifices. Thus does tradition in India perpetuate the past.

The public audience chamber is a striking example of Rajputan architecture of the early nineteenth century. Its lovely, green marble pillars are said to have aroused the envy of the Mongol kings in Delhi to such an extent that the rulers ordered them to be covered with plaster to hide their beauty.

GALTA PASS

From Galta Pass, five miles from Jaipur, the visitor can get a splendid panoramic view of the city. Here, also, he may find interesting old rock temples, with their rude sculptures of the ancient gods. And in the valley beyond the temples are to be found many hermit-like priests, and groups of large, solemn, gray monkeys. Galta Pass is a bit of ancient India transplanted into the present, and it offers the inquisitive traveler a rare treat in an exotic atmosphere.

Courtesy Methodist Book Concern

THE FRIDAY MOSQUE, DELHI

DELHI

Delhi, the capital of India, is built upon the site of many former cities. It is surrounded by the ruins of ancient towns, forts, and buildings, about some of which very little is known. Tradition tells us that it was seven times the seat of an imperial capital before the coming of the British. New Delhi was built after 1911, when the capital was transferred from Calcutta.

The older cities suffered greatly at the hands of various invaders and were frequently looted and burned. The ruthless Persian conqueror, Nadir Shah, ordered such an invasion in 1739. His men massacred the inhabitants, took a tremendous amount of treasures as loot, and carried off the famous Peacock Throne and the Koh-i-noor diamond. In spite of these depredations, however, the Mongol stronghold of Shahjahanabad still survives as the thickly populated older section of Delhi today, a city of magnificent structures and vivid history.

Here are to be found the fort and palace built in 1638 by Shah Jehan, the celebrated creator of the Taj Mahal. Entering by the imposing Lahore gate, the visitor finds himself in a high-vaulted approach which opens into a large square, to either side of which were once fine arcades, gay with the richest wares of the Orient.

On the east stands the imperial drum-house, through whose gate only the greatest of the nobility could pass while mounted. It gives admission to the palace proper. Here the visitor finds the vast public audience hall with its splendid red-sandstone pavilion, its colonnades, and its raised alcove where the emperor sat to dispense justice. In the Diwan-i-Khas, or private audience chamber, stands a beautiful marble pavilion, which once sparkled with the finest jewels of the Orient. Through the entire length of the palace runs a marble watercourse, which was designed to cool the air in the rooms through which it passed. This air-conditioned palace, with its carved and inlaid marblework, its ceilings of gold and silver leaf, and its gem-studded thrones, must have been the envy of every oriental potentate.

THE JUMNA MUSJID

Within sight of the fort stands the Jumna Musjid, the principal place of worship for the Mohammedan population of Delhi. Built in 1644 of red sandstone and white marble, it is remarkable for the geometrical symmetry of its domes and minarets. On holy days thousands of devout Mohammedans gather before this great edifice, bowing and prostrating themselves in unison. It is a sight which the visitor will not soon forget.

Behind the Jumna Musjid is the famous ivory palace. Here the traveler may watch the making of exquisite ornaments and trinkets. Delhi is noted for its carved-ivory work, which is said to be some of the finest in the world.

The Chandni Chank, or silver bazaar, is another of Delhi's famous places. It is a fine, broad street, where may be purchased some of the best of India's gold and silver articles. In this artistic center many historic events took place. Here the streets ran red with blood when Nadir Shah commenced his massacre of a hundred thousand Delhi citizens.

Not far from the government offices in New Delhi lies the Ridge, scene of the most severe fighting during the time of the Sepoy Mutiny. Here are to be found Flagstaff Tower, chief post of the attacking force, and Hindu Rao's House, the key position of the gallant defenders. From the Mutiny Memorial, with its lists of regiments and their losses, a fine view of the city may be obtained.

ARCHITECTURAL WONDERS

A short distance outside of Delhi stands a remarkable structure known as the Kutb Minar. This masterpiece of thirteenth-century construction, thought by some to be a victory tower, is 238 feet high. It is 47 feet in diameter at the base and tapers upward in five graceful, balconied stories of different-colored sandstone. The top, which may be reached in a climb of 379 steps, was probably used by muezzins when calling the faithful to prayer.

Near at hand are the ruins of a very fine old mosque. Within the original court of this building stands the famous Iron Pillar, a forged bar of pure iron, about 24 feet in height. Brought here from Muttra in 1052, this amazing pillar has defied all the forces of decay for nearly sixteen hundred years.

In India, where much attention is given to the after life, many vast and beautiful monuments are erected in memory of the deceased. Where else in the world could be found such an imposing tomb as that of Humayun? The emperor himself selected the site, and the mausoleum was completed in 1565. It is built of rose-colored sandstone and marble and surmounted by a stately dome of white marble. Here, in one of the dimly lighted compartments which surround the central chamber, the last of the Mongol rulers yielded his sword to the British after the recapture of Delhi from the Sepoys.

While Delhi is filled with splendors of the past, it also at the present time is the seat of a modern government and enjoys all the conveniences of Western culture. Old and new—progressive and primitive—mingle here to create never ending surprises.

PESHAWAR

From Delhi in the center of northern India, to Peshawar, final outpost of the northwest frontier, it is almost five hundred miles. But the two cities are separated by more than mere miles. A world of differences in culture, climate, race, and attitude divides them; for Peshawar is a border town, containing some of the rougher elements of fear, distrust, greed, and violence, in contrast to the highly cultured city of Delhi.

Peshawar is the most important military station in India. For centuries invaders have entered the country through the mountain passes just beyond the city, and it is not unlikely that any future attacks will come by the same route. There is no settled peace on the northwest border, and being in Peshawar is dangerous. The Khyber and Kohat passes, long famous, are sometimes closed because of skirmishes between British forces and the wild native tribesmen. But on Tuesdays and Fridays, when the visitor is sometimes permitted to approach the border, nothing is more interesting than to watch the arrival of the camel caravans which bring with them into India so many of the treasures of Asia.

Srinagar, although situated in the valley of the Jhelum river, is over five thousand feet above sea level. In the winter deep snows make most of the roads temporarily impassable, and the visitor would do well to be there some time between May and October. At this season of the year the climate is delightfully mild during the day and cool at night.

Just beyond the city lies the Dal Lake, surrounded by beautiful terraced gardens, among which the Shalimar Bagh is world famous. The numerous floating gardens and houseboats which dot the blue waters of this mountain-encircled lake add variety to a prospect that would charm the eye of any lover of beauty. The scenery is magnificent and compares favorably with that of Switzerland. The mountains, rivers, lakes, plains, trees, and flowers make Kashmir an artist's paradise.

THE CITY OF KIPLING'S "KIM"

Lahore, the capital of the Punjab, is situated about three hundred and fifty miles northeast of Delhi. It is an important center of commerce and trade; and although it contains many fine public buildings, its chief charm is to be found in the colorful life of its bazaars and streets. Rudyard Kipling, who worked here in a newspaper office for five years, immortalized the city and its immediate surroundings in his famous story of *Kim*.

At the intersection of two roads a little beyond the Town Hall stands that historical piece of artillery known as the Zam Zamma Gun. Although it was originally cast in Lahore, it fell into the hands of Ranjit Singh and was not returned to the city until 1818 after it had been damaged at the siege of Multan. It was to this cumbersome old weapon that Kipling referred when he spoke of the gun around which "Kim" was accustomed to play.

Lahore, like many other splendid Indian cities, has its share of magnificent monuments and tombs. Among these are the mausoleums dedicated to the memories of Jahangir, Nur Jahan, and Anarkali. The latter, according to a popular legend, was one of the very beautiful ladies attached to Akbar's court. One day, however, the mighty emperor saw in a mirror the reflection of a smile exchanged between her and his son, Jahangir. Enraged by what he fancied to be a slur on the honor of the harem, Akbar commanded that she be bricked up alive. This terrible order was obeyed by his trembling servants, and the maiden perished there.

Then Jahangir, stricken with grief but powerless to save her life, later built her the tomb which stands in this place today. The sarcophagus which contains Anarkali's body is made of pure marble of extraordinary beauty and workmanship. It is, according to some authorities, one of the finest pieces of carving in the world.

THE SHALIMAR GARDENS

Like many illustrious rulers who followed them, the Indian kings often moved their courts away from the crowded cities during the heat of the summer and established themselves in cooler and quieter retreats in the country. A few miles outside of Lahore stands the Shalimar, or garden of pleasure, which Shah Jehan designed for himself as one of these places of refuge. It is composed of three large terraces, the highest of which was reserved for the ladies. The second, or middle terrace, was used by the emperor himself, and the third was open to men. Even today, although shorn of many of its marble adornments and bereft of the Mongol pomp and ceremony, the Shalimar remains a very beautiful resort. Its delicately built pavilions, its broad green lawns divided by watercourses where fountains play, and its groves of fruit trees, make the garden an attractive place to visit.

THE GOLDEN TEMPLE

Amritsar was founded in 1574. The original temple which was built here by Ram Das was destroyed in the turbulent times that followed. In 1802, however, the city was captured by the Sikh leader, Ranjit Singh, who built the Fort of Govindgarh and restored the temple, using sheets of gilt copper on its beautiful domes.

The Golden Temple rises from the center of the sacred pool, supported by a platform some 65 feet square. It is approached from beneath an archway on the west side by a white marble bridge over 200 feet in length. The lower portion of the temple is of white marble to a height of six feet. The remaining exterior is encased in gilt copper sheets upon whose glittering surfaces appear religious inscriptions.

Permission may usually be obtained from the manager of the Golden Temple to visit the Temple Treasury on the mainland. This building has a very beautiful marble gateway, and its roof is supported by 31 silver pillars. It contains some magnificent jewelry, golden canopies, maces, and other valuable articles used on ceremonial occasions.

AGRA, THE DREAM CITY OF INDIA

If an imaginary line were to be extended southeastward from the Golden Temple of Amritsar and through the Palace of Shah Jehan in Delhi, it would eventually come fairly close to the world-famous Taj Mahal of Agra. Of all the cities in India, Agra is perhaps the most interesting, because of the beauty and number of its Mogul buildings.

Several visits should be made to the Taj, since its appearance changes completely with varying light. In the morning the marble of the huge, white, central dome gleams like a great jewel. In the morning, also, the visitor can get a truer idea of its size. The building seems to grow as one approaches it, and the exquisite marble inlay and carved work upon the walls become apparent. Almost beyond conception is the fineness and detail of the decorations on a building of this size.

The Taj is probably the best-known monument in the world. It was commenced in 1630 and finished in 1652. Costing something in the neighborhood of fifteen million dollars, it was erected by Shah Jehan as a tomb for Mumtaz Mahal, his favorite wife. The emperor, himself, is buried here beside his empress, and their actual tombs lie in a vault below the floor of the Taj.

The Taj stands in a setting worthy of the jewel it contains. An immense arched gateway guards the approach to the grounds and is a worthy structure on its own merits. From the windows located in the stairway and upper story of this entrance a good view of the mausoleum may be obtained. Graceful cypress trees flank the long, rectangular, marble watercourse, which stretches away toward the Taj, and when the fountains in the pool are not playing, beautiful reflections add to the magnificence of the scene.

Within sight of the Taj Mahal stands the Fort of Agra, used by the British during the Mutiny of 1857 and containing many important Mogul buildings. Among these are the famous Pearl Mosque with its beautiful arched roof and marble pillars; the Gem Mosque, where Shah Jehan was once imprisoned by his son; and the Jasmine Tower from which, in 1666, the Emperor gazed from his deathbed at the completed Taj.

The Juma Musjid, the Mohammedan place of worship in Agra, is very fine, although it is somewhat smaller than that of Delhi. There are also in Agra two beautiful tombs which the traveler will not want to miss. The tomb of Mumtaz Mahal's grandfather, like that of Chini-ka-Rauza, contains much very excellent marble carving, and although both are entirely different in size and design, each has a distinctive beauty of its own.

About five miles from Agra the visitor will find the last resting-place of Akbar, the great Mongol emperor. His large red-sandstone tomb with its marble dome is a very impressive structure. The vaulted ceiling was originally frescoed in rich blue and gold, and part of this has been restored. At the head of the tomb there is a short marble column upon which once rested the famous Koh-i-noor diamond.

FATEHPUR

A pleasant automobile ride of about thirty minutes will take the visitor from Agra to the deserted city of Fatehpur in Sikri. The city was built by Akbar in 1569 to celebrate his victories and the birth of his son, Jahangir. It was abandoned after the emperor's death in 1605 because of its unhealthfulness and lack of a good water supply.

Although he was a Mohammedan, Akbar was tolerant of other religions, and among his many wives were at least one Christian and one Hindu. Each of his wives had her own luxurious quarters —a miniature palace within a palace—in which she lived with her attendants. The apartments were so arranged that the discreet emperor could visit any one of his wives without the knowledge of the others.

LUCKNOW, SCENE OF THE MUTINY

East and slightly south of Agra is Lucknow, one of the largest cities in northern India. It is a comparatively modern city, and although it contains many fine public buildings and parks, it is remembered chiefly as the site of much bitter fighting

SACRED WATERS

Southeast of Lucknow and about eighty miles from Benares is Allahabad, one of the holy places of India. Situated at the junction of the Ganges and Jumna rivers, it is doubly sanctified in the eyes of devout Hindus. Each February it is the scene of an immense religious festival known as the Magh Mela, and Hindus flock to it from all over India. A pilgrimage to these sacred waters is considered obligatory, and devotees believe that bathing in them will wash away the sins of a lifetime.

Courtesy Methodist Book Concern

BATHING GHATS (OR LANDING PLACE) AT BENARES, INDIA

Courtesy The Art Institute of Chicago

VISHNU TEMPLE AT BENARES

ONE OF THE OLDEST CITIES OF THE WORLD

Not far from the sacred city of Allahabad lies the even more sacred city of Benares. Situated on the left bank of the Ganges, it has been the religious capital of India from time immemorial. It has in all ages been the home of sanctity and the resort of religious teachers and philosophers. Although Benares is undoubtedly one of the most ancient of cities, it has been destroyed on several occasions by Mohammedan invaders, and very few buildings remain which date back beyond the time of Akbar.

With perhaps three thousand years of tradition behind it, Benares is one of the most picturesque cities of the Orient. Besides the innumerable shrines and temples that crowd the city's streets and line the entire three-mile stretch of the river bank, there is in the holy city all the daily ritual of human life to be observed. The religious side of Indian life is best seen at the bathing ghats which flank the river.

By the side of Dasashwamedh Ghat stands Jai Singh's Observatory, similar to that which the visitor saw in Jaipur. Further to the south is the Temple of Jagannath with its three curious copper images. Going northward along the river again, the visitor will come upon the Yalsain and Manikarna Ghats, the principal burning ghats of the city.

MOSQUE OF AURANGZEB AND GOLDEN TEMPLE

Beyond the handsome palaces of Gwalior and Bhonsla stands the famous mosque which was built by the Mogul emperor, Aurangzeb. Its twin minarets, the ascent of which is both difficult and dangerous, afford a magnificent view of the city, for they rise to a height of 142 feet above the upper level of the river bank. The mosque, which is extraordinarily beautiful, is constructed partly from the materials of a former temple.

Although comparatively small, the eighteenth-century Golden Temple of Benares is famous for its symmetry of design. The

Courtesy The Art Institute of Chicago

SHOAY LAGONE PAGODA AT RANGOON, BURMA

roof, which is capped by an ornate dome of gilded copper, gives the temple its name. The structure is flanked on two sides by spires; one of gilt copper, the other of carved sandstone. The contrast of color and the splendor of the cupolas, pinnacles, and niches, combine to form a very striking picture. The temple is dedicated to Visweswara, whose emblem, a plain black marble column, is deposited behind a silver door in a shrine below the gilt spire.

At Sarnath, a few miles from Benares, is located an ancient Buddhist city. Excavations have brought to light not only the secrets of two great stupas (towers), but the remains of many Buddhist monasteries which flourished there more than fifteen hundred years ago. The stump of Asoka's Pillar is one of the most interesting monuments among the excavations. It dates from the third century B.C.; and on its polished sandstone surface may be seen the well known Edict of Asoka, warning the monks and nuns of Sarnath against creating a split in the Buddhist church.

THE LARGEST CITY IN INDIA

Calcutta, the largest city and the commercial center of India, lies 120 miles inland and is approached from the sea by the Hooghly river. It was founded in 1690 by Job Charnock of the East India Company. Commanding the only outlet to the sea for the vast produce of Bengal and the adjacent provinces, the city soon grew to great size and today maintains its superiority over other Indian cities.

Calcutta is built around the Maidan, or large park, upon which no buildings are allowed to encroach. The only buildings now on the Maidan are Fort William and the beautiful Victoria Memorial. Surrounding it, however, are the many stores, hotels, government buildings, official residences, and commercial districts of a modern city.

Places of interest in Calcutta include the High Court, built in 1872 after the Town Hall of Ypres; the Hindu bathing ghats along the river front; and the celebrated Kalighat Temple, dedicated to the goddess Kali, consort of Siva, the Destroyer. The visitor will be especially interested in the Zoological Gardens, with their fine collection of animals; Fort William, in which is quartered a part of the garrison of Calcutta; and the General Post Office, which occupies part of the site of Old Fort William, in

Courtesy Methodist Book Concern

VICTORIA MEMORIAL BUILDING, CALCUTTA

the northeastern corner of which will be found the actual Black Hole of Calcutta. Here also are the Royal Botanical Gardens, founded in 1786 and containing the great Banyan Tree, whose branches and down-shoots cover ground 1,000 feet in circumference.

About three hundred miles southwest of Calcutta lies Puri (or Jagganath), one of the most sacred towns in India. Situated on the seacoast, besides being a place of pilgrimage, Puri is a popular holiday and health resort. The town is of great antiquity and is the scene of the world-famous Jagganath car procession. Its remarkable temple, Vishnu's greatest shrine, stands on rising ground in the center of the town.

"ON THE ROAD TO MANDALAY"

Rangoon, the capital and principal port of Burma, lies 25 miles from the sea on the Rangoon River. The most prominent feature of the city is the Shwe Dagon Pagoda, the largest and most sacred pagoda in Asia. This great shrine of Buddhism is about two miles inland from the river and rests on an elevated terrace. It is approached by a long flight of steps, at the foot of which are two gigantic Leogryphs, weird composite animals. A carved teakwood

Courtesy The Art Institute of Chicago

QUEEN SOOFYALAT'S SILVER PAGODA, BURMA

roof covers these steps, forming an arcade in which may be found numerous shops where flowers, gongs, gold leaf, and other articles connected with worship may be bought.

Every visitor to Burma should make an effort to see Mandalay, the famous city immortalized in Kipling's poem. The boat trip from Rangoon is 350 miles up the great Irrawaddy River. One finds a tropical city of flowers, sweet odors, modern conveniences, and old-world mystery. It was the last capital of the kings of Burma; and it was here that the cruel but weak King Thebaw was captured by the British in 1885.

The center of the city is occupied by the fort, built in the form of a square. Its sides are over a mile long and it is surrounded by a wall 26 feet high and a moat of water which is 75 yards across. On each side of this huge square are thirteen teakwood watch towers, built in Burmese style and elaborately decorated. The moat is crossed by five wooden bridges and there are twelve gates in each of the four walls.

Within the fort are the Royal Palace with its gardens, artificial canals and lakes; its magnificent Hall of Audience and Lion Throne; and the lovely Lily Throne. Outside the fort are many monasteries and groups of pagodas.

Courtesy The Art Institute of Chicago

SHWE DAGONE PAGODA, RANGOON

Above the town, rises Mandalay Hill, covered from its base to its summit with religious buildings. One of these, the Dat Daw, on the southern slope, contains Buddha relics of great interest. The Hill is an excellent place from which to view the whole city. Southeast of the Hill are the 730 pagodas, or Kuthodaw, where Thebaw's father recorded the holy books of Buddha on 729 stones, over each of which was erected a small, domed building to preserve it from the weather. The 730th pagoda is larger than the others and is situated in the center of the group. Visitors should not fail to see the Zegyo Bazaar, which is one of the chief centers of colorful, Burmese life. Here are gathered representatives of such distant tribes as the Chins, the Shans, and the Kachins.

THE PEARL OF THE ORIENT

Ceylon, often referred to as the "pearl of the Orient," is a beautiful tropical island, resting in the clear blue waters of the Indian Sea, just a few miles off the southeastern coast of the Indian peninsula. It is joined to the mainland by a series of shoals known as "Adam's Bridge." The island is surrounded by a coral beach, which rises in the southern and eastern sections to jungle-covered slopes and mountain peaks. One of the loftiest and most impressive of these is called "Adam's Peak" and is considered holy.

Most of the inhabitants of the island today are Singhalese. The Singhalese are Buddhists, who, throughout the history of the island, have contributed much in the way of culture and fine buildings. Hindus, Christians, and Mohammedans comprise the remainder of the population.

Colombo, the capital of Ceylon, is one of the busiest ports of the East. Unlike those of most large oriental cities, the streets of Colombo are comparatively clean, and ragged beggars, wandering cattle, and wretched urchins are seldom to be encountered. Places of interest here include the Pettah, or native business quarter; the interesting Buddhist temple at Kelaniya; the Cinnamon Gardens, in the residential section; the Museum; and Victoria Park.

Anuradhapura is situated in the northern part of Ceylon and is on the main route between Madras and Colombo. It is the best known of the "Buried Cities of Ceylon" and is famous for its ancient and interesting Buddhist ruins, more than 2,000 years old. Like every other Buddhist city, Anuradhapura was practically a monastery, the inhabitants devoting their entire lives to contemplation and attaining the state of contentment known as Nirvana. The wonderful ruins here, with beautiful designs and painstaking carving, comprise all the evidence of these people that remains.

India! Burma! Ceylon! These are magic names which seem to call from out of the past, urging the traveler eastward into the land of mystery, tragedy, and splendor. Who can resist the spell of the Orient? Strange places—unusual people—weird customs—all beckon to the outsider. The lure of the unknown is a powerful magnet, drawing the visitor with an ever increasing force to the history of yesterday, the knowledge of today, and the dreams of tomorrow. To the occidental in India, the old is forever new. Those who have never been to India are irresistibly drawn there. Those who have been there and gone away, will always want to return.